OpenStack Networking Cookbook

Harness the power of OpenStack Networking for public
and private clouds using 90 hands-on recipes

Sriram Subramanian

Chandan Dutta Chowdhury

[PACKT] open source*
PUBLISHING   community experience distilled

BIRMINGHAM - MUMBAI

OpenStack Networking Cookbook

First published: October 2015

Production reference: 1030207

Published by Packt Publishing Ltd.
Livery Place
35 Livery Street
Birmingham B3 2PB, UK.

ISBN 978-1-78528-610-0

www.packtpub.com

Credits

Authors
Sriram Subramanian
Chandan Dutta Chowdhury

Reviewers
Daniel Aquino
Yan Haifeng
Sayali Lunkad
Sarath Chandra Mekala
Madhusudan H V

Commissioning Editor
Kartikey Pandey

Acquisition Editor
Vivek Anantharaman

Content Development Editor
Divij Kotian

Technical Editor
Bharat Patil

Copy Editor
Tasneem Fatehi

Project Coordinator
Nikhil Nair

Proofreader
Safis Editing

Indexer
Mariammal Chettiyar

Graphics
Jason Monteiro

Production Coordinator
Nilesh R. Mohite

Cover Work
Nilesh R. Mohite

About the Authors

Sriram Subramanian is an experienced professional with over 18 years of experience in building networking and network management products. Since 2011, he has been working with Juniper Networks leading engineering teams responsible for OpenStack Neutron plugins, VMware integration, and Network management products. He is a technologist with a passion for virtualization and cloud networking. He blogs regularly at `http://www.innervoice.in/blogs` and loves experimenting with new technologies and programming.

I would like to dedicate this book to my family. I want to thank my wife, Kala, for her support during this entire project. Her *give your best* attitude motivates me to strive harder in managing my time and energy effectively. I also want to thank Appa and Amma for their patience and blessings, and a special thank you to my daughter, Navya, and our Labrador, Neige, for the *joie de vivre* they bring to my life.

I extend a special thank you to my employer, Juniper Networks, and specifically my manager, Rakesh Manocha. The leadership team at Juniper has created an environment where individuals can pursue excellence through innovation. It has helped me expand my knowledge and capabilities beyond my imagination.

I would like to express my gratitude to my publishers, Packt Publishing, and the reviewers who provided invaluable feedback.

Finally, a big thank you to Chandan for being a great coauthor and helping me learn a whole lot more about OpenStack.

Chandan Dutta Chowdhury is a tech lead at Juniper Networks Pvt. Ltd. working on OpenStack Neutron plugins. He has over 11 years of experience in the deployment of Linux-based solutions. In the past, he has been involved in developing Linux-based clustering and deployment solutions. He has contributed to setting up and maintaining a private cloud solution in Juniper Networks. He loves to explore technology and writes a blog at https://chandanduttachowdhury.wordpress.com.

I would like to dedicate this book to my parents, Manju and Kiran Moy Dutta Chowdhury. They have been a source of inspiration and support throughout my life.

I am thankful to my coauthor and manager, Sriram, who has motivated me to pursue challenges that I thought were beyond my reach. He has always provided me with encouraging and constructive feedback.

I would like to thank Juniper Networks for providing a supportive environment and great opportunities to learn and explore new technology.

I would like to thank Packt Publishing for their guidance and feedback.

About the Reviewers

Daniel Aquino currently holds the position of a system architect at Nasdaq. This role involves challenging and interesting problems in automation, and the deployment of infrastructure and applications at scale for both public and private cloud platforms. OpenStack is one of the cloud computing platforms that he is currently exploring.

Yan Haifeng is a software engineer in HP's Cloud. He has participated in the development of OpenStack when he was still an undergraduate in a laboratory of South China Agricultural University. Before HP, he worked for Vipshop (building an enterprise private cloud platform) and ChinaNetCenter (building a public cloud and managed cloud for customers), both based on OpenStack.

Haifeng blogs at `http://yanheven.github.io/`.

> Thanks to my first boss, Larf (Chen zhanqi) in Vipshop, who gave me the chance to participate in building a private cloud for Vipshop, and Chen Shake, who encouraged me a lot and guided me on the road to cloud computing.

Sayali Lunkad is 23 years old and was born and brought up in India. She is currently living in Germany. She graduated with a bachelor's degree in computer science in 2014 from the Pune Institute of Computer Technology. She was a former intern in the Outreach Program for Women (now known as the Outreachy Program) working with the OpenStack foundation while still completing her degree course. After completing her bachelor's degree, she was freelancing for about one year, mainly working on open source projects such as OpenStack. She is a core reviewer for OpenStack. She is currently working at SUSE Linux as an OpenStack developer.

> I would like to thank my family, especially my mother, Smita Lunkad, for always having faith in me and being extremely supportive.

Sarath Chandra Mekala holds a master's degree in communication systems from the Indian Institute Of Technology, Madras. He currently works as a technical lead at Juniper Networks and is responsible for integrating various Juniper devices such as EX and QFX switches and SRX/VSRX firewall devices with leading Open Source Cloud Orchestration Solutions such as OpenStack and CloudStack.

Sarath has over 12 years of experience working on Java & J2EE based Network Management Systems. He has a wide array of skills spanning over web and server side programming, which he keeps cramming with new technologies and skills all the time.

Sarath is multi-faceted and he prides himself as an intermediate level professional photographer, an avid sci-fi & fantasy reader, an aquarist, a budding gardener, a blogger, and a gastronomist.

Sarath blogs at `http://sarathblogs.blogspot.in/`

I would like to thank my wife, Kalyani, for encouraging me along and my son, Abhiram, for the joy he brings to my life.

Thanks to Sriram and Chandan for tagging me up for the review and the team at Packt Publishing for their support.

Madhusudan H V works as a Staff Engineer at Juniper Networks. He has more than 11 years of experience in developing enterprise grade telecom and networking management applications. He loves coding and focuses on developing new applications that help solve day-to-day problems of network and datacenter administrators.

Madhusudan is passionate about networking, virtualization, and cloud domains. He is a VMware Certification Professional (VCP) and Cisco Certified Network Associate (CCNA).

Madhusudan is the author of a cloud-related technical blog at `http://fastclouds.net/`.

Thanks to Sriram Subramanian for his guidance and support in my experiments with new technologies. I would also like to thank my wife, Nanditha, and my son, Alok, for supporting me in reviewing this book.

www.PacktPub.com

Support files, eBooks, discount offers, and more

For support files and downloads related to your book, please visit www.PacktPub.com.

Did you know that Packt offers eBook versions of every book published, with PDF and ePub files available? You can upgrade to the eBook version at www.PacktPub.com and as a print book customer, you are entitled to a discount on the eBook copy. Get in touch with us at service@packtpub.com for more details.

At www.PacktPub.com, you can also read a collection of free technical articles, sign up for a range of free newsletters and receive exclusive discounts and offers on Packt books and eBooks.

https://www2.packtpub.com/books/subscription/packtlib

Do you need instant solutions to your IT questions? PacktLib is Packt's online digital book library. Here, you can search, access, and read Packt's entire library of books.

Why Subscribe?

- ▶ Fully searchable across every book published by Packt
- ▶ Copy and paste, print, and bookmark content
- ▶ On demand and accessible via a web browser

Free Access for Packt account holders

If you have an account with Packt at www.PacktPub.com, you can use this to access PacktLib today and view 9 entirely free books. Simply use your login credentials for immediate access.

Table of Contents

Preface

OpenStack is an open source platform that leverages compute, network, and storage solutions to create private and public clouds. In the last couple of years, the adoption of OpenStack has increased dramatically and is being embraced by enterprises around the world.

Networking is one of the pillars of OpenStack. A solid understanding of OpenStack Networking will help you implement a rich suite of services in your OpenStack cloud. This book helps you develop the practical knowledge of a wide range of OpenStack Networking concepts.

This book starts with building blocks such as Network, Subnet, and Port. It then proceeds to cover OpenStack Networking technologies, such as Routers, Firewalls, and so on. Advanced topics such as the configuration of load balancers, VPN service to provide site-to-site connectivity, and development of a simple ML2 driver are also covered to help you build and manage the best networks for your OpenStack cloud.

This book will cover you the following topics:

- ► How to build and manage virtual switching, routing, and firewall-based networks in OpenStack using Neutron
- ► How to develop plugins and drivers for Neutron to enhance the built-in networking capabilities
- ► How to monitor and automate OpenStack networks using tools such as Ceilometer and Heat

What this book covers

Chapter 1, Getting Started with OpenStack Networking, introduces you to the building blocks of OpenStack Networking, namely Network, Subnet, and Port.

Chapter 2, Using Open vSwitch for VLAN-based Networks, shows you how to build and manage OpenStack networks using VLANs and Open vSwitch.

Chapter 3, Exploring Other Network Types in Neutrons, takes you through the different types of OpenStack networks with the help of a practical example.

Chapter 4, Exploring Overlay Networks with Neutron, shows you how to build and manage the VXLAN-based and GRE-based networks in OpenStack.

Chapter 5, Managing IP Addresses in Neutron, helps you understand the IP address allocation and DHCP-based address assignment features in OpenStack Neutron.

Chapter 6, Using Routing Services in Neutron, explores how to leverage OpenStack routing capabilities to connect multiple networks.

Chapter 7, Using Neutron Security and Firewall Services, shows you how to implement security groups and Firewall as a service in OpenStack in order to secure your cloud networks.

Chapter 8, Using HAProxy for Load Balancing, takes you through the techniques to implement load balancing as a service in OpenStack using HAProxy.

Chapter 9, Monitoring OpenStack Networks, shows you how to monitor your OpenStack networks using Ceilometer.

Chapter 10, Writing Your Own ML2 Mechanism Driver, gives you a foundation on how to write your own custom ML2 mechanism driver for Neutron.

Chapter 11, Troubleshooting Tips for Neutron, highlights the different OpenStack networking problems that you can run into and their solutions.

Chapter 12, Advanced Topics, covers advanced topics, such as VPN as a Service and Networking using Heat template.

What you need for this book

To use this book, you will need computers or servers that have hardware virtualization capabilities.

Kilo is the most recent release of OpenStack and is recommended to try out the recipes in this book.

OpenStack supports different models of deployment and each chapter provides a high level setup that is relevant for the corresponding recipes. You can also use DevStack for most of the recipes, but we recommend creating a distributed OpenStack setup for in-depth learning.

Who this book is for

This book is aimed at network and system administrators who want to deploy and manage the OpenStack-based cloud and IT infrastructure. If you have a basic knowledge of OpenStack and virtualization, this book will help you leverage the rich functionality of OpenStack Networking in your cloud deployments.

Sections

In this book, you will find several headings that appear frequently (Getting ready, How to do it, How it works, There's more, and See also).

To give clear instructions on how to complete a recipe, we use these sections, as follows:

Getting ready

This section tells you what to expect in the recipe, and describes how to set up any software or any preliminary settings required for the recipe.

How to do it...

This section contains the steps required to follow the recipe.

How it works...

This section usually consists of a detailed explanation of what happened in the previous section.

There's more...

This section consists of additional information about the recipe in order to make the reader more knowledgeable about the recipe.

See also

This section provides helpful links to other useful information for the recipe.

Conventions

In this book, you will find a number of text styles that distinguish between different kinds of information. Here are some examples of these styles and an explanation of their meaning.

Code words in text, database table names, folder names, filenames, file extensions, pathnames, dummy URLs, user input, and Twitter handles are shown as follows: "We can include other contexts through the use of the `include` directive."

A block of code is set as follows:

```
[ml2]
. . .
dhcp_agents_per_network = 2
```

Any command-line input or output is written as follows:

```
openstack@controller:~$ cat author_openrc.sh
export OS_TENANT_NAME=cookbook
export OS_USERNAME=author
export OS_PASSWORD=password
export OS_AUTH_URL=http://controller:35357/v2.0
```

New terms and **important words** are shown in bold. Words that you see on the screen, for example, in menus or dialog boxes, appear in the text like this: "In the left navigation menu, click on **Identity** and then **Projects**."

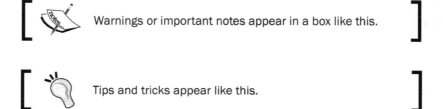

> Warnings or important notes appear in a box like this.

> Tips and tricks appear like this.

Reader feedback

Feedback from our readers is always welcome. Let us know what you think about this book—what you liked or disliked. Reader feedback is important for us as it helps us develop titles that you will really get the most out of.

To send us general feedback, simply e-mail feedback@packtpub.com, and mention the book's title in the subject of your message.

If there is a topic that you have expertise in and you are interested in either writing or contributing to a book, see our author guide at www.packtpub.com/authors.

Customer support

Now that you are the proud owner of a Packt book, we have a number of things to help you to get the most from your purchase.

Downloading the example code

You can download the example code files from your account at `http://www.packtpub.com` for all the Packt Publishing books you have purchased. If you purchased this book elsewhere, you can visit `http://www.packtpub.com/support` and register to have the files e-mailed directly to you.

Downloading the color images of this book

We also provide you with a PDF file that has color images of the screenshots/diagrams used in this book. The color images will help you better understand the changes in the output. You can download this file from `https://www.packtpub.com/sites/default/files/downloads/6100OS_ColorImages.pdf`.

Errata

Although we have taken every care to ensure the accuracy of our content, mistakes do happen. If you find a mistake in one of our books—maybe a mistake in the text or the code—we would be grateful if you could report this to us. By doing so, you can save other readers from frustration and help us improve subsequent versions of this book. If you find any errata, please report them by visiting `http://www.packtpub.com/submit-errata`, selecting your book, clicking on the **Errata Submission Form** link, and entering the details of your errata. Once your errata are verified, your submission will be accepted and the errata will be uploaded to our website or added to any list of existing errata under the Errata section of that title.

To view the previously submitted errata, go to `https://www.packtpub.com/books/content/support` and enter the name of the book in the search field. The required information will appear under the **Errata** section.

Piracy

Piracy of copyrighted material on the Internet is an ongoing problem across all media. At Packt, we take the protection of our copyright and licenses very seriously. If you come across any illegal copies of our works in any form on the Internet, please provide us with the location address or website name immediately so that we can pursue a remedy.

Please contact us at `copyright@packtpub.com` with a link to the suspected pirated material.

We appreciate your help in protecting our authors and our ability to bring you valuable content.

Questions

If you have a problem with any aspect of this book, you can contact us at `questions@packtpub.com`, and we will do our best to address the problem.

1
Getting Started with OpenStack Networking

In this chapter, we will show you the following set of recipes covering the different ways to create and manage the core Neutron entities, namely Network, Subnet, and Port:

- ▶ Creating a Subnet and Network using Horizon
- ▶ Viewing the details of a Network using Horizon
- ▶ Associating a Network to an instance using Horizon
- ▶ Creating a Network using OpenStack CLI
- ▶ Creating a Subnet using OpenStack CLI
- ▶ Creating a Port without an associated instance using OpenStack CLI
- ▶ Associating a Port to an instance using OpenStack CLI
- ▶ Configuring the networking quota in OpenStack

Introduction

Businesses are increasingly adopting cloud-based solutions for their IT requirements. This move to cloud started with the server virtualization where a hardware server ran as a virtual machine on a hypervisor.

The server hardware connects to the Network switches using Ethernet and IP to establish Network connectivity. However, as servers move from physical to virtual, the Network boundary also moves from the physical network to the virtual network. As the cloud platforms leverage virtualization, it is important that they support the physical and virtual networking effectively.

OpenStack is an open source cloud platform that helps build public and private clouds at scale. In OpenStack, the name for the OpenStack networking project is Neutron. The functionality of Neutron can be classified as core and service. In the rest of the book, the terms Neutron and OpenStack networking are used interchangeably.

The OpenStack networking core functionality refers to the Layer 2 (L2) Network connectivity and basic IP address management for virtual machines. Neutron provides the core functionality using entities such as Network, Subnet, and Port. This chapter will provide you with recipes about managing these entities. The OpenStack networking service functionality deals with the Layer 3 (L3) to Layer 7 (L7) capabilities as defined in the OSI Network model.

Neutron also works with the telemetry module called Ceilometer in order to let the cloud operators monitor the health of the OpenStack Networks.

In order to implement the recipes covered in this chapter, you will need an OpenStack setup, as described here:

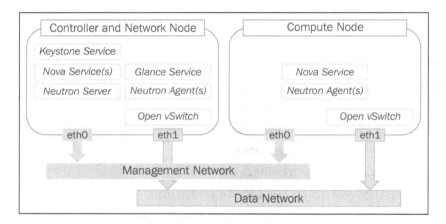

This setup has one compute node and one node for the controller and networking services. For this chapter, you can also set up a single all-in-one environment. This book is based on OpenStack on the Ubuntu platform. For other platforms, such as Red Hat, the dashboard may have a different theme but there should not be any difference in the functionality.

Creating a Subnet and Network using Horizon

Network and Subnet are the fundamental networking entities in OpenStack. Using these two entities, virtual machines or instances are provided with Network connectivity. The creation of a Subnet and Network go hand in hand. Both OpenStack CLI and Horizon support the creation of a Subnet and Network. This recipe explains how to create a Subnet and Network using Horizon.

Getting ready

In order to create a Network and Subnet, you will need the following information, minimally:

- The Network name
- The Subnet name
- The IP address range for the Subnet—the range should be in CIDR format

How to do it...

1. Log in to the OpenStack Horizon dashboard.
2. In the left navigation menu, click on **Project** | **Network** | **Networks**.
3. Now click on the **+ Create Network** button. The following screen will be displayed:

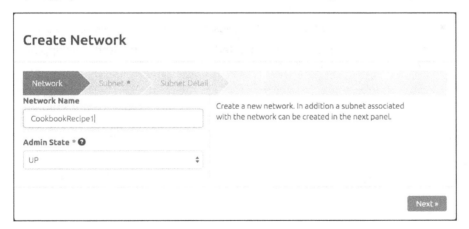

4. Enter the **Network Name** and click **Next**.
5. The next screen lets you create the Subnet that will be part of the Network.

6. Enter the **Subnet Name** and the address range in CIDR format, as shown in the following screenshot:

7. Click **Next**. In the next screen, all the fields are optional, so click on **Create**.

8. Once the Network and Subnet are created successfully, the entry will appear in the **Networks** table, as shown here:

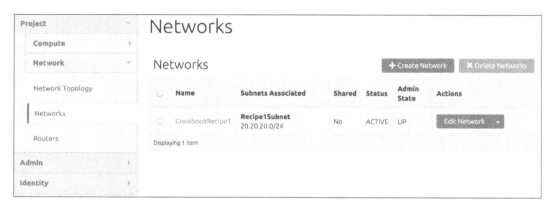

The preceding steps covered the most commonly used workflow to create a Network and Subnet using Horizon.

How it works...

The Network and Subnet entities represent two basic Networking functionalities. A Network defines the Layer 2 (L2) boundary for all the instances that are associated with it. All the virtual machines in a Network are a part of the same L2 broadcast domain. The Subnet, on the other hand, is the range of IP addresses that are assigned to the virtual machines on the associated Network. OpenStack Neutron configures the DHCP server with this IP address range and it starts one DHCP server instance per Network, by default. OpenStack Neutron also allocates one IP to act as the gateway IP unless the user provides a specific IP address for the gateway.

There's more...

As you can see from the UI, it is possible to create a Network without a Subnet. You can choose between the IPv4 or IPv6 addressing schemes. The **Subnet Details** section allows operators to enable or disable DHCP for the Network. Optionally, you can also specify the DNS servers and IP pools.

Viewing the details of a Network using Horizon

Once a Network and Subnet have been created, you can use Horizon to view useful details such as the ID, Network Type, and Gateway IP. You can also view the topology of the Network that you just created.

Getting ready

For this recipe, you need to know the name of the Network whose details you want to view.

How to do it...

1. Log in to the OpenStack Horizon dashboard using a user ID with an administrative role.
2. In the left navigation menu, click on **Project** | **Network** | **Networks**.

3. On the right-hand side, you will see a list of all the Networks. In the following screenshot, you can see two Networks:

4. To view the details of a particular Network, click on the **Name** of the Network:

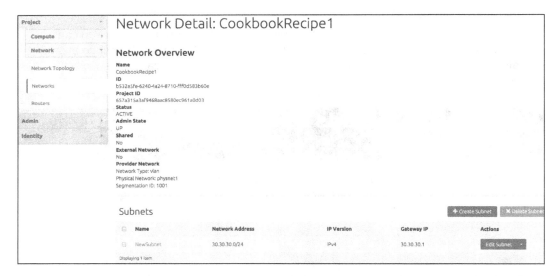

5. In the preceding screen, the key fields to note are **Network Type**, **Segmentation ID**, and **Gateway IP** for the Subnet.

6. To view the topology, click on **Network Topology** in the left navigation panel:

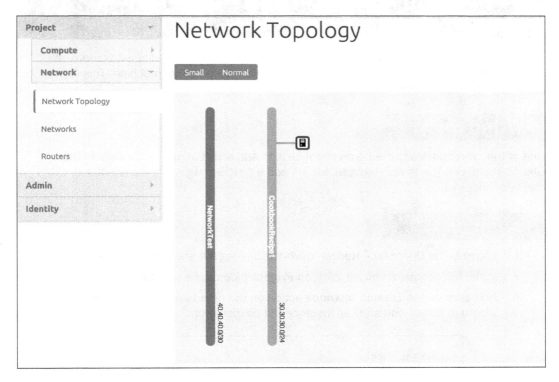

7. As you can see, the two Networks are shown as vertical color-coded bars. The Subnets belonging to the Network are indicated at the end of the bars.

How it works...

When you create a Network, the Horizon dashboard makes a REST API call to Neutron to create a Network. During the installation, the OpenStack administrator configures Neutron with a tenant Network type. This Network type is used by Neutron to create the Network.

> Note that if you create and view the Network with a non-administrative role, some of the fields may not be displayed.

While creating the Subnet, we did not select any gateway IP, so Neutron will automatically select the first IP address in the Subnet and configure this as the gateway IP for that Subnet.

Associating a Network to an instance using Horizon

Once the Network and Subnet are created, the next step for the end user is to create an instance or virtual machine and associate the Network to the virtual machine. This recipe shows you how to accomplish this.

Getting ready

One of the prerequisites to create an instance is to add a virtual machine image to the Glance image service. In our example, we will add a CirrOS image and use this image to create an instance.

How to do it...

1. Log in to the OpenStack Horizon dashboard using the appropriate credentials.

2. In the left navigation menu, click on **Project | Compute | Instances**.

3. Now click on the **Launch Instance** action on the right-hand side of the screen. The wizard to create and start an instance will be displayed:

4. Enter a name for the instance, choose a **Flavor**, select a source as **Boot from image**, and choose the desired image:

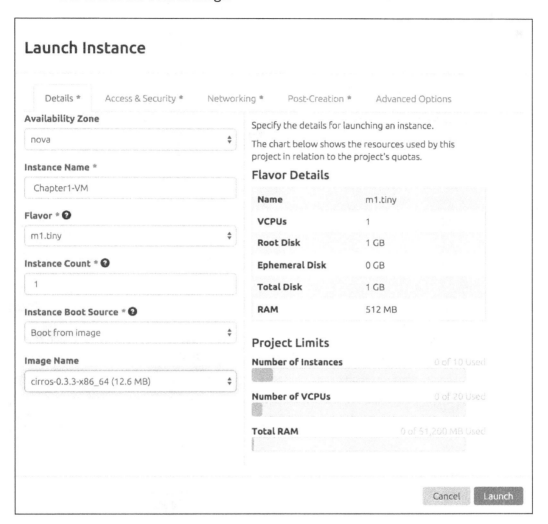

5. To associate the instance to a Network, click on the **Networking** tab at the top. You should see a screen where the **Selected networks** field is empty:

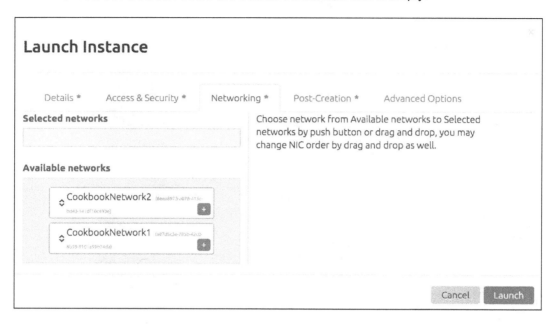

6. In the **Available networks** field, click on the **+** sign next to the Network to which the instance needs to be associated. Then click on **Launch**:

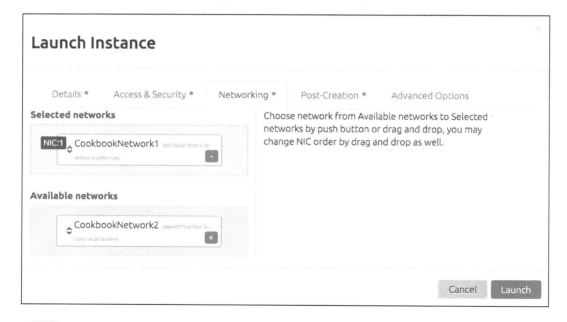

7. This should result in the creation and booting up of your instance and the Instances table is updated to show you the instance that was just created:

This recipe showed you that as a part of instance creation, the Horizon GUI allows users to choose the Network to which the instance needs to be associated.

How it works...

As part of the instance creation process, the user chooses the Network to which the instance will be associated. The instance creation and scheduling is the responsibility of Nova and it sends a create Port request to Neutron in order to associate the instance to the selected Network.

In response to the create Port request, Neutron will ensure that the virtual Network on the hypervisor server is configured so as to provide connectivity to the virtual machine. For the very first instance created on the Network, the Neutron server will also start a DHCP process on the Network node. This happens when DHCP is enabled on the corresponding Network. Once a virtual machine boots up, it will send a DHCP request. In response to this request, the DHCP server for that Network will respond with an IP address.

There's more...

If there is exactly one Network for a given tenant, then the dashboard automatically selects this Network when an instance is created. Additionally, note that the tenants can associate more than one Network to an instance. This will create multiple interfaces in the virtual machine.

Creating a Network using OpenStack CLI

We have seen how to use the Horizon dashboard to create a Network. Let's now do the same with OpenStack CLI. Several CLI commands offer additional capabilities when compared to the dashboard. So it is good to develop a sound knowledge of the CLI commands.

Getting ready

You will need the following information to create a Network using CLI:

- ▶ The login credentials for SSH to a node where the Neutron client packages are installed (usually the controller node)
- ▶ A shell RC file that initializes the environment variables for CLI

How to do it...

The next set of steps will show you how to use the Neutron CLI commands to create a Network:

1. Using the appropriate credentials, SSH into the OpenStack node where the Neutron client software packages are installed.

2. Source the shell RC file to initialize the environment variables required for the CLI commands:

    openstack@controller:~$ source author_openrc.sh

3. The contents of a typical shell RC file are as follows:

    openstack@controller:~$ cat author_openrc.sh

    export OS_TENANT_NAME=cookbook

    export OS_USERNAME=author

    export OS_PASSWORD=password

    export OS_AUTH_URL=http://controller:35357/v2.0

    openstack@controller:~$ openstack

4. The command to create a Network is neutron net-create, and in the simplest form, the only argument required is the Network name:

```
openstack@controller:~$ neutron net-create CookbookNetwork2
Created a new network:
+---------------------------+--------------------------------------+
| Field                     | Value                                |
+---------------------------+--------------------------------------+
| admin_state_up            | True                                 |
| id                        | 3fba8a42-ef06-4137-a1b9-e055f6fa4310 |
| name                      | CookbookNetwork2                     |
| provider:network_type     | vlan                                 |
| provider:physical_network | physnet1                             |
| provider:segmentation_id  | 1004                                 |
| router:external           | False                                |
| shared                    | False                                |
| status                    | ACTIVE                               |
| subnets                   |                                      |
| tenant_id                 | 657a315a3af9468aac8580ec961a0d03     |
+---------------------------+--------------------------------------+
```

5. You can view all the Networks created using the `neutron net-list` command:

```
openstack@controller:~$ neutron net-list
+--------------------------------------+----------------+-----------------------------------------------------+
| id                                   | name           | subnets                                             |
+--------------------------------------+----------------+-----------------------------------------------------+
| a87d5c3a-785b-42c0-8b59-8101a99b74da | CookbookNetwork1 | 3fe9dd8f-ae99-4fd0-bd3b-1349bbc04055 50.50.50.0/28 |
| 20a5d319-6c86-4654-bf84-a5d0dc3f7b62 | NetworkTest    | 16abf572-bd8f-463c-9838-1756e64e556e 40.40.40.0/30 |
| b532a5fe-6240-4a24-8710-fff0d583b60e | CookbookRecipe1 | 82d8c23b-eead-4d1b-bf8c-cace79e4aaad 30.30.30.0/24 |
| 3fba8a42-ef06-4137-a1b9-e055f6fa4310 | CookbookNetwork2 |                                                     |
+--------------------------------------+----------------+-----------------------------------------------------+
```

6. One of the interesting command-line options for the neutron net-create command is the `--tenant-id` option. This option allows users with an administrative role to create a Network for another tenant. The following screenshot shows you how an administrative user (for an administrative project or tenant) creates a Network for a cookbook tenant:

```
openstack@controller:~$ neutron net-create --tenant-id 195fd2454f9a4c379eeaf688f2cd03f7 AdminCreatedNetwork
Created a new network:
+---------------------------+--------------------------------------+
| Field                     | Value                                |
+---------------------------+--------------------------------------+
| admin_state_up            | True                                 |
| id                        | 38a2b79d-a471-4ef6-8137-2f9179d92b39 |
| name                      | AdminCreatedNetwork                  |
| provider:network_type     | vlan                                 |
| provider:physical_network | physnet1                             |
| provider:segmentation_id  | 1005                                 |
| router:external           | False                                |
| shared                    | False                                |
| status                    | ACTIVE                               |
| subnets                   |                                      |
| tenant_id                 | 195fd2454f9a4c379eeaf688f2cd03f7     |
+---------------------------+--------------------------------------+
```

7. The tenant ID argument works only when the user specifies the unique tenant ID. However, sometimes it is convenient to use the tenant name. The following command automates the conversion from the tenant to the tenant ID. The keyword, `cookbook`, is the tenant name used for this command:

```
openstack@controller:~$ neutron net-create --tenant-id `keystone tenant-list \
| awk '/ cookbook / {print $2}'` NetCreatedUsingTenantName
Created a new network:
+---------------------------+--------------------------------------+
| Field                     | Value                                |
+---------------------------+--------------------------------------+
| admin_state_up            | True                                 |
| id                        | 888697a3-823f-4276-a4a1-34cbb8ebbdd5 |
| name                      | NetCreatedUsingTenantName            |
| provider:network_type     | vlan                                 |
| provider:physical_network | physnet1                             |
| provider:segmentation_id  | 1006                                 |
| router:external           | False                                |
| shared                    | False                                |
| status                    | ACTIVE                               |
| subnets                   |                                      |
| tenant_id                 | 195fd2454f9a4c379eeaf688f2cd03f7     |
+---------------------------+--------------------------------------+
```

How it works...

When the user executes the `neutron net-create` command, the user name and tenant name attributes are taken from the shell environment variables that were initialized at the beginning. Neutron creates the Network with this user and tenant (or project). However, once the `--tenant-id` option is used, the Network is created on behalf of the tenant whose ID is specified.

There's more...

Users can specify several other arguments while creating Networks. These options are `provider:network_type`, `--provider:segmentation_id`, and `router:external`. While we will be taking a closer look at these parameters in the subsequent chapters, it is important to note that some of these options are available only if users have the administrative privilege.

To view the details of a specific Network, you can use the `neutron net-show` command.

Creating a Subnet using OpenStack CLI

Similar to the CLI commands to create a Network, the next recipe will explore the CLI command to create a Subnet. The key aspect of the CLI commands for Subnet creation is that a **Network Name** is a mandatory attribute.

Getting ready

You will need the following information to get started:

- The login credentials for SSH to a node where the Neutron client packages are installed
- A shell RC file that initializes the environment variables for CLI

How to do it...

The next set of steps will show you how to use Neutron CLI to create a Subnet:

1. Using the appropriate credentials, SSH into the OpenStack node where the Neutron client software packages are installed.
2. Source the shell RC file to initialize the environment variables required for the CLI commands as seen in the previous recipe.

3. The command to create a Subnet is `neutron subnet-create` and the mandatory arguments are the Network name and IP address range in the CIDR format. However, it is a good practice to specify a name for the Subnet. For simplicity, we will choose the Network, **CookbookNetwork2**, that was created earlier because it does not have any associated Subnet yet:

```
openstack@controller:~$ neutron subnet-create --name CookbookSubnet CookbookNetwork2 40.40.41.0/24
Created a new subnet:
+-------------------+--------------------------------------------------------+
| Field             | Value                                                  |
+-------------------+--------------------------------------------------------+
| allocation_pools  | {"start": "40.40.41.2", "end": "40.40.41.254"}         |
| cidr              | 40.40.41.0/24                                          |
| dns_nameservers   |                                                        |
| enable_dhcp       | True                                                   |
| gateway_ip        | 40.40.41.1                                             |
| host_routes       |                                                        |
| id                | 70498800-8644-4f0d-a901-832624130466                  |
| ip_version        | 4                                                      |
| ipv6_address_mode |                                                        |
| ipv6_ra_mode      |                                                        |
| name              | CookbookSubnet                                         |
| network_id        | 3fba8a42-ef06-4137-a1b9-e055f6fa4310                  |
| tenant_id         | 657a315a3af9468aac8580ec961a0d03                      |
+-------------------+--------------------------------------------------------+
```

4. Now, when we execute the `neutron net-list` command, we will see that `CookbookNetwork2` has an associated Subnet that we just created:

```
openstack@controller:~$ neutron net-list
+--------------------------------------+-----------------+--------------------------------------------------------+
| id                                   | name            | subnets                                                |
+--------------------------------------+-----------------+--------------------------------------------------------+
| a87d5c3a-785b-42c0-8b59-8101a99b74da | CookbookNetwork1| 3fe9dd8f-ae99-4fd0-bd3b-1349bbc04055 50.50.50.0/28     |
| b532a5fe-6240-4a24-8710-fff0d583b60e | CookbookRecipe1 | 82d8c23b-eead-4d1b-bf8c-cace79e4aaad 30.30.30.0/24     |
| 3fba8a42-ef06-4137-a1b9-e055f6fa4310 | CookbookNetwork2| 70498800-8644-4f0d-a901-832624130466 40.40.41.0/24     |
+--------------------------------------+-----------------+--------------------------------------------------------+
```

5. Users can view the list of Subnets using the `neutron subnet-list` command:

```
openstack@controller:~$ neutron subnet-list
+--------------------------------------+----------------+---------------+-------------------------------------------------+
| id                                   | name           | cidr          | allocation_pools                                |
+--------------------------------------+----------------+---------------+-------------------------------------------------+
| 3fe9dd8f-ae99-4fd0-bd3b-1349bbc04055 | CBSubnet1      | 50.50.50.0/28 | {"start": "50.50.50.2", "end": "50.50.50.14"}   |
| 82d8c23b-eead-4d1b-bf8c-cace79e4aaad | NewSubnet      | 30.30.30.0/24 | {"start": "30.30.30.2", "end": "30.30.30.254"}  |
| 70498800-8644-4f0d-a901-832624130466 | CookbookSubnet | 40.40.41.0/24 | {"start": "40.40.41.2", "end": "40.40.41.254"}  |
+--------------------------------------+----------------+---------------+-------------------------------------------------+
```

How it works...

When the user executes the `neutron subnet-create` command, Neutron creates a Subnet with the specified IP address range and other parameters. Neutron also associates the Subnet with the specified Network.

Creating a Port without an associated instance using the OpenStack CLI

Port is another building block in OpenStack Neutron. You will not find a way to create a Port using the **Horizon** dashboard. As we saw earlier in the *Associating a Network to an instance using Horizon* recipe, a Port is created implicitly as a part of the create instance operation from the dashboard. However, using CLI, some advanced networking configuration can be accomplished. This recipe shows you how to create a Port using OpenStack CLI.

Getting ready

You will need the following information to get started:

 ▸ The login credentials for SSH to a node where the Neutron client packages are installed

 ▸ A shell RC file that initializes the environment variables for CLI

How to do it...

The next set of steps will show you how to use Neutron CLI to create a Port:

1. Using the appropriate credentials, SSH into the OpenStack node where the Neutron client software packages are installed.

2. Source the shell RC file to initialize the environment variables required for the CLI commands as seen in the previous recipe.

3. The command to create a Port is `neutron port-create` and the only mandatory parameter is the Network name. However, it is a good practice to specify a name for the Port:

```
openstack@controller:~$ neutron port-create --name CLIPortCreate CookbookNetwork2
Created a new port:
+-----------------------+------------------------------------------------------------------------------------+
| Field                 | Value                                                                              |
+-----------------------+------------------------------------------------------------------------------------+
| admin_state_up        | True                                                                               |
| allowed_address_pairs |                                                                                    |
| binding:host_id       |                                                                                    |
| binding:profile       | {}                                                                                 |
| binding:vif_details   | {}                                                                                 |
| binding:vif_type      | unbound                                                                            |
| binding:vnic_type     | normal                                                                             |
| device_id             |                                                                                    |
| device_owner          |                                                                                    |
| fixed_ips             | {"subnet_id": "70498800-8644-4f0d-a901-832624130466", "ip_address": "40.40.41.4"}  |
| id                    | 880814d4-3b7a-4448-bd60-1dca68883060                                               |
| mac_address           | fa:16:3e:32:20:84                                                                  |
| name                  | CLIPortCreate                                                                      |
| network_id            | 3fba8a42-ef06-4137-a1b9-e055f6fa4310                                               |
| security_groups       | a92b7adc-0ae9-4a0c-a100-809695a9113c                                               |
| status                | DOWN                                                                               |
| tenant_id             | 657a315a3af9468aac8580ec961a0d03                                                   |
+-----------------------+------------------------------------------------------------------------------------+
```

4. Note that the Port has been assigned a MAC address as well as an IP address.

5. You can use the `neutron port-list` command to view a list of all the Ports in the system:

```
openstack@controller:~$ neutron port-list
+--------------------------------------+--------------+-------------------+------------------------------------------------------------------------------------------+
| id                                   | name         | mac_address       | fixed_ips                                                                                |
+--------------------------------------+--------------+-------------------+------------------------------------------------------------------------------------------+
| 581fabd4-2be5-4d87-9234-9a8703e175f2 |              | fa:16:3e:d0:0d:5c | {"subnet_id": "82d8c23b-eead-4d1b-bf8c-cace79e4aaad", "ip_address": "30.30.30.3"}         |
| 69faea20-9c35-443d-bd5b-7215e56e28bf |              | fa:16:3e:9a:45:4c | {"subnet_id": "82d8c23b-eead-4d1b-bf8c-cace79e4aaad", "ip_address": "30.30.30.2"}         |
| 0dad51ea-acc1-41be-a7f6-2b61ac8B5697 |              | fa:16:3e:fb:8f:15 | {"subnet_id": "16abf572-bd8f-463c-9838-1756e64e556e", "ip_address": "40.40.40.2"}         |
| 880814d4-3b7a-4448-bd60-1dca60883060 | CLIPortCreate| fa:16:3e:32:20:84 | {"subnet_id": "70498800-8644-4f0d-a901-832624130466", "ip_address": "40.40.41.4"}         |
+--------------------------------------+--------------+-------------------+------------------------------------------------------------------------------------------+
```

How it works...

A Port primarily represents an endpoint in a Network. The most common Ports in an OpenStack environment are the virtual interfaces in a virtual machine.

When the `neutron port-create` command is executed, OpenStack Neutron allocates a unique MAC address to the Port. The Network name argument effectively helps Neutron in identifying a Subnet and then Neutron assigns an IP address to the Port from the list of available IP addresses in the Subnet.

The `post-create` request is also the most common trigger to configure the physical and virtual Networks using the appropriate drivers.

Associating a Port to an instance using OpenStack CLI

The previous recipe showed you how to create a Port using CLI. The next recipe shows you how we can use an existing Port as part of the instance creation command.

Getting ready

For this recipe, you will have to identify the Port that you want to associate with an instance. For the instance creation itself, the software image needs to be identified.

How to do it...

The next set of steps will show you how to use the Nova and Neutron CLI commands to create an instance that uses an existing Port:

1. Using the appropriate credentials, SSH into the OpenStack node where the Neutron and Nova client software packages are installed.

2. Source the shell RC file to initialize the environment variables required for the CLI commands as seen in the earlier recipes.

3. Execute the `neutron port-list` command and identify the ID of the Port that you want to use to create an instance. Make a note of the MAC and IP addresses assigned to the Port:

```
openstack@controller:~$ neutron port-list
+--------------------------------------+--------------+-------------------+------------------------------------------------------------------------------------+
| id                                   | name         | mac_address       | fixed_ips                                                                          |
+--------------------------------------+--------------+-------------------+------------------------------------------------------------------------------------+
| e18666b5-a31a-4105-b333-744962109969 |              | fa:16:3e:01:a7:90 | {"subnet_id": "6f10a8ca-8e1b-4af5-9635-aebdf443bf84", "ip_address": "40.40.41.2"}  |
| ee6f30a1-6851-435a-89cd-a8e7390325a4 | CLIPortCreate| fa:16:3e:b3:a4:e6 | {"subnet_id": "6f10a8ca-8e1b-4af5-9635-aebdf443bf84", "ip_address": "40.40.41.4"}  |
+--------------------------------------+--------------+-------------------+------------------------------------------------------------------------------------+
```

4. The CLI command to create an instance is `nova boot`. This command supports an argument called `--nic` that allows us to specify a Port ID that we want to associate with the instance:

   openstack@controller:~$ nova boot --flavor m1.tiny --image cirros-0.3.3-x86_64 --nic port-id=ee6f30a1-6851-435a-89cd-a8e7390325a4 CLIPortVM

5. Note that the virtual machine name used in the command is `CLIPortVM`. If we execute the `nova show` command now, we can see the details about the instance:

```
openstack@controller:~$ nova show CLIPortVM
+--------------------------------------+------------------------------------------------------------+
| Property                             | Value                                                      |
+--------------------------------------+------------------------------------------------------------+
| CookbookNetwork2 network             | 40.40.41.4                                                 |
| OS-DCF:diskConfig                    | MANUAL                                                     |
| OS-EXT-AZ:availability_zone          | nova                                                       |
| OS-EXT-SRV-ATTR:host                 | controller                                                 |
| OS-EXT-SRV-ATTR:hypervisor_hostname  | controller                                                 |
| OS-EXT-SRV-ATTR:instance_name        | instance-00000007                                          |
| OS-EXT-STS:power_state               | 1                                                          |
| OS-EXT-STS:task_state                | -                                                          |
| OS-EXT-STS:vm_state                  | active                                                     |
| OS-SRV-USG:launched_at               | 2015-02-17T06:29:26.000000                                 |
| OS-SRV-USG:terminated_at             | -                                                          |
| accessIPv4                           |                                                            |
| accessIPv6                           |                                                            |
| config_drive                         |                                                            |
| created                              | 2015-02-17T06:29:15Z                                       |
| flavor                               | m1.tiny (1)                                                |
| hostId                               | 630438cef66f12cfe02120da9c3012a225c8a498cf8d5b306a6602e4   |
| id                                   | 2d424124-1517-4d00-a808-5c34c0125623                       |
| image                                | cirros1 (8aa1a365-15b1-4c19-b072-f64638d15df7)             |
| key_name                             | -                                                          |
| metadata                             | {}                                                         |
| name                                 | CLIPortVM                                                  |
| os-extended-volumes:volumes_attached | []                                                         |
| progress                             | 0                                                          |
| security_groups                      | default                                                    |
| status                               | ACTIVE                                                     |
| tenant_id                            | 0f15f3fea4b84eb89b558447a87402e6                           |
| updated                              | 2015-02-17T06:29:26Z                                       |
| user_id                              | b3cd9cf9539d47bdb61144c6efedd332                           |
+--------------------------------------+------------------------------------------------------------+
```

6. In the preceding output, you can see that the IP address of the Port created using CLI has been assigned to the instance.

7. Log in to the Horizon dashboard and navigate to **Network Topology**, as discussed in the *Viewing the details of a Network using Horizon* recipe. In **Network Topology**, move the mouse pointer over the icon representing the instance and click on **Open Console** as shown here:

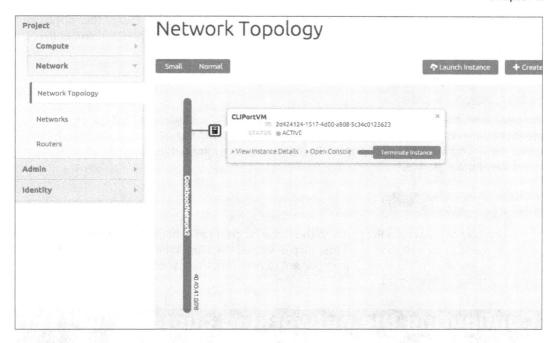

8. In the resulting window, log in to the instance. In our example, we will be using the CirrOS default username and password for the login.

   At the shell prompt of the instance, type `ifconfig eth0`. This command will show the virtual interface for this instance. The command output shows the MAC and IP addresses that are assigned to the virtual interface:

```
080/vnc_auto.html?token=467f0785-8fb4-4103-a99d-a423bf2b0f85&title=CLIPortVM(2d424124-1517-4d00-a...

                      Connected (unencrypted) to: QEMU (Instance-00000007)

$ ifconfig
eth0      Link encap:Ethernet  HWaddr FA:16:3E:B3:A4:E6
          inet addr:40.40.41.4  Bcast:40.40.41.15  Mask:255.255.255.240
          inet6 addr: fe80::f816:3eff:feb3:a4e6/64 Scope:Link
          UP BROADCAST RUNNING MULTICAST  MTU:1500  Metric:1
          RX packets:23 errors:0 dropped:0 overruns:0 frame:0
          TX packets:89 errors:0 dropped:0 overruns:0 carrier:0
          collisions:0 txqueuelen:1000
          RX bytes:2449 (2.3 KiB)  TX bytes:5084 (4.9 KiB)

lo        Link encap:Local Loopback
          inet addr:127.0.0.1  Mask:255.0.0.0
          inet6 addr: ::1/128 Scope:Host
          UP LOOPBACK RUNNING  MTU:16436  Metric:1
          RX packets:46 errors:0 dropped:0 overruns:0 frame:0
          TX packets:46 errors:0 dropped:0 overruns:0 carrier:0
          collisions:0 txqueuelen:0
          RX bytes:4192 (4.0 KiB)  TX bytes:4192 (4.0 KiB)

$ _
```

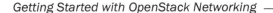

This recipe demonstrated how to associate a Port to an instance. At the end of the recipe, we can see that the MAC and IP addresses for this virtual interface (eth0) match those of the Port that we used in the nova boot command.

How it works...

We have seen that Neutron assigns an IP address and MAC address to a Port during their creation. When users execute the nova boot command with the --nic option, then Nova takes the IP and MAC addresses of the Port and uses this information to configure the virtual interface of the instance.

There's more...

This technique of creating a Port prior to the instance creation is helpful if a specific IP address needs to be assigned to an instance or virtual machine. While we will cover this in another recipe later in the book, it is important to note that this capability is not available using the Horizon dashboard.

Configuring the networking quota in OpenStack

Quotas are limits defined in OpenStack to ensure that the system resources and capacity are used in a systematic manner. Different users can be given different quota limits based on their requirement and priority. In this recipe, we will show you how to configure a quota related to networking at a project level and for the whole system.

Getting ready

The setting up and enforcement of the quota are done at the project level. If any user in the project tries to exceed the allotted quota, the system will reject the corresponding request. To configure the quota-related parameters, you need to have a good idea about the capacity, scale, and performance requirements of your OpenStack-based cloud.

How to do it...

The following steps will show you how to configure the networking-related quota:

1. Log in to the OpenStack Horizon dashboard using a user ID with an administrative role.

2. In the left navigation menu, click on **Identity** and then **Projects**. In the **Actions** column, select **Modify Quota** for the tenant of your choice, as follows:

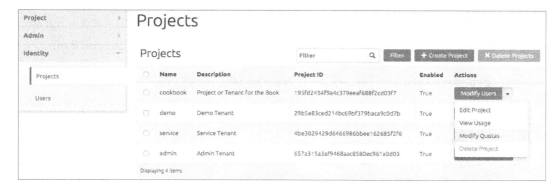

3. In the resulting window, the networking-related quotas are defined as shown in the following screenshot. Make the changes and click **Save**.

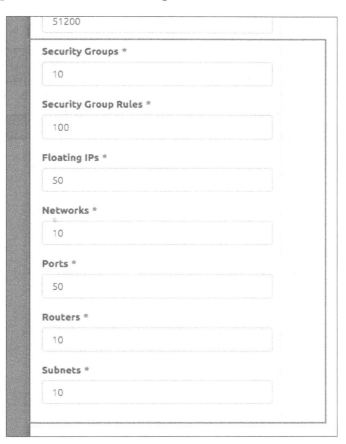

4. In order to change the networking-related quota at the whole system level, you need to change the settings in the Neutron server configuration file.

5. With the appropriate credentials, SSH into the node where the Neutron server is running.

6. Open the Neutron configuration file using your desired editor. For example, the command for vi editor will be as follows:

```
openstack@controller:~$ sudo vi /etc/neutron/neutron.conf
```

7. In the configuration file, look for a section starting with [quotas]. All the quota-related settings start with quota_. Edit these settings as required and save the file.

8. The Neutron server needs to be restarted for these settings to take effect. Restart the Neutron server using the following command:

```
sudo service neutron-server restart
```

How it works...

All the quota settings are stored on a per project (tenant) basis. During the creation of a project using CLI or Horizon, OpenStack (Keystone) fetches the system-wide default quotas from the configuration files and associates them to the project (or tenant). Hereafter, even if the system-wide quotas are changed, the project-level quotas do not change automatically. However, the project-level quotas can be changed anytime using Horizon or CLI, and these changes take effect immediately.

All the OpenStack commands and API calls are checked against the project-level quotas. If any commands or API calls violate the limits, they will be rejected with an appropriate error.

2
Using Open vSwitch for VLAN-Based Networks

In this chapter, we will demonstrate how Open vSwitch can be used to create and manage VLAN-based Networks for OpenStack tenants. The following recipes will be covered in this chapter:

- ► Configuring Neutron to use the Open vSwitch mechanism driver
- ► Configuring Neutron to use the VLAN type driver
- ► Configuring the VLAN range to be used for the Networks
- ► Viewing the VLAN allotted for a Network
- ► Creating a Network with a specific VLAN
- ► Viewing the virtual interface information on the compute node
- ► Viewing the virtual interface information on the Network node

Introduction

As discussed in the first chapter, virtualization and cloud computing are pushing the network boundary from the physical network to the virtual network. The non-virtualized physical servers are connected to the physical network switches for connectivity. The shift from physical to virtual networking implies that the virtual machines should be connected to the virtual switches for connectivity.

In order to allow the multiple networking technologies to interoperate, Neutron uses the concept of plugins. The **Modular Layer 2** (**ML2**) is a type of core plugin that supports multiple drivers so that the plugin functionality can be extended and customized. The ML2 plugin comprises of type drivers and mechanism drivers.

Open vSwitch, popularly referred to as OVS, is one of the implementations of the virtual switches for the Linux platforms. It is an open source, production quality, virtual switch that supports the rich networking protocols and features.

In order to implement these recipes, you will need an OpenStack setup as described here:

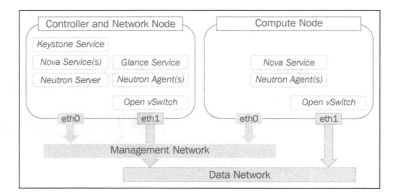

This setup has one compute node and one node for the controller and networking services. For this chapter, you can also use a single all-in-one OpenStack setup.

As discussed in the previous chapter, the core functionality of Neutron is to provide **Layer 2** (**L2**) connectivity. Neutron provides this functionality through the use of a core plugin. All the recipes of this chapter assume that ML2 is the core plugin in the Neutron configuration file.

Configuring Neutron to use the Open vSwitch mechanism driver

The ML2 plugin can support many mechanisms to provide the core functionality. We will see how Open vSwitch can act as a mechanism driver for the ML2 plugin.

Getting ready

Using OVS as the mechanism driver requires changes to the ML2 plugin configuration file. We also have to configure OVS with a tenant network type and physical network alias.

How to do it...

The following steps will show you how to configure Open vSwitch as the mechanism driver for the ML2 plugin:

1. With the appropriate credentials, SSH into the node where the Neutron server is running. In our setup, it will be the Controller and Network node.

2. Open the Neutron ML2 plugin configuration file using your desired editor. For example, the command for vi editor will be as follows:

    ```
    openstack@controller:~$ sudo vi /etc/neutron/plugins/ml2/ml2_conf.
    ini
    ```

3. In the `[ml2]` section of the file, configure ML2 to use OVS as the mechanism driver:

    ```
    [ml2]

    ...

    mechanism_drivers = openvswitch
    ```

4. In the `[ovs]` section of the file, configure OVS with the tenant network type and physical bridge mapping:

    ```
    [ovs]

    ...

    tenant_network_type = vlan

    bridge_mappings = physnet1:br-eth1
    ```

5. In the previous step, `br-eth1` represents the actual Open vSwitch instance that is bound to a physical interface and `physnet1` represents the alias for the OVS instance.

6. The OVS instance, `br-eth1`, can be created using the following steps (assuming that the `eth1` interface is used for the data traffic):

    ```
    openstack@controller:~$ sudo ovs-vsctl add-br br-eth1

    openstack@controller:~$ sudo ovs-vsctl add-port br-eth1 eth1
    ```

7. Restart the Neutron and Open vSwitch services on the Controller and Network nodes of our setup, using the following commands:

    ```
    openstack@controller:~$ sudo service neutron-server restart

    openstack@controller:~$ sudo service openvswitch-switch restart

    openstack@controller:~$ sudo service neutron-openvswitch-agent
    restart
    ```

8. Repeat these steps for the compute node in the setup.

9. The next few steps will show you the changes that are needed on the Network node so that the Neutron agents can use the OVS-related drivers.

10. Edit the `[DEFAULT]` section of the DHCP agent configuration file located at `/etc/neutron/dhcp_agent.ini` as follows:

    ```
    [DEFAULT]

    ...

    interface_driver = neutron.agent.linux.interface.
    OVSInterfaceDriver
    ```

Edit the `[DEFAULT]` section of the L3 agent configuration file located at `/etc/neutron/l3_agent.ini` as follows:

```
[DEFAULT]

...

interface_driver = neutron.agent.linux.interface.
OVSInterfaceDriver
```

11. Edit the `[securitygroup]` section of the ML2 plugin configuration file located at `/etc/neutron/plugins/ml2/ml2_conf.ini` as follows:

```
[securitygroup]

...

firewall_driver =
   neutron.agent.linux.iptables_firewall.
OVSHybridIptablesFirewallDriver
```

12. Restart the Neutron-related services as mentioned in step 7.

How it works...

As part of its startup, the Neutron server will load the core plugin, which in our case is the ML2 plugin. As the ML2 plugin allows multiple ways to implement the physical and virtual networks, it uses the `mechanism_drivers` attribute to load the desired drivers. The previous steps showed you how to configure OVS as the mechanism driver for ML2. The OVS mechanism driver needs additional information such as the bridge name and physical interface mapping so as to provide network connectivity. Hence, these mappings are also a part of the mechanism driver configuration.

Configuring Neutron to use the VLAN type driver

The ML2 plugin needs to be configured in order to use VLAN as the network type for all the tenant networks.

Getting ready

The ML2 plugin has a configuration file setting that needs to be updated so that the tenants can use VLAN as the tenant network type.

How to do it...

The following steps will show you how to configure VLAN as the type driver and tenant network type:

1. With the appropriate credentials, SSH into the node where the Neutron server is running. In our setup, it will be the Controller and Network node.

2. Open the Neutron ML2 plugin configuration file using your desired editor. For example, the command for vi editor will be as follows:

   ```
   openstack@controller:~$ sudo vi /etc/neutron/plugins/ml2/ml2_conf.
   ini
   ```

3. In the [ml2] section of the file, configure VLAN as the type driver and network type:

   ```
   [ml2]

   ...

   type_drivers = vlan
   tenant_network_types = vlan
   ```

4. Restart the Neutron and Open vSwitch services on the Controller and Network node of our setup, using the following commands:

   ```
   openstack@controller:~$ sudo service neutron-server restart
   openstack@controller:~$ sudo service openvswitch-switch restart
   openstack@controller:~$ sudo service neutron-plugin-openvswitch-
   agent restart
   ```

5. The first three steps have to be repeated for the compute node in our setup as shown previously. The command to restart OVS on the compute node is:

   ```
   openstack@compute:~$ sudo service openvswitch-switch restart
   ```

How it works...

During the startup, the Neutron server will load the core plugin, which in our case is the ML2 plugin. As the ML2 plugin allows multiple types of networks, it uses type_drivers to check which network type drivers to load. Finally, each tenant with a non-administrative role can use only certain network types. The tenant_network_types attribute indicates the network types.

Configuring the VLAN range to be used for the networks

In order to use VLAN as the network type, Neutron requires a range of VLAN identifiers. Each OpenStack Network will be associated with a unique VLAN identifier. This recipe shows you how to configure this range of VLAN IDs.

Getting ready

The valid range for a VLAN ID is 1-4095. However, based on your OpenStack environment and the physical network, it is possible to use a subset of this range.

How to do it...

Configuring the VLAN ID range is a setting in the plugin configuration file. The following steps will show you how to set this range:

1. With the appropriate credentials, SSH into the node where the Neutron server is running.

2. Open the Neutron ML2 plugin configuration file using your desired editor. For example, the command for vi editor will be as follows:

    ```
    openstack@controller:~$ sudo vi /etc/neutron/plugins/ml2/ml2_conf.
    ini
    ```

3. In the `[ml2_type_vlan]` section of the file, configure the VLAN range:

    ```
    [ml2_type_vlan]

    ...

    network_vlan_ranges = physnet1:1001:1200
    ```

4. For this recipe, we have used a VLAN ID range of 1001 to 1200.

5. The keyword `physnet1` represents the alias for the physical network. This refers to the OVS bridge that is bound to the physical Network adapter on the node.

6. These steps have to be repeated for all the nodes in your OpenStack setup including all the compute and Network nodes.

How it works...

When a network is created, Neutron will check the tenant network type first. In the case of the VLAN networks, Neutron will fetch the first unused VLAN ID from the range that was configured. This VLAN ID is then associated to the Network and also marked as used.

Viewing the VLAN allotted for a Network

Open vSwitch configures the VLAN ID on the virtual port associated with a virtual machine instance. The underlying physical network must also be configured so as to allow the data traffic for the same VLAN ID. Hence, the knowledge of the VLAN ID allotted for a Network is very useful, especially while troubleshooting networking problems. This recipe shows you how to view the VLAN ID allotted for a Network.

Getting ready

The VLAN ID information is available only to users with an administrative role. Hence, for this recipe, you will need the appropriate credentials.

How to do it...

The following steps will show you how to view the VLAN ID allotted for a Network:

1. Log in to the OpenStack Horizon dashboard using a user ID with an administrative role.

2. In the left navigation menu, click on **Admin | System | Networks**.

3. On the right-hand side, you will get a list of all the Networks in the setup, as shown in the following screenshot:

4. To view the details of a particular Network, click on the name of the Network.

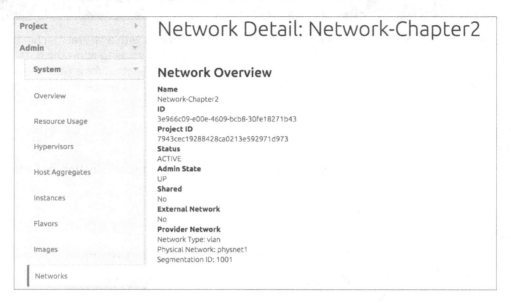

5. In the preceding screenshot, we can observe that **Network Type** is **vlan**.

6. **Segmentation ID** represents the VLAN ID allotted for this particular Network. Therefore, we can see that the VLAN ID of **1001** has been assigned to this Network.

7. The same information can be viewed using the `neutron net-show` command of the Neutron CLI, as follows:

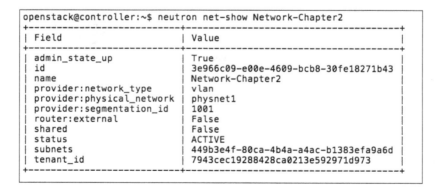

```
openstack@controller:~$ neutron net-show Network-Chapter2
+----------------------------+--------------------------------------+
| Field                      | Value                                |
+----------------------------+--------------------------------------+
| admin_state_up             | True                                 |
| id                         | 3e966c09-e00e-4609-bcb8-30fe18271b43 |
| name                       | Network-Chapter2                     |
| provider:network_type      | vlan                                 |
| provider:physical_network  | physnet1                             |
| provider:segmentation_id   | 1001                                 |
| router:external            | False                                |
| shared                     | False                                |
| status                     | ACTIVE                               |
| subnets                    | 449b3e4f-80ca-4b4a-a4ac-b1383efa9a6d |
| tenant_id                  | 7943cec19288428ca0213e592971d973     |
+----------------------------+--------------------------------------+
```

How it works...

When a Network is created, Neutron computes the first free VLAN ID from the range that was configured in the configuration file. This VLAN ID is stored as a segmentation ID in the Neutron database.

Creating a Network with a specific VLAN

When the user creates a Network, the VLAN ID is automatically assigned to it. However, there can be situations when a Network is required to use a specific VLAN. This can happen when the physical network is preconfigured to carry a certain type of traffic using a specific VLAN ID.

Getting ready

You will need the following information to create a Network with a specific VLAN:

▸ The project (tenant) name for which the Network needs to be created

▸ A VLAN ID from the range configured in the ML2 configuration file

How to do it...

The following steps will show you how to create a Network with a specific VLAN ID:

1. Log in to the OpenStack Horizon dashboard using a user ID with an administrative role.

2. In the left navigation menu, click on **Admin | System and Networks**.

3. On the right-hand side, we will get a list of all the Networks. As we logged in with an administrative role, we should be able to view all the networks across all the projects:

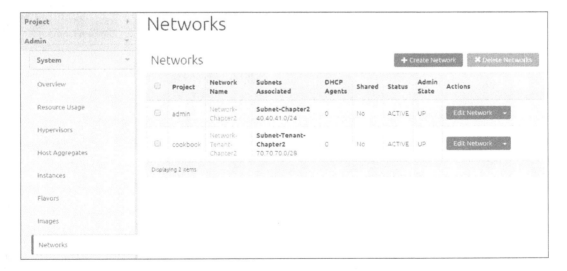

4. Click on the **+ Create Network** button to display the **Create Network** screen for the administrators. Note that this screen is different from the one shown for tenants, which is as follows:

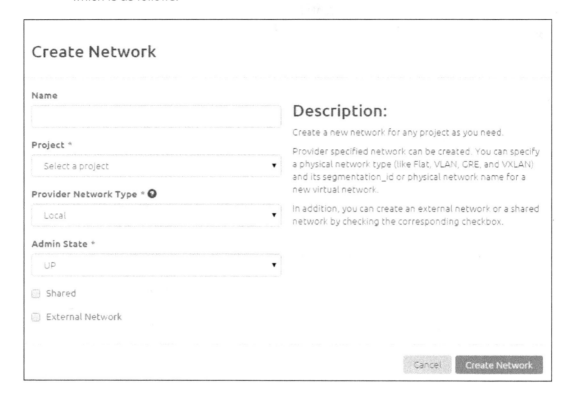

5. Enter a name for the Network. Select a **Project** and select **VLAN** as **Provider Network Type**. Once you choose **VLAN** as the Network type, the screen will prompt you to provide more details as shown here:

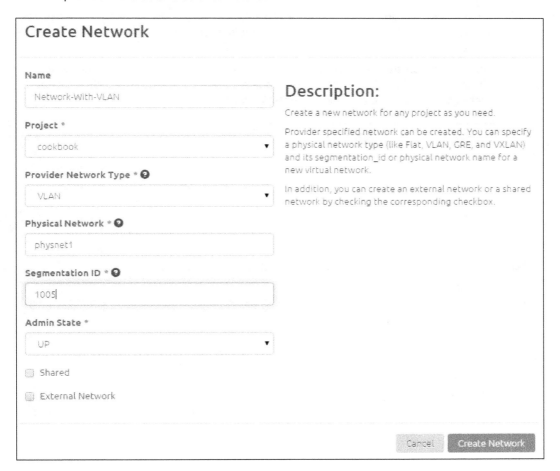

6. Enter `physnet1` as the value for **Physical Network**. This was the alias that was used when configuring OVS as the mechanism driver in the recipe titled *Configuring Neutron to use the Open vSwitch mechanism driver*.

7. In the **Segmentation ID** field, enter a VLAN ID from the range that was configured for Neutron. Note that if you enter a VLAN ID that is already in use, the create network request will fail.

8. Now click on **Create Network**. Once the network creation succeeds, the network will show in the list. Note that this mechanism creates a Network without a subnet. Therefore, you will see that the **Subnets Associated** column is empty:

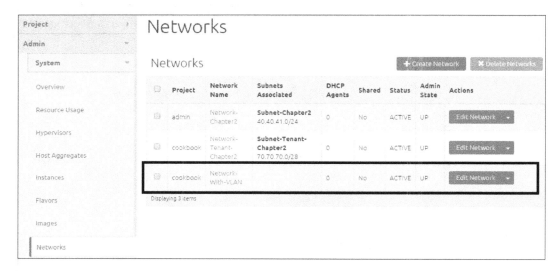

9. Click on the Network name of the newly created Network to view its details. You can see that the **Segmentation ID** that we entered has been used to create the Network:

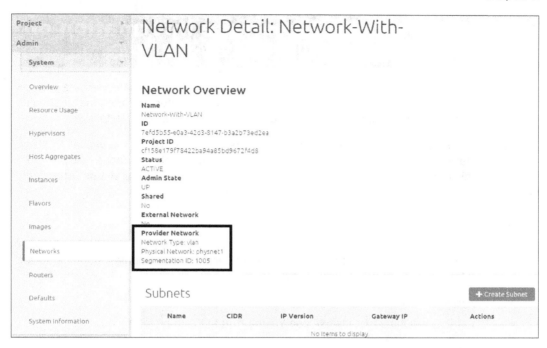

Users can use the **+ Create Subnet** button to add a Subnet to this Network. The preceding steps showed you how a user with an administrative role could create a Network with a specific VLAN.

How it works...

When a network is created as shown in this recipe, the Neutron server validates the segmentation ID against the VLAN ID range configured in Neutron. If the segmentation ID falls within the range, Neutron will check whether the segmentation ID is already in use or not. If the ID is not in use, then the Network creation will succeed.

Viewing the virtual interface information on the compute node

As tenants, users can create a Network, Subnet, and Instances. However, the underlying physical and virtual network details are hidden from them. This is important because the tenants should focus on their business requirements instead of the specific implementation details.

However, the OpenStack administrators need to understand the physical and virtual networking details. This is required in order to troubleshoot any problems faced by the tenants. In this recipe, we will show you how an administrator can view the **virtual interface** (**VIF**) information for an instance running on a compute node.

Getting ready

As this recipe is described from the point of view of an administrator troubleshooting a tenant problem, the following information is required:

▸ The Tenant Network name

▸ The virtual machine instance whose VIF information is to be identified

How to do it...

The following steps will show you how to find the VIF information on a compute node:

1. Log in to the OpenStack Horizon dashboard using a user ID with an administrative role.

2. In the left navigation menu, click on **Admin | System | Instances**. On the right-hand side, you will see a list of all the virtual machine instances.

3. Click the checkbox next to the virtual machine instance whose VIF details you want to see. Using the drop-down menu at the end of the row, select **Console**:

4. This should show the VNC console for the selected instance. Log in to the instance and execute the following command:

   ```
   $ ifconfig
   ```

5. You should see an output similar to the following screen. Note down the IP address, `70.70.70.2` in this case, and the MAC address (`fa:16:3e:76:cb:e5`):

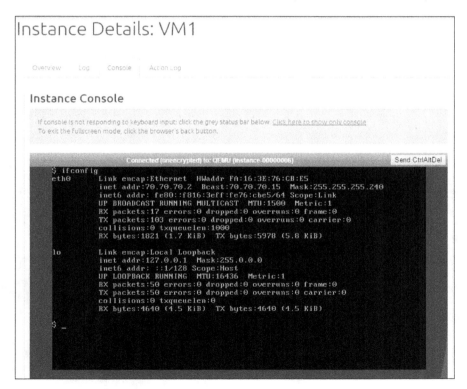

6. In the left navigation menu, click on **Admin | System | Networks**. Click on the name of the Network to which the instance belongs. This will display the Network Detail for that Network. Note the **Segmentation ID** (VLAN ID), which is **1002** in our example:

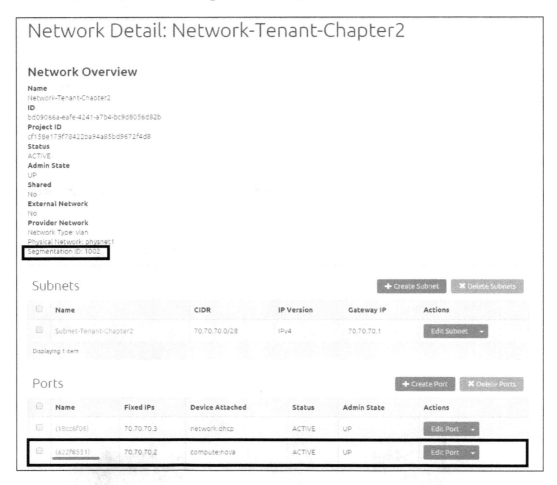

7. You can also see the list of the OpenStack ports for that Network. Our virtual machine instance had an IP address of **70.70.70.2** and there is a Port corresponding to this IP address. Click on the Port Name to view the Port Detail. Note that the MAC and IP addresses match our virtual machine:

8. Pay attention to the ID of the port, especially the first 11 characters, **a22f8551-57**.

9. Now, log in to the compute node of your setup with the appropriate credentials and execute the following command:

```
openstack@compute1:~$ sudo ovs-vsctl show
```

10. You should see an output as follows. The key thing to note is the OVS port named `qvoa22f8551-57`. As you can see, this port name matches the ID of the OpenStack port used for our virtual machine instance:

```
openstack@compute1:~$ sudo ovs-vsctl show
e2305089-6db0-423e-b2d7-b4200a3c0110
    Bridge "br-eth1"
        Port "br-eth1"
            Interface "br-eth1"
                type: internal
        Port "phy-br-eth1"
            Interface "phy-br-eth1"
                type: patch
                options: {peer="int-br-eth1"}
        Port "p2p1"
            Interface "p2p1"
    Bridge br-int
        fail_mode: secure
        Port "int-br-eth1"
            Interface "int-br-eth1"
                type: patch
                options: {peer="phy-br-eth1"}
        Port "qvoa22f8551-57"
            tag: 3
            Interface "qvoa22f8551-57"
        Port br-int
            Interface br-int
                type: internal
    ovs_version: "2.1.3"
```

11. The tag used for our `qvoa22f8551-57` port is 3. This is the tag used in OVS. When OVS forwards the packets from our virtual machine to the outside world, it must tag it with the VLAN ID of 1002 (Segmentation ID). We can verify this using the `ovs-ofctl dump-flows br-int` command. This command prints all the network flow information for the specific Open vSwitch instance. See the following highlighted output:

```
openstack@compute1:~$ sudo ovs-ofctl dump-flows br-int
NXST_FLOW reply (xid=0x4):
cookie=0x0, duration=2846589.807s, table=0, n_packets=184, n_bytes=14630,
idle_age=1410, hard_age=65534, priority=1 actions=NORMAL

cookie=0x0, duration=2525.210s, table=0, n_packets=5, n_bytes=909, idle_age=1434,
priority=3,in_port=2,dl_vlan=1002 actions=mod_vlan_vid:3,NORMAL

cookie=0x0, duration=2846166.773s, table=0, n_packets=329244, n_bytes=32975201,
idle_age=4, hard_age=65534, priority=2,in_port=2 actions=drop

cookie=0x0, duration=2846589.677s, table=23, n_packets=0, n_bytes=0, idle_age=65534,
hard_age=65534, priority=0 actions=drop
```

How it works...

The OpenStack entities such as Network, port, and others are assigned a unique ID when they are created. These unique IDs are reused while configuring the physical and virtual network so that troubleshooting is easier.

In the preceding example, we identified the port ID for the instance and using this ID, we were able to view the OVS and VLAN information on the compute node. These are usually the foremost steps in identifying the networking problems on a compute node.

Viewing the virtual interface information on the Network node

The previous recipe showed you how to identify the VIF information on the compute node. Now let's turn our attention to the Network node.

While a virtual machine is instantiated on a compute node, the DHCP server for the entire tenant Network is started on the Network node. As multiple tenant networks can have overlapping IP addresses, the Network node uses the concept of namespaces to isolate one Network from the other.

Getting ready

As this recipe is described from the point of view of an administrator troubleshooting a tenant problem, the following information is required:

  ▸   The tenant Network name
  ▸   The virtual machine instance whose VIF information is to be identified

How to do it...

The previous recipe showed you how to view the ports associated with a Network on the Network Detail screen. This recipe shows you how to look for the DHCP-related information on the Network node:

1. In the left navigation menu, click on **Admin | System | Networks**. Click on the name of the Network to view the details of the network to which the virtual machine instance belongs.

2. In the details of the Network, we can see the Ports associated with this Network. The DHCP Port for the selected network is highlighted as follows:

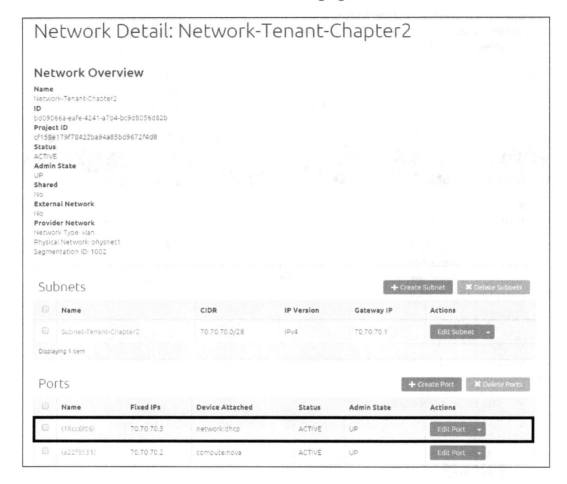

3. Click on the Port name to view the DHCP Port Detail. Note that the DHCP **IP address** is **70.70.70.3** and the Port ID starts with **18cc6f06-2b** as highlighted here:

4. Now log in to the network node of your setup (the Controller and Network node of our setup for this chapter) with the appropriate credentials and execute the following command:

   openstack@controller:~$ ip netns

   qdhcp-bd09066a-eafe-4241-a7b4-bc9d8056d82b

5. The output of the `ip netns` command lists all the Linux namespaces created on the node. In our setup, we can see a namespace called `qdhcp-bd09066a-eafe-4241-a7b4-bc9d8056d82b`. This name is generated by Neutron by adding `qdhcp` and the unique ID for the Network.

6. To view the networking information and applications running in a namespace, we will need to start a command shell in the namespace. You can do this using the following command:

   openstack@controller:~$ `sudo ip netns exec qdhcp-bd09066a-eafe-4241-a7b4-bc9d8056d82b /bin/bash`

7. Once this command is successful, you will get a new shell prompt. All the commands executed at this shell prompt are restricted to that namespace. Let's type the following `ifconfig` command at the prompt:

```
root@controller:~# ifconfig
lo        Link encap:Local Loopback
          inet addr:127.0.0.1  Mask:255.0.0.0
          inet6 addr: ::1/128 Scope:Host
          UP LOOPBACK RUNNING  MTU:65536  Metric:1
          RX packets:0 errors:0 dropped:0 overruns:0 frame:0
          TX packets:0 errors:0 dropped:0 overruns:0 carrier:0
          collisions:0 txqueuelen:0
          RX bytes:0 (0.0 B)  TX bytes:0 (0.0 B)

tap18cc6f06-2b Link encap:Ethernet  HWaddr fa:16:3e:6c:44:46
          inet addr:70.70.70.3  Bcast:70.70.70.15  Mask:255.255.255.240
          inet6 addr: fe80::f816:3eff:fe6c:4446/64 Scope:Link
          UP BROADCAST RUNNING  MTU:1500  Metric:1
          RX packets:79 errors:0 dropped:0 overruns:0 frame:0
          TX packets:13 errors:0 dropped:0 overruns:0 carrier:0
          collisions:0 txqueuelen:0
          RX bytes:5404 (5.4 KB)  TX bytes:1575 (1.5 KB)
```

8. In the output of the `ifconfig` command, we can see an interface called `tap18cc6f06-2b`. You will notice that `18cc6f06-2b` matches the first few characters of the DHCP port ID that we noted in step 3.

9. Neutron uses `dnsmasq` to provide DHCP services. We can confirm that the `dnsmasq` process is using the `tap18cc6f06-2b` interface with the `ps` command as shown here:

```
root@controller:~# ps -ef | grep dnsmasq
nobody    2776     1  0 20:57 ?        00:00:00 dnsmasq --no-hosts --no-resolv --
strict-order --bind-interfaces --interface=tap18cc6f06 -2b --except-interface=lo --
pid-file=/var/lib/neutron/dhcp/bd09066a-eafe-4241-a7b4-bc9d8056d82b/pid --dhcp-
hostsfile=/var/lib/neutron/dhcp/bd09066a-eafe-4241-a7b4-bc9d8056d82b/host --addn-
hosts=/var/lib/neutron/dhcp/bd09066a-eafe-4241-a7b4-bc9d8056d82b/addn_hosts --dhcp-
optsfile=/var/lib/neutron/dhcp/bd09066a-eafe-4241-a7b4-bc9d8056d82b/opts --leasefile-
ro --dhcp-range=set:tag0,70.70.70.0 ,static,86400s --dhcp-lease-max=16 --conf-file=
--domain=openstacklocal
root      4476  4436  0 21:12 pts/15   00:00:00 grep --color=auto dnsmasq
```

10. Next, we will check how the `tap18cc6f06-2b` interface is connected to the external physical network. For this, we will exit the namespace shell prompt and execute the following `ovs-vsctl show` command on the controller shell:

```
openstack@controller:~$ sudo ovs-vsctl show
622ef8a8-c58e-492c-81d0-b95cea7badc0
    Bridge "br-eth1"
        Port "phy-br-eth1"
            Interface "phy-br-eth1"
                type: patch
                options: {peer="int-br-eth1"}
        Port "eth1"
            Interface "eth1"
        Port "br-eth1"
            Interface "br-eth1"
                type: internal
    Bridge br-int
        fail_mode: secure
        Port "tap18cc6f06-2b"
            tag: 1
            Interface "tap18cc6f06 -2b"
                type: internal
        Port "int-br-eth1"
            Interface "int-br-eth1"
                type: patch
                options: {peer="phy-br-eth1"}
        Port br-int
            Interface br-int
                type: internal
    Bridge br-ex
        Port "eth2"
            Interface "eth2"
        Port br-ex
            Interface br-ex
                type: internal
    ovs_version: "2.1.3"
```

11. As seen in the preceding output, the `tap18cc6f06-2b` interface is bound to the OVS bridge, `br-eth1`. This in turn uses the `eth1` physical interface of the network node.

12. As seen in the previous recipe, we can execute the `ovs-ofctl dump-flows br-int` command to confirm that the DHCP port is also using VLAN 1002 that was assigned to the tenant network.

How it works...

Namespaces are constructs in Linux that allows the users to create a copy of a full TCP/IP network stack including interfaces and routing tables. In the OpenStack networking, one DHCP server is started for each Network and an IP address from the corresponding subnet is assigned to the DHCP server. As the tenant networks can have similar or overlapping IP addresses, Neutron uses namespaces to isolate each DHCP server.

As we saw in the previous recipe, Neutron uses unique IDs to identify the physical and virtual network information. The namespace name contained the unique ID of the tenant network. Moreover, the interface used by the DHCP server contained the unique ID of the Network port.

3
Exploring Other Network Types in Neutron

OpenStack Networking supports different types of network in order to provide rich functionality and flexibility. In this chapter, we will show you the following set of recipes that cover a few specific network types supported in OpenStack:

- ► Configuring Neutron to use the Linux bridge mechanism driver
- ► Viewing the virtual interface information for Linux bridge on the compute node
- ► Configuring Neutron to use a Flat Network type
- ► Creating a Flat Network using Horizon
- ► Creating a shared Network using Horizon
- ► Creating an external Network using Horizon
- ► Setting up a simple web application – an introduction
- ► Setting up a simple web application – setting up OpenStack Networks
- ► Setting up a simple web application – creating instances

Introduction

In the previous chapter, we saw how OpenStack supports Open vSwitch as the mechanism for a VLAN network type. Similar to Open vSwitch, Linux bridge is a software bridge in a Linux host that is capable of providing virtual network connectivity to instances.

In this chapter, we will see how to implement a network type called Flat Network. We will also see how to provide an external (say, the Internet) access to virtual machines (VMs).

Finally, we will apply the concepts learned in this chapter to deploy a simple web application.

In order to implement these recipes, you will need an OpenStack setup as described here:

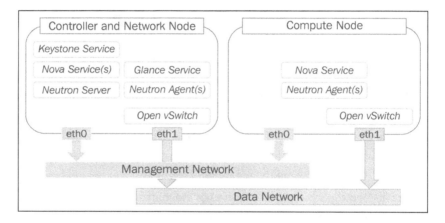

This setup has one compute node and one node for controller and networking services. For this chapter, you can also have a single all-in-one environment.

As discussed in the previous chapter, the core functionality of Neutron is to provide a **Layer 2** (**L2**) connectivity. Neutron provides this functionality through the use of a core plugin. All the recipes of this chapter assume that ML2 is the core plugin in the Neutron configuration file.

Configuring Neutron to use the Linux bridge mechanism driver

The ML2 plugin can support many mechanisms in order to provide the core functionality. We will see how a Linux bridge can act as a mechanism driver for the ML2 plugin. This recipe shows you how to configure an ML2 plugin with a Linux bridge as the mechanism driver.

Getting ready

Configuring ML2 to use a Linux bridge as the mechanism driver requires changes to the ML2 plugin configuration file. We will also have to configure the Linux bridge with a tenant network type and the alias for the Linux bridge that is bound to the physical network adapter of the node.

How to do it...

The following steps will show you how to configure Linux as the mechanism driver for the ML2 plugin:

1. With the appropriate credentials, SSH into the node where the Neutron server is running. In our setup, it will be the Controller and Network node.

2. Open the Neutron ML2 plugin configuration file using your desired editor. For example, the command for vi editor will be as follows:

    openstack@controller:~$ sudo vi /etc/neutron/plugins/ml2/ml2_conf.ini

3. In the [ml2] section of the file, configure ML2 to use the Linux bridge as the mechanism driver:

    ```
    [ml2]
    . . .
    mechanism_drivers = linuxbridge
    ```

4. In the [linux_bridge] section of the file, configure the Linux bridge with the tenant network type and physical interface mapping:

    ```
    [linux_bridge]
    tenant_network_type = vlan
    physical_interface_mappings = physnet1:eth1
    ```

5. In the previous step, physnet1 represents the alias and eth1 represents the physical interface that is added to the Linux bridge instance.

6. Restart the Neutron server and Linux bridge agent on Controller and Network node of our setup using the following commands:

    ```
    openstack@controller:~$ sudo service neutron-server restart
    openstack@controller:~$ sudo service neutron-plugin-linuxbridge-agent restart
    ```

7. Steps 2 to 5 have to be repeated for the compute node in our setup. On the compute node only the Linux bridge agent needs to be restarted.

8. On the Network node, a few changes are needed so that the Neutron agents can use Linux bridge-related drivers.

9. Edit the [DEFAULT] section of the DHCP agent configuration file located at /etc/neutron/dhcp_agent.ini on the network node, as follows:

```
[DEFAULT]
…
interface_driver = neutron.agent.linux.interface.
BridgeInterfaceDriver
```

10. Edit the [DEFAULT] section of the L3 agent configuration file located at /etc/neutron/l3_agent.ini on the network node in the following way:

```
[DEFAULT]
…
interface_driver = neutron.agent.linux.interface.
BridgeInterfaceDriver
```

11. Edit the [securitygroup] section of the ML2 plugin configuration file located at /etc/neutron/plugins/ml2/ml2_conf.ini, as follows:

```
[securitygroup]
…
firewall_driver = neutron.agent.linux.iptables_firewall.
IptablesFirewallDriver
```

12. Restart the Linux Bridge agent on the Network node by executing service neutron-plugin-linuxbridge-agent restart.

How it works...

At the start of the Neutron server, it will load the core plugin, which in our case is ML2. As the ML2 plugin allows you to implement physical networks in multiple ways, it uses the mechanism_drivers attribute to load the desired drivers. The preceding steps showed you how to configure a Linux bridge as the mechanism driver for ML2. The Linux bridge mechanism driver needs additional information such as the bridge name and physical interface mapping in order to provide network connectivity. Hence, these mappings are also a part of the mechanism driver configuration.

Viewing the virtual interface information for Linux bridge on the compute node

Users can create Networks, Subnets, and instances as tenants. However, the underlying physical and virtual network details are hidden from them. This is important because tenants should focus on their business requirements instead of specific implementation details.

However, administrators of the cloud platforms that have been built using OpenStack need to understand the physical and virtual networking details. This is required in order to troubleshoot any problems faced by the tenants. In this recipe, we will show you how an administrator can view the virtual interface (VIF) information for an instance that is running on a compute node.

Getting ready

As this recipe is described from the point of view of an administrator who is troubleshooting a tenant problem, the following information is required:

▸ The tenant network name

▸ The VM instance whose VIF information is to be identified

How to do it...

The following steps will show you how to view the VIF information on a compute node when using the Linux bridge:

1. Log in to the OpenStack Horizon dashboard using a user ID with an administrative role.

2. In the left navigation menu, navigate to **Admin | System | Instances**. On the right-hand side, you will see a list of all the VM instances.

3. Click on the checkbox next to the VM instance whose VIF details you want to see. Using the drop-down menu at the end of the row, select **Console**, as follows:

4. This should show the VNC console for the selected instance. Log in to the instance and execute the following command:

   ```
   $ ifconfig
   ```

5. You should see an output similar to the following screen. Note down the IP address, `70.70.70.2` in this case, and the MAC address, (`FA:16:3E:3E:F0:EB`), as shown in the following screenshot:

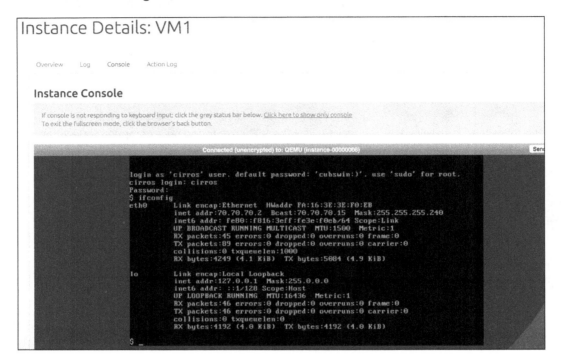

6. In the left navigation menu, navigate to **Project** | **Admin** | **Networks**. Click on the name of the Network to which the instance belongs. This will display the Network Detail for this Network. Note the **Segmentation ID** (VLAN ID), which is **1002** in our example:

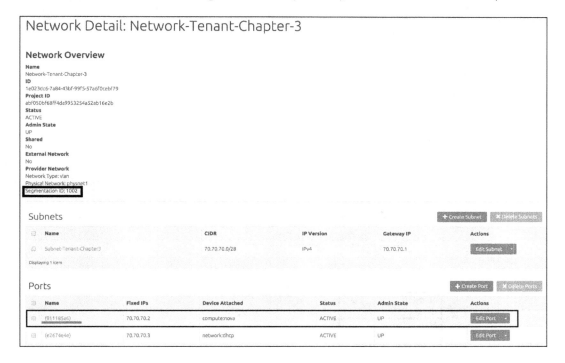

7. You can also see the list of the OpenStack ports for this Network. Our VM instance has an IP address of **70.70.70.2** and there is a Port corresponding to this IP address. Click on the Port Name to view the Port Detail. Note that the MAC and IP addresses match our VM:

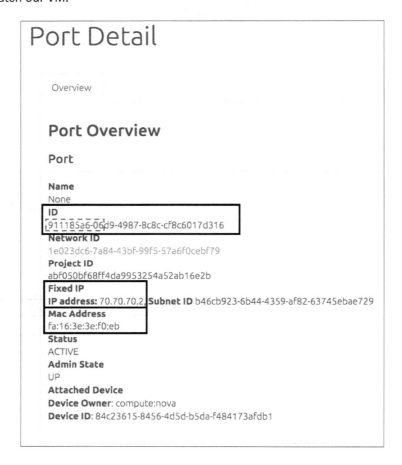

8. Pay attention to the ID of the port, especially the first 11 characters: **911185a6-06**.

9. Now log in to the compute node of your setup with the appropriate credentials and execute the following command:

```
openstack@compute:~$ brctl show
```

10. You should see an output as follows:

```
bridge name      bridge id             STP enabled      interfaces
brq1e023dc6-7a   8000.080027532e74     no               eth1.1002
                                                         tap911185a6-06
```

The preceding output shows two important things. The Linux bridge name, `brq1e023dc6-7a`, is derived from the ID of the Network and the `Tap` interface name, `tap911185a6-06`, is derived from the OpenStack Port used for our VM. The `Tap` interface is the entity that connects the virtual interface on the instance to the Linux bridge.

The output of the `brctl` command also shows that `eth1.1002` is the physical interface on the Linux bridge. This notation indicates that the traffic on that Linux bridge will be sent out on the `eth1` physical interface with a VLAN tag of `1002`.

How it works...

In the preceding example, we identified the Port ID for the instance, and using this ID, we were able to view the Linux bridge and VLAN information on the compute node. These are usually the foremost steps in identifying the networking problems on a compute node.

We also saw that the Linux bridge name is derived from the ID of the OpenStack Network. This implies that when a Linux bridge is used as the mechanism driver, one bridge will be created for every OpenStack Network. The Linux bridge-based configuration on a compute node is pictorially depicted here:

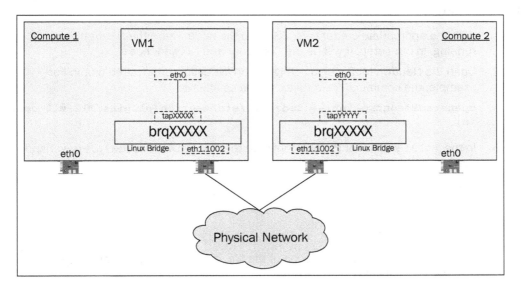

There's more...

This recipe showed you how to identify the virtual interface on the compute node. On the Network node, there is no change due to the Linux bridge being a mechanism driver. You can refer to the recipe titled *Viewing the virtual interface information on the Network node* in *Chapter 2, Using Open vSwitch for VLAN-Based Networks*, to view the virtual interface on a Network node.

Configuring Neutron to use a Flat network type

A Flat Network is another network type that is supported by the OpenStack Neutron ML2 plugin. Flat Networks are useful when tenant network isolation is not a mandatory requirement. Another scenario for a Flat Network type could be the access to centralized storage for all the instances using a dedicated physical interface.

Getting ready

To use Flat Networks, the ML2 plugin's type driver and related settings need to be updated. Just as VLAN, the Flat Network type can work with an OVS or Linux bridge mechanism driver. In our example, we will use the Linux bridge mechanism driver.

How to do it...

The following steps will show you how to configure the Flat Network as the type driver and tenant network type:

1. With the appropriate credentials, SSH into the node where the Neutron server is running. In our setup, it will be the Controller and Network node.

2. Open the Neutron ML2 plugin configuration file using your desired editor. For example, the command for vi editor will be as follows:

    ```
    openstack@controller:~$ sudo vi /etc/neutron/plugins/ml2/ml2_conf.
    ini
    ```

3. In the [ml2] section of the file, configure the Flat Network as the type driver and network type:

    ```
    [ml2]
    . . .
    type_drivers = flat
    tenant_network_types = flat
    ```

4. In the [ml2_type_flat] section of the file, configure the physical network names with the Flat Networks that are created:

    ```
    [ml2_type_flat]
    ...
    flat_networks = physnet1
    ```

5. As we used the Linux bridge as the mechanism driver, ensure that the Linux bridge physical interface mappings are configured appropriately. Refer to the first recipe of this chapter.

6. Restart the Neutron server and Linux bridge agent on Controller and Network Node of our setup using the following commands:

```
openstack@controller:~$ sudo service neutron-server restart
```

```
openstack@controller:~$ sudo service neutron-plugin-linuxbridge-agent restart
```

7. Steps 2 to 4 have to be repeated for the compute node in our setup. The command to restart the networking services on the compute node is as follows:

```
openstack@controller:~$ sudo service neutron-plugin-linuxbridge-agent restart
```

How it works...

At the start of the Neutron server, it will load the core plugin, which in our case is ML2. As the ML2 plugin allows multiple types of networks, it uses `type_drivers` to see which network drivers to be loaded. Finally, each tenant with a non-administrative role can use only certain network types. The `tenant_network_types` attribute indicates the network types.

A Flat Network is used when the L2 isolation between different tenant networks is not required. In this scenario, all the instances are a part of the same network. However, they can be a part of different subnetworks.

Creating a Flat Network using Horizon

In the case of a VLAN network type, we saw that the physical interface was separated in logical interfaces such as `eth1.1002`, `eth1.1003`, and so on. Moreover, each of these logical interfaces was placed on a Linux bridge corresponding to the OpenStack network.

In contrast, Flat Networks are created by placing the physical interfaces directly on the Linux bridge. This means that you can have only one Flat Network per physical interface on the compute node. Due to this reason, only the users with an administrative role are allowed to create a Flat Network.

Getting ready

In order to create a Flat Network and Subnet, you will need the following information, minimally:

- The Network name
- The Subnet name and IP address range
- The physical network name—this information was configured in the ML2 plugin configuration file

How to do it...

The following steps will show you how to create a Flat Network using Horizon:

1. Log in to the OpenStack Horizon dashboard using a user ID with an administrative role.

2. In the left navigation menu, navigate to **Admin | System | Networks**.

3. Click on the **+ Create Network** button to display the following **Create Network** screen for administrators:

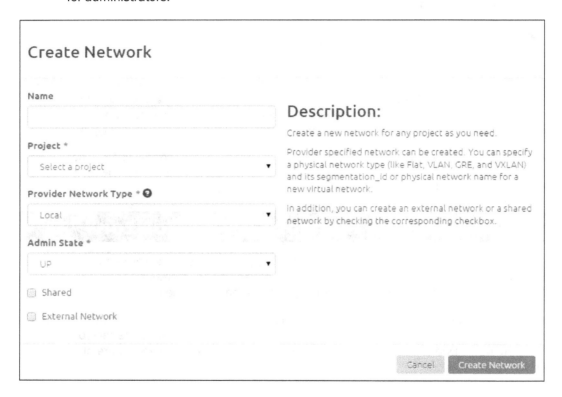

4. Enter a name for the Network. Select a Project to assign the Network to a specific tenant.

5. Select **Flat** as **Provider Network Type**. Once you choose **Flat** as the Network type, the screen will prompt you to provide more details, as shown in the following screenshot:

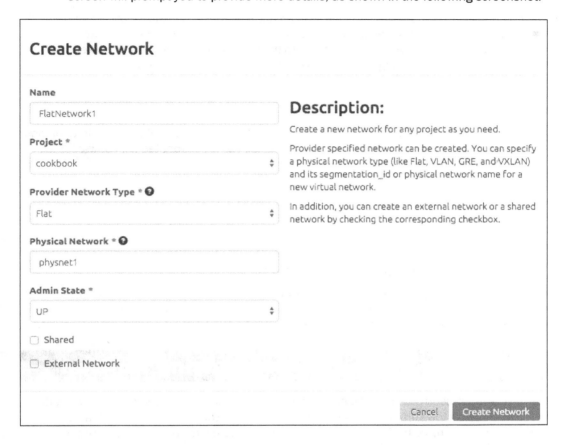

6. Enter `physnet1` as the value for **Physical Network**. This was the alias used when configuring the Flat Network as the type driver in the previous recipe.

7. Now click on **Create Network**. Once the network creation succeeds, the network will show in the list.

8. Note that this mechanism creates a Network without a Subnet. Therefore, the next step is to create a Subnet for this Network. This step can be performed as a normal user associated with the Project to which this Network was added.

How it works...

The preceding steps showed how a user with an administrative role can create a Flat Network and assign it to a Project. When the tenant creates an instance using this Flat Network, Neutron will map the physical network name to the corresponding mechanism driver. The mechanism driver (Linux bridge or Open vSwitch) will then provision the virtual network.

There's more...

If your compute node has additional physical interfaces, then it is possible to create additional Flat Networks. To do this, the ML2 configuration file needs to be updated as follows:

```
[ml2_type_flat]
...
flat_networks = physnet1,physnet2
...
[linux_bridge]
...
physical_interface_mappings = physnet1:eth1,physnet2:eth2
```

In the **Create Network** window, the administrative user can choose `physnet2` for the second Flat Network. The previous example assumes that the Linux bridge is the mechanism driver but a similar configuration can be done for OVS as well.

Creating a Shared Network using Horizon

We have already seen situations where only the administrative users can create a Network. For example, only the administrators can create a Flat Network or a Network with a specific VLAN ID. In addition, we have seen that the administrative users can assign a Network to a particular tenant.

OpenStack also allows administrators to share a Network among all the tenants. This recipe shows you how to accomplish this.

Getting ready

In order to create a shared network, you will need the following information:

- The Network name
- The Network type—for this recipe we will use a Flat Network
- The physical Network name—this information was configured in the ML2 plugin configuration file

How to do it...

The following steps will show you how to create a Flat Network using Horizon:

1. Log in to the OpenStack Horizon dashboard using a user ID with an administrative role.

2. In the left navigation menu, navigate to **Admin | System | Networks**.

3. Click on the **+ Create Network** button to display the following **Create Network** screen for administrators:

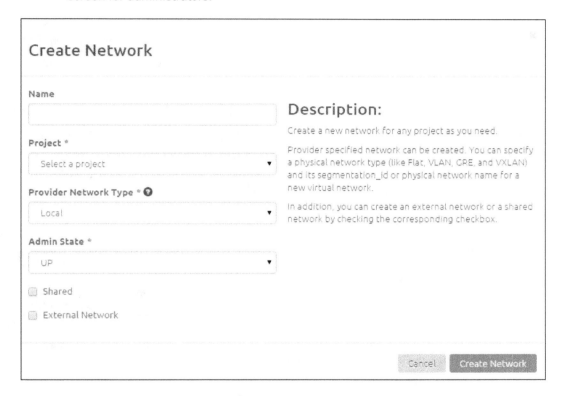

4. Enter a name for the Network. Select a **Project** to assign the Network to a specific tenant.

5. Select **Provider Network Type** as desired. For this recipe, we will choose **Flat** networks as **Provider Network Type**. Once you choose **Flat** as the Network type, the screen will prompt you to provide more details, as shown in the following screenshot:

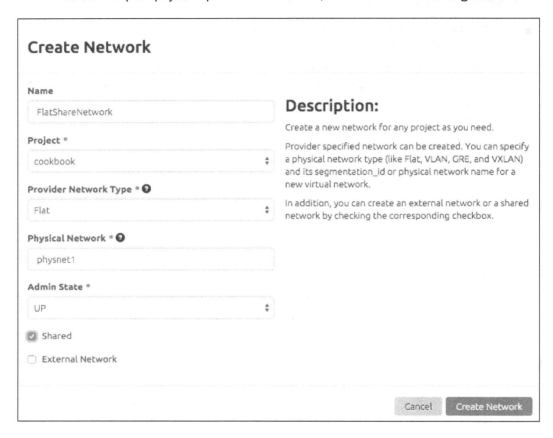

6. Enter `physnet1` as the value for **Physical Network**. This was the alias used when configuring the Flat Network as the type driver in the previous recipe.

7. Check the **Shared** checkbox.

8. Now click on **Create Network**. Once the network creation has succeeded, the network will show in the list.

How it works...

A shared network is available to all the tenants independent of the project that was chosen during creation. All the tenants can use the shared network to create VM instances. However, only the administrative user of the project that was chosen during creation can edit or delete the shared Network. Similarly, only the administrative user of the project can add a Subnet to the shared Network.

Creating an External Network using Horizon

External Networks have a unique role to play with OpenStack Networking. As we have seen, the DHCP server assigns an IP address from the Subnet to each VM instance. These IP addresses are reachable only in the Network because tenant isolation is required. However, many common deployments require that the VM instances have access to outside networks including the Internet and also be reachable from the outside network.

The main purpose of the external Networks is to allow the VMs to access networks outside the data center and Internet. They also allow the VMs to be accessed from the outside network.

Getting ready

As the external Networks have a special behavior associated with them, only users with an administrative role can create them. Besides the standard input such as the Network name and so on, it is important to identify the IP address range to be used for the external Network. This recipe assumes that the L3 agent on the Network node has been configured with the correct bridge information for the External Network access.

How to do it...

The following steps will show you how to create an external Network using Horizon:

1. Log in to the OpenStack Horizon dashboard using a user ID with an administrative role.
2. In the left navigation menu, navigate to **Admin | System | Networks**.

3. Click on the **+ Create Network** button to display the following **Create Network** screen for administrators:

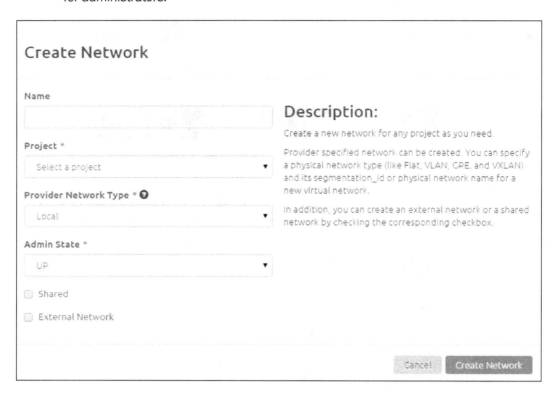

4. Enter a name for the Network. Select a project to assign the Network to a specific tenant.

5. Select **Provider Network Type** as desired. For this recipe, we will choose **Flat** networks as **Provider Network Type**. Once you choose **Flat** as the Network type, the screen will prompt you to provide more details, as shown in the following screenshot:

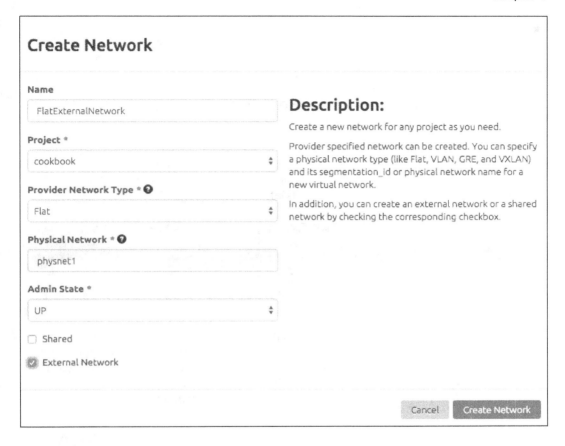

6. Enter `physnet1` as the value for **Physical Network**. This was the alias used when configuring the Flat Network as the type driver in the previous recipe.

7. Check the **External Network** checkbox.

8. Now click on **Create Network**. Once the network creation has succeeded, the network will show in the list.

9. The next important step is to create a Subnet for the newly created external Network.

How it works...

As described Earlier, external Networks are used in cases where the VM instances need an outside network access. External Networks can be used directly to attach the instances, and in this case, their behavior is the same as any other Network. However, the main use case for an External Network is in conjunction with the OpenStack router. We will describe this in detail in *Chapter 6, Using Routing Services in Neutron*.

In either situation, an important element needs to be kept in mind. While creating a Subnet for an External Network, the Gateway IP needs to be carefully selected. This is because this IP address is already configured on the physical routers that will provide Internet access. Therefore, we cannot let OpenStack choose a Gateway IP arbitrarily.

Setting up a simple web application – an introduction

Now that we have seen several scenarios to create Networks and instantiate the VMs, let's take a practical example and apply this knowledge.

In this 3-recipe series, you will learn how to use the OpenStack Networking capabilities to create a simple web application. In the first recipe, we will just introduce the components of the web application and desired network connectivity. The next two recipes will show you how to implement this using OpenStack. For simplicity, we will not focus on the exact software running in the VMs. We will just name the VMs as per our requirement.

Getting ready

A simple web application consists of a database and web application server. While both the database and web server are capable of being executed on the same server, for a good scale and performance, it is better to keep them on different servers.

The following image depicts the networking connections between the VMs in our web application. The **DB-VM** runs the database engine and **Web-VM** runs the web server:

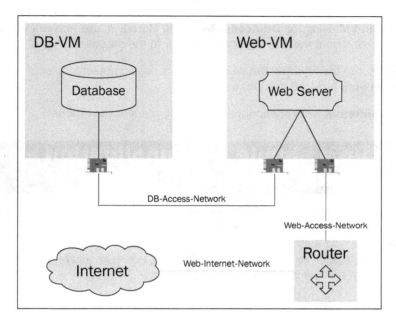

How to do it...

The following steps will show you what kind of OpenStack networks need to be set up in order to accomplish this:

1. We will create a tenant Network for the Web Server to the Database connection called **DB-Access-Network**. The important thing for this Network will be to limit the number of IP addresses in the Subnet.

2. Next, we will create another tenant network for the **Web Server** to the **Router** called **Web-Access-Network**. Once again, we will limit the number of IP addresses in the Subnet.

3. The last network will be an External Network called **Web-Internet-Network** to provide Internet access to the Web Server.

How it works...

The database stores critical information. So, the network access to the **DB-VM** is available only from the **Web-VM** using the **DB-Access-Network**. Moreover, this network will also carry the database queries from the web application server to the database engine.

In order to connect to the Internet, the Web Server needs to connect to a local router. The **Web-Access-Network** provides this connectivity.

Finally, the **Web-Internet-Network** connects the local router to the Internet.

Setting up a simple web application – setting up OpenStack Networks

The previous recipe defined the different types of networks that we need to create in order to set up our web application. This recipe shows you the specific steps that are required to create the Networks and Subnets. We will refer to the earlier recipes about the Network and Subnet creation instead of going through it step by step. However, this recipe will highlight the important steps that are specific for the web application.

Getting ready

We will need to create three networks to connect the database, web application server, and Internet. The following steps assume that the Linux bridge is the mechanism driver and VLAN is the type driver configured in Neutron. This is important as the step to create an External Network requires the type of Network.

For this recipe, we will use the following information to create the networks:

Network name	Subnet name	Network address range	Allocation pools
DB-Access-Network	DB-Access-Subnet	192.168.20.0/29	192.168.20.2,192.168.20.4
Web-Access-Network	Web-Access-Subnet	192.168.30.0/29	192.168.30.2,192.168.30.4
Web-Internet-Network	Web-Internet-Subnet	10.10.1.0/24	10.10.1.1,10.10.1.2

We will also need the Gateway IP address for the external Network.

How to do it...

The following steps will show you how to create the three networks required for the web application:

1. Follow the steps mentioned in the recipe titled *Creating a Subnet and Network using Horizon* in *Chapter 1, Getting Started with OpenStack Networking*. Use the Network name, Subnet name, and Network address from the preceding table for DB-Access-Network.

2. Before clicking on the **Create** button to create the Network, enter `192.168.20.2,192.168.20.4` in the **Allocation Pools** field, as shown in the following screenshot. Note that there should not be any space after the comma:

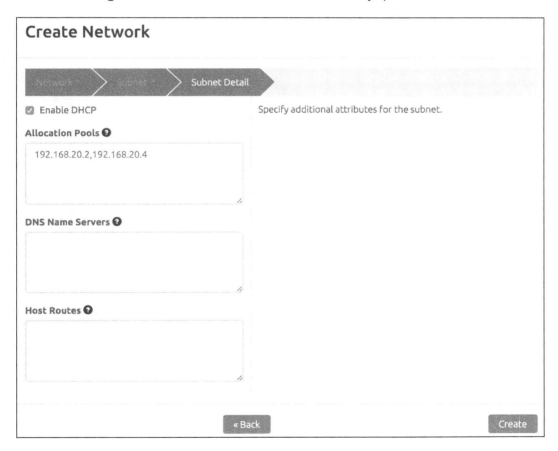

3. Click on the **Create** button to create DB-Access-Network.

4. Repeat these steps for Web-Access-Network. Once again, use the information in the preceding table.

5. The next step is to create the external Network called Web-Internet-Network. As this is an external Network, you will need administrative privileges.

6. Follow the steps mentioned in the recipe titled *Creating External Networks using Horizon* in this chapter. Ensure that the Project is the same as that of the previous two Networks.

7. The next step after the creation of Web-Internet-Network is to add the Subnet. For this, click on the name of the network to view the details. Then, click on **+ Create Subnet** as shown here:

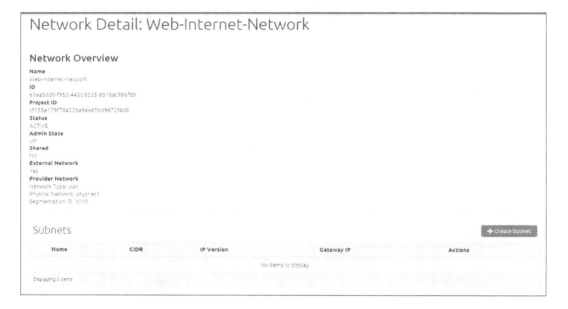

8. Enter **Subnet Name**, **Network Address**, and **Gateway IP** for the Subnet, as shown in the following screenshot. Then click on **Next**:

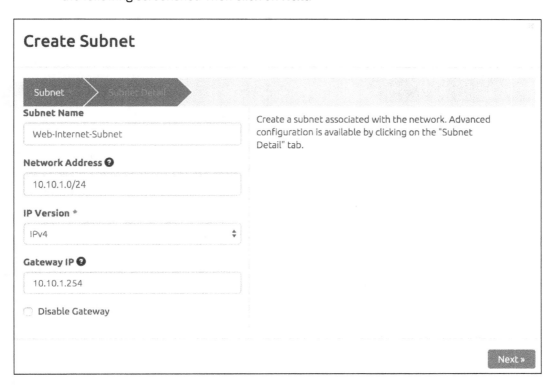

9. In the **Subnet Detail** section, enter **Allocation Pools** as shown here and click on **Create**:

These steps should result in three networks being shown when you select **Project |
Network | Networks**, as follows:

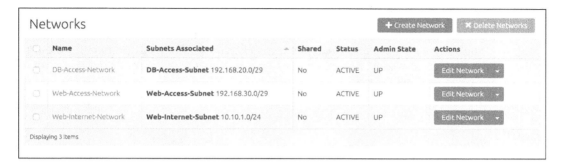

As mentioned earlier, the External Networks are used in conjunction with the OpenStack
routers. After the creation of the three networks, the next step is to create an OpenStack
router. We need to associate Web-Access-Subnet as an interface on this router and use Web-
Internet-Network as the gateway for this router. This will enable Internet access for the web
application server. The sixth chapter will cover the steps in detail.

How it works...

As a specific tenant creates the web application, he also creates the two tenant networks,
namely DB-Access-Network and Web-Access-Network. Access to the Internet is controlled and
hence, the administrator creates the external Network called Web-Internet-Network on behalf
of the tenant. Thus, the tenant effectively has all the three networks made available to him.

Setting up a simple web application – creating instances

With all the networks created, the final step is to create the two instances. The main step
during an instance creation is to choose the correct Network for each of the VMs.

Getting ready

You will require the appropriate OS images for the Database VM as well as the Web VM.

How to do it...

The following steps will show you how to create the two VM instances for the web application:

1. Create an instance called DB-VM by following the steps of the recipe titled *Associating a Network to an instance using Horizon* in *Chapter 1, Getting Started with OpenStack Networking*. Ensure that **DB-Access-Network** is chosen in the **Selected networks** field, as follows:

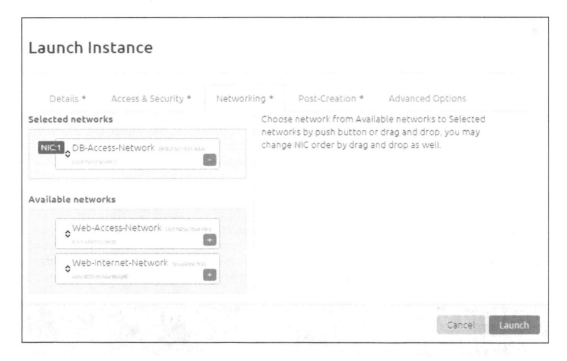

2. Create another instance called `Web-VM` by following the steps of the recipe titled *Associating a Network to an instance using Horizon* in *Chapter 1, Getting Started with OpenStack Networking*. Ensure that both **DB-Access-Network** and **Web-Access-Network** are chosen in the **Selected networks** field, as shown in the following screenshot:

3. Once the instances are active, the instances list will look as follows:

These steps complete the setting up of the web application using two VMs and three OpenStack Networks.

How it works...

DB-VM and **Web-VM** will exchange the database-related messages over **DB-Access-Network**. The web traffic from and to the Internet will travel over **Web-Access-Network** and **Web-Internet-Network**.

4

Exploring Overlay Networks with Neutron

In this chapter, we will cover the following recipes:

- ▶ Configuring Neutron to use a VXLAN type driver
- ▶ Configuring a VNI Range for VXLAN Networks
- ▶ Viewing a VNI assigned to a Neutron Network
- ▶ Creating a Network with a specific VNI
- ▶ Viewing the virtual interface information on the compute node for VXLAN tunnels
- ▶ Viewing the virtual interface information on the network node for VXLAN tunnels
- ▶ Configuring Neutron to use a GRE type driver
- ▶ Viewing a virtual interface on the compute node for GRE tunnels

Introduction

The OpenStack Neutron provides you with various ways to implement virtual networks in order to connect the virtual machine instances started by tenants. At a broad level, these network types can be classified in two categories—networks based on VLANs and networks based on overlays or tunnels.

In the case of overlay networks, the virtual switch on the Hypervisor encapsulates the data packets from the VM in an IP packet and sends it to the destination Hypervisor. The virtual switch on the destination Hypervisor then de-encapsulates and delivers the data packet to the destination VM instance. The encapsulation process adds an identifier or a tunnel key to mark and identify the packets belonging to different virtual networks.

The OpenStack Neutron provides two ways to implement the overlay or tunnel-based virtual networks, namely VXLAN and GRE. In this chapter, we will see how to implement virtual networks using overlays and the ML2 plugin in Neutron.

In order to implement these recipes, we will be using the following OpenStack setup with two nodes, one acting as the controller and network node and another as the compute node:

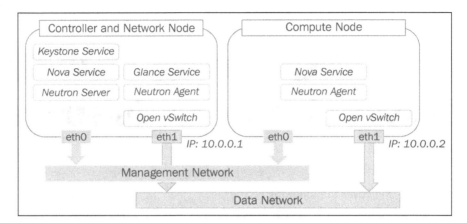

Configuring Neutron to use a VXLAN type driver

Virtual eXtensible LAN (**VXLAN**) is one of the overlaying drivers supported by the Neutron ML2 plugin. The process of tunneling involves encapsulating the data packets from the VM in a UDP packet. The VXLAN encapsulation process adds a special key called **Virtual Network Identifier** (**VNI**) in order to identify the network to which the data packet belongs.

The OVS instance on the Hypervisor is responsible for encapsulating the data packets coming out of the VM. The Neutron ML2 plugin provides the OVS instance with all the information that is required to implement a virtual network using VXLAN. For example, the plugin provides information such as the VNI and IP address for the **Virtual Tunnel End Point** (**VTEP**) to the OVS instance. The VTEP IPs on the source and destination compute or network node are used while encapsulating the VXLAN packet.

Getting ready

For this recipe, you will need the following information:

▶ The SSH login credentials for the OpenStack nodes
▶ The VTEP IP to be used for the node

How to do it...

The following steps will show you how to configure Neutron to use a VXLAN type driver:

1. With the appropriate credentials, SSH into the node where the Neutron server is running. In our setup, it will be the controller and network node.

2. Open the Neutron ML2 plugin configuration file using your desired editor. For example, the command for the vi editor will be as follows:

   ```
   openstack@controller:~$ sudo vi /etc/neutron/plugins/ml2/ml2_conf.
   ini
   ```

3. In the [ml2] section of the file, configure VXLAN as type_driver and tenant_ network_type:

   ```
   [ml2]

   ...

   type_drivers = vxlan

   tenant_network_types = vxlan

   mechanism_drivers = openvswitch
   ```

4. In the [ovs] section, set local_ip to the VTEP IP address. OVS uses this IP to carry all the tunneled traffic. In our setup, the VTEP IP for the controller node is 10.0.0.1:

   ```
   [ovs]

   local_ip = 10.0.0.1
   ```

5. In the [agent] section, set tunnel_types to vxlan:

   ```
   [agent]

   tunnel_types = vxlan
   ```

6. Restart the Neutron server and Open vSwitch Agent on the controller and network node of our setup using the following commands:

   ```
   openstack@controller:~$ sudo service neutron-server restart

   openstack@controller:~$ sudo service neutron-plugin-openvswitch-
   agent restart
   ```

7. The first five steps have to be repeated for all the compute and network nodes. Remember to update local_ip on the compute nodes with the correct value. Restart the OVS agent on the compute and network nodes:

   ```
   openstack@controller:~$ sudo service neutron-plugin-openvswitch-
   agent restart
   ```

How it works...

In this recipe, we configured the Neutron ML2 plugin to create virtual networks with a VXLAN type. We also configured Neutron to use Open vSwitch to implement the virtual network.

The Neutron OVS L2 agent is responsible for configuring the local OVS instance on the compute and network nodes. The L2 agent runs as a daemon on the compute and network nodes. This daemon communicates with the Neutron server using **Remote Procedure Call** (**RPC**) to get the details of the virtual networks, as shown in the following image:

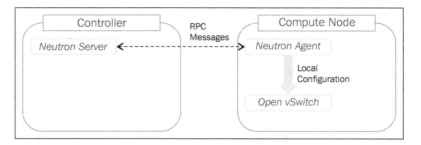

OVS encapsulates the data packets from the VM using an outer UDP and IP packet. The outer IP packet uses the IP address configured as `local_ip` in the Neutron configuration file.

There's more...

Due to the encapsulation of the Layer 2 (L2) data packet in a Layer 3 (L3) packet, the size of the network packet increases. Hence, you may need to adjust the MTU settings on the underlying physical network.

Configuring a VNI Range for VXLAN Networks

In this recipe, we will see how to configure Neutron with the ML2 plugin in order to use a **VXLAN Network Identifier** (**VNI**) range. The ML2 plugin allows the customization of the range of VNI numbers in order to uniquely identify the virtual networks. VXLAN can support up to 16 million unique VNIs.

Getting ready

For this recipe, you will need the following information:

► The SSH login credentials for the OpenStack controller node

► The VNI range to configure for the VXLAN-based virtual networks

How to do it...

The following steps will show you how to configure the VNI range for the ML2 plugin:

1. With the appropriate credentials, SSH into the node where the Neutron server is running. In our setup, it will be the controller and network node.

2. Open the Neutron ML2 plugin configuration file using your desired editor. For example, the command for the vi editor will be as follows:

    ```
    openstack@controller:~$ sudo vi /etc/neutron/plugins/ml2/ml2_conf.ini
    ```

    In the `[ml2_type_vxlan]` section of the file, set `vni_ranges` to the appropriate range list. Multiple ranges can be provided using comma-separated values:

    ```
    [ml2_type_vxlan]
    vni_ranges = 1001:2000,3001:4000,5001:6000
    ```

3. Finally, restart the Neutron server on the controller node using the following command:

    ```
    openstack@controller:~$ sudo service neutron-server restart
    ```

How it works...

In this recipe, we configured the ML2 plugin in order to use the given range of VNIs while creating virtual networks based on VXLAN tunnels. When Neutron receives a request to create a virtual network, it allocates a VNI from this range to create the VXLAN-based virtual network. A range is described with the lower value and higher value separated by `:`.

Viewing a VNI assigned to a Neutron Network

In this recipe, we will see how to view the VNI assigned to a VXLAN-based virtual network. Knowing the VNI that is assigned to a virtual network is very useful to troubleshoot communication problems between the VMs or other network services.

Getting ready

For this recipe, you will need the following information:

▶ The SSH login credentials for the node where the Neutron client packages are installed

▶ A shell RC file that initializes the environment variables for CLI

How to do it...

The following steps will show you how you can view the VNI using the OpenStack CLI:

1. Log in to a node with access to OpenStack.

2. Source your RC file to set up access credentials as an administrator.

3. You can view all the Networks created using the `neutron net-list` command:

```
openstack@controller:~$ neutron net-list -c id -c name
+--------------------------------------+---------+
| id                                   | name    |
+--------------------------------------+---------+
| 0048b37d-916b-4aeb-b95a-9630d270cf85 | private |
| d6288489-bc92-4345-8b99-a5a5bade9f5f | public  |
+--------------------------------------+---------+
```

4. Use the `neutron net-show` command to view further details for any network. In case the Network name is not unique, use its ID instead of the name:

```
openstack@controller:~$ neutron net-show public
+---------------------------+--------------------------------------+
| Field                     | Value                                |
+---------------------------+--------------------------------------+
| admin_state_up            | True                                 |
| id                        | d6288489-bc92-4345-8b99-a5a5bade9f5f |
| name                      | public                               |
| provider:network_type     | vxlan                                |
| provider:physical_network |                                      |
| provider:segmentation_id  | 1002                                 |
| router:external           | True                                 |
| shared                    | False                                |
| status                    | ACTIVE                               |
| subnets                   | 6d23f27c-4805-47cf-a3e2-dc43cc8f0990 |
| tenant_id                 | 25135f04f33941abaf2f5d545a716b2c     |
+---------------------------+--------------------------------------+
```

We can also achieve the same using Horizon. The steps are as follows:

1. Log in to Horizon as an administrative user.

2. In the left navigation menu, navigate to **Admin | Networks**. This will list all the available virtual networks as shown in the following screenshot:

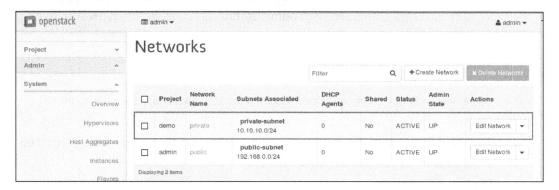

3. Click on the Network name for the network that you want to view:

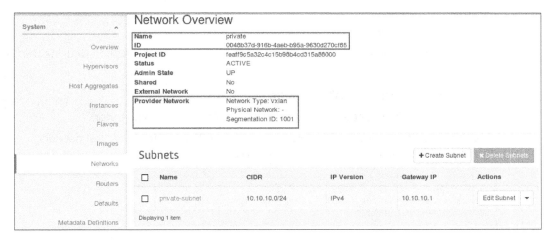

4. This will open the network overview screen for the selected Network, which shows details such as **Network Type**, **Segmentation ID**, and so on.

How it works...

When the Neutron server receives a request to create a virtual network, it automatically allocates a VNI from the configured VNI range to use with the newly created virtual network. In this recipe, we looked at the ways to find the VNI associated with a virtual network.

Creating a Network with a specific VNI

In this recipe, we will see how to create a VXLAN-based virtual network using a specific VNI. Normally, Neutron would automatically allocate a VNI for a VXLAN-based virtual network from the range of available VNIs, but there are situations when users need a network with a specific VNI. In such cases, an OpenStack administrator can create a virtual network with a manually assigned VNI.

Getting ready

For this recipe, you will need to access OpenStack as an administrator. You will also need the following information:

▶ The SSH login credentials for the node where the Neutron client packages are installed

▶ An administrative level access to OpenStack

▶ The Network name

▶ A VNI for the virtual network

How to do it...

The following steps will show you how to create a virtual network with a specific VNI using the OpenStack CLI:

1. Log in to a node with access to OpenStack.

2. Source your RC file to set up the access credentials as an administrator.

3. Use the following `neutron net-create` command to create the virtual network with a specific VNI, for example, using VNI 1010:

```
openstack@controller:~$ neutron net-create --provider:network_type=vxlan\
--provider:segmentation_id=1010 Chapter4_VXLAN_with_VNI
Created a new network:
+---------------------------+--------------------------------------+
| Field                     | Value                                |
+---------------------------+--------------------------------------+
| admin_state_up            | True                                 |
| id                        | 2fad8b41-77a2-4049-951c-7bfbbfb6a4f7 |
| name                      | Chapter4_VXLAN_with_VNI              |
| provider:network_type     | vxlan                                |
| provider:physical_network |                                      |
| provider:segmentation_id  | 1010                                 |
| router:external           | False                                |
| shared                    | False                                |
| status                    | ACTIVE                               |
| subnets                   |                                      |
| tenant_id                 | feaff9c5a32c4c15b98b4cd315a88000     |
+---------------------------+--------------------------------------+
```

We can also achieve the same result using a Horizon interface in the following way:

1. Log in to Horizon as an administrative user.

2. Navigate to **Admin | Networks**.

3. Click on **+ Create Network** and provide the desired **Name. Provider Network Type** should be set to **VXLAN** and **Segmentation ID** should be set to the required VNI:

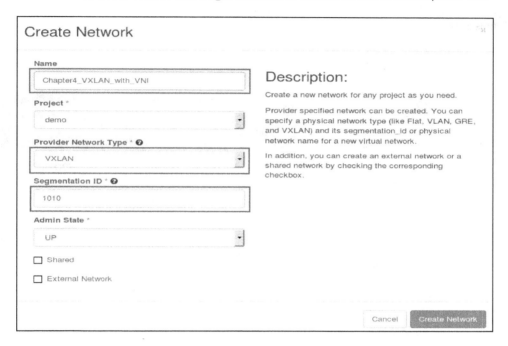

4. Click on **Create Network**. This should create the virtual network with the provided VNI. Once it has been created, verify the network details by navigating to the **Admin | Network Name** link for the newly created virtual network:

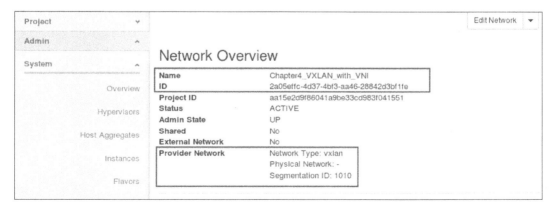

5. This will open the **Network Overview** screen for the selected network, which shows details such as **Network Type**, **Segmentation ID**, and so on.

How it works...

In this recipe, we looked at creating a virtual network with a specific VNI. This procedure overrides the automatic allocation of a VNI for a virtual network and requires administrative access.

An unused VNI in the range configured as a part of the VXLAN type driver should be used to create the virtual network.

Viewing the virtual interface information on the compute node for VXLAN tunnels

When a tenant launches a VM and attaches it to a virtual network, a virtual network interface is created on the compute node, which connects the VM to the OVS instance.

In this recipe, we will identify the virtual network interface, which attaches a VM to the OVS instance on the VXLAN network.

We will also look at the OVS configuration, which makes the communication between the VM and other members on the virtual network possible.

Getting ready

For this recipe, you should have the following information:

▸ The SSH login credentials for the node where the Neutron client packages are installed

▸ User-level access to OpenStack

▸ The name of the VM for which you want to identify the virtual interface

How to do it...

The following steps will show you how to identify an interface connecting a VM to a virtual network:

1. Log in to a node with access to OpenStack.

2. Import the OpenStack RC file to set up the user-level access credentials.

3. Use the `nova list` commands to identify the VM instance, virtual network, and IP associated with it. In this case, the VM is `vm1` with an IP of `20.20.20.2` on the `Chapter4_VXLAN_with_VNI` virtual network, as shown in the following screenshot:

```
openstack@controller:~$ nova list
+--------------------------------------+------+--------+------------+-------------+-----------------------------------+
| ID                                   | Name | Status | Task State | Power State | Networks                          |
+--------------------------------------+------+--------+------------+-------------+-----------------------------------+
| fea2267c-8b90-467d-9f42-bf8017a30dee | vm1  | ACTIVE | -          | Running     | Chapter4_VXLAN_with_VNI=20.20.20.2 |
+--------------------------------------+------+--------+------------+-------------+-----------------------------------+
```

4. Next, we will use the `neutron port-list` command to find the port ID for the virtual interface associated with this VM, based on the VM IP that we determined in the previous step:

```
openstack@controller:~$ neutron port-list |grep 20.20.20.2| cut -f2 -d" "
2d538755-d5f9-49a6-9088-8f07d3e98875
```

5. Now, we will log in to the compute node and check out the OVS configuration.

6. We can use the `ovs-vsctl show` command to look at the ports created on the OVS instance. The OVS port name is composed of a part of the Neutron Port ID. In the following listing, `qvo2d538755-d5` is the port corresponding to our virtual interface ID of `2d538755-d5f9-49a6-9088-8f07d3e98875`. It is connected to the `br-int` bridge and is configured with `tag: 1` to mark all the packets entering this interface with VLAN 1:

```
openstack@compute1:~$ sudo ovs-vsctl show
0f159554-44fe-4003-b2d1-e6f0281edbdc
    Bridge br-int
        fail mode: secure
        Port "qvo2d538755-d5"
            tag: 1
            Interface "qvo2d538755-d5"
        Port br-int
            Interface br-int
                type: internal
        Port patch-tun
            Interface patch-tun
                type: patch
                options: {peer=patch-int}
```

7. Next, we will look at the flow configuration on OVS on the `br-tun` bridge, which sends the packets to the other Hypervisors through the VXLAN tunnels using the `ovs-ofctl dump-flow br-tun` command:

```
openstack@compute1:~$ sudo ovs-ofctl dump-flows br-tun
NXST_FLOW reply (xid=0x4):
 cookie=0x0, duration=3340.706s, table=0, n_packets=109, n_bytes=6867,
idle_age=2948, priority=1,in_port=1 actions=resubmit(,2)
 cookie=0x0, duration=3339.526s, table=0, n_packets=17, n_bytes=1958,
idle_age=2948, priority=1,in_port=2 actions=resubmit(,4)
 cookie=0x0, duration=3340.636s, table=0, n_packets=5, n_bytes=390,
idle_age=3332, priority=0 actions=drop
 cookie=0x0, duration=3340.569s, table=2, n_packets=12, n_bytes=1042,
idle_age=2948, priority=0,dl_dst=00:00:00:00:00:00/01:00:00:00:00:00
actions=resubmit(,20)
 cookie=0x0, duration=3340.502s, table=2, n_packets=97, n_bytes=5825,
idle_age=2962, priority=0,dl_dst=01:00:00:00:00:00/01:00:00:00:00:00
actions=resubmit(,22)
 cookie=0x0, duration=3340.435s, table=3, n_packets=0, n_bytes=0,
idle_age=3340, priority=0 actions=drop
 cookie=0x0, duration=3109.941s, table=4, n_packets=17, n_bytes=1958,
idle_age=2948, priority=1,tun_id=0x3f2 actions=mod_vlan_vid:1,resubmit
(,10)
 cookie=0x0, duration=3340.368s, table=4, n_packets=0, n_bytes=0,
idle_age=3340, priority=0 actions=drop
 cookie=0x0, duration=3340.301s, table=10, n_packets=17, n_bytes=1958,
idle_age=2948, priority=1 actions=learn
(table=20,hard_timeout=300,priority=1,NXM_OF_VLAN_TCI
[0..11],NXM_OF_ETH_DST[]=NXM_OF_ETH_SRC[],load:0->NXM_OF_VLAN_TCI
[],load:NXM_NX_TUN_ID[]->NXM_NX_TUN_ID[],output:NXM_OF_IN_PORT
[]),output:1
 cookie=0x0, duration=3340.234s, table=20, n_packets=0, n_bytes=0,
idle_age=3340, priority=0 actions=resubmit(,22)
 cookie=0x0, duration=3110.008s, table=22, n_packets=85, n_bytes=4628,
idle_age=2962, dl_vlan=1 actions=strip_vlan,set_tunnel:0x3f2,output:2
 cookie=0x0, duration=3340.167s, table=22, n_packets=12, n_bytes=1197,
idle_age=3110, priority=0 actions=drop
```

8. In the highlighted section of the output, we can see that the configuration strips the local VLAN 1 from the packets going out of the compute node and adds a tunnel key (VNI), `0x3f2`. The VNI of `0x3f2` is the hexadecimal equivalent of 1010, which was used to create the OpenStack network.

How it works...

When a VM is launched, OpenStack creates a virtual interface and attaches it to the OVS instance on the Hypervisor through a Linux bridge. For this discussion, we will focus on the OVS connectivity. The OVS instance on the Hypervisor has two bridges, `br-int` for communication in the Hypervisor and `br-tun`, which is used to communicate with the other Hypervisors using the VXLAN tunnels. Let's have a look at the following screenshot:

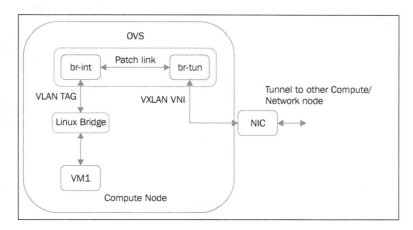

The OVS bridge, `br-int`, uses VLANs to segregate the traffic in the Hypervisors. These VLANs are locally significant to the Hypervisor. Neutron allocates a unique VNI for every virtual network. For any packet leaving the Hypervisor, OVS replaces the VLAN tag with the VNI in the encapsulation header. OVS uses `local_ip` from the plugin configuration as the source VTEP IP for the VXLAN packet.

Viewing the virtual interface information on the network node for VXLAN tunnels

The network node hosts network services such as DHCP, DNS, and so on for each virtual network. These services need to communicate with the other members on the virtual network. The network node runs an OVS instance to connect to the virtual network.

In this recipe, we will look at the DHCP service running on the Network node and identify the virtual network interface, which connects this service to the virtual network.

Getting ready

For this recipe, you will need the following information:

▶   The SSH login credentials for the controller and network node

How to do it...

The following steps will show you how to identify an interface connecting a network service to the virtual network. In this recipe, we will look at the network interface for the DHCP service:

1. Log in to a node with access to OpenStack.

2. Next, we will find the DHCP server process that is associated with our virtual network. OpenStack uses `dnsmasq` to provide the following DNS and DHCP services on the virtual network:

```
openstack@controller:~$ ps aux|grep dnsmasq|grep 2fad8b41-77a2-4049-951c-7bfbbfb6a4f7
nobody    26450  0.0  0.0  28204  1040 ?        S    00:07   0:00 dnsmasq --no-hosts
--no-resolv --strict-order --bind-interfaces --interface=tap32a8ae83-27 --except-interface=lo
--pid-file=/opt/stack/data/neutron/dhcp/2fad8b41-77a2-4049-951c-7bfbbfb6a4f7/pid
--dhcp-hostsfile=/opt/stack/data/neutron/dhcp/2fad8b41-77a2-4049-951c-7bfbbfb6a4f7/host
--addn-hosts=/opt/stack/data/neutron/dhcp/2fad8b41-77a2-4049-951c-7bfbbfb6a4f7/addn_hosts
--dhcp-optsfile=/opt/stack/data/neutron/dhcp/2fad8b41-77a2-4049-951c-7bfbbfb6a4f7/opts
--leasefile-ro --dhcp-authoritative --dhcp-range=set:tag0,20.20.20.0,static,86400s
--dhcp-lease-max=256 --conf-file= --domain=openstacklocal
```

3. From the previous step, we find that the `dnsmasq` process is bound to a virtual interface, `tap32a8ae83-27`. We can now look at the OVS configuration in order to identify the virtual interface port:

```
openstack@controller:~$ sudo ovs-vsctl show
0f159554-44fe-4003-b2d1-e6f0281edbdc
    Bridge br-int
        fail_mode: secure
        Port "qr-3458162c-e5"
            tag: 1
            Interface "qr-3458162c-e5"
                type: internal
        Port patch-tun
            Interface patch-tun
                type: patch
                options: {peer=patch-int}
        Port "tap32a8ae83-27"
            tag: 2
            Interface "tap32a8ae83-27"
                type: internal
        Port br-int
            Interface br-int
                type: internal
```

4. From the OVS configuration, we can see that the virtual network interface, `tap32a8ae83-27`, is connected to `br-int` and configured with `tag: 2` to tag all the incoming packets from the DHCP server with VLAN 2.

5. Next, we will look at the flow configuration on OVS on the `br-tun` bridge, which sends the packets to the other Hypervisors through the VXLAN tunnels using the `ovs-ofctl dump-flow br-tun` command:

```
openstack@controller:~$ sudo ovs-ofctl dump-flows br-tun
NXST_FLOW reply (xid=0x4):
 cookie=0x0, duration=35681.277s, table=0, n_packets=38, n_bytes=3676,
idle_age=31287, priority=1,in_port=1 actions=resubmit(,2)
 cookie=0x0, duration=31677.968s, table=0, n_packets=91, n_bytes=5150,
idle_age=31287, priority=1,in_port=2 actions=resubmit(,4)
 cookie=0x0, duration=35681.202s, table=0, n_packets=0, n_bytes=0,
idle_age=35681, priority=0 actions=drop
 cookie=0x0, duration=35681.128s, table=2, n_packets=15, n_bytes=1818,
idle_age=31287, priority=0,dl_dst=00:00:00:00:00:00/01:00:00:00:00:00
actions=resubmit(,20)
 cookie=0x0, duration=35681.059s, table=2, n_packets=23, n_bytes=1858,
idle_age=31441, priority=0,dl_dst=01:00:00:00:00:00/01:00:00:00:00:00
actions=resubmit(,22)
 cookie=0x0, duration=35680.991s, table=3, n_packets=0, n_bytes=0,
idle_age=35680, priority=0 actions=drop
 cookie=0x0, duration=35665.028s, table=4, n_packets=0, n_bytes=0,
idle_age=35665, priority=1,tun_id=0x3e9 actions=mod_vlan_vid:1,resubmit
(,10)
 cookie=0x0, duration=31449.234s, table=4, n_packets=91, n_bytes=5150,
idle_age=31287, priority=1,tun_id=0x3f2 actions=mod_vlan_vid:2,resubmit
(,10)
 cookie=0x0, duration=35680.922s, table=4, n_packets=0, n_bytes=0,
idle_age=35680, priority=0 actions=drop
 cookie=0x0, duration=35680.853s, table=10, n_packets=91, n_bytes=5150,
idle_age=31287, priority=1 actions=learn
(table=20,hard_timeout=300,priority=1,NXM_OF_VLAN_TCI
[0..11],NXM_OF_ETH_DST[]=NXM_OF_ETH_SRC[],load:0->NXM_OF_VLAN_TCI
[],load:NXM_NX_TUN_ID[]->NXM_NX_TUN_ID[],output:NXM_OF_IN_PORT
[]),output:1
 cookie=0x0, duration=35680.782s, table=20, n_packets=0, n_bytes=0,
idle_age=35680, priority=0 actions=resubmit(,22)
 cookie=0x0, duration=31449.306s, table=22, n_packets=2, n_bytes=140,
idle_age=31441, dl_vlan=2 actions=strip_vlan,set_tunnel:0x3f2,output:2
 cookie=0x0, duration=31677.895s, table=22, n_packets=0, n_bytes=0,
idle_age=31677, dl_vlan=1 actions=strip_vlan,set_tunnel:0x3e9,output:2
 cookie=0x0, duration=35680.709s, table=22, n_packets=21, n_bytes=1718,
idle_age=31449, priority=0 actions=drop
```

6. From the flow configuration, we can see that when the packet is sent out through the VXLAN tunnel, OVS strips the local VLAN tag and instead uses a tunnel ID to identify the virtual network.

How it works...

Network services such as the DHCP server are started for each virtual network as soon as the first VM that is attached to the virtual network is launched. To provide the DHCP service, the DHCP agent node attaches a dnsmasq process to a virtual network interface attached to an OVS instance running on the network node. The OVS instance uses two bridges, br-int and br-tun, as described in the previous recipe, to connect the network service to the virtual network.

Configuring Neutron to use a GRE type driver

As described earlier, tunneled networks can also be implemented using the **Generic Routing Encapsulation** (**GRE**) protocol. GRE is a general-purpose point-to-point encapsulation protocol. The GRE header contains a 32-bit *key* which is used to identify a flow or virtual network in a tunnel.

This recipe shows you how to configure the OpenStack Neutron in order to use GRE for virtual networking.

Getting ready

For this recipe, we will need the following information:

- ▶ An SSH-based access to the OpenStack controller node
- ▶ The IP address for the tunnel endpoint
- ▶ A range of tunnel IDs

How to do it...

The following steps will show you how to configure the GRE type driver for the ML2 plugin:

1. With the appropriate credentials, SSH into the node where the Neutron server is running. In our setup, it will be the controller and network node.

2. Open the Neutron ML2 plugin configuration file using your desired editor. For example, the command for the vi editor will be as follows:

   ```
   openstack@controller:~$ sudo vi /etc/neutron/plugins/ml2/ml2_conf.ini
   ```

3. In the [ml2] section of the file, configure GRE as the type driver and tenant network type:

   ```
   [ml2]

   ...

   type_drivers = gre
   ```

```
tenant_network_types = gre

mechanism_drivers = openvswitch
```

4. In the `[ml2_type_gre]` section, update `tunnel_id_range` to the range of the tunnel IDs that can be used for the virtual networks:

    ```
    [ml2_type_gre]

    tunnel_id_ranges = 1:1000
    ```

5. In the `[ovs]` section, set `local_ip` to the IP address of the network card that you want to use in order to carry the tenant data traffic:

    ```
    [ovs]

    local_ip = 10.0.0.1
    ```

6. In the `[agent]` section, set `tunnel_types` to `gre`:

    ```
    [agent]

    tunnel_types = gre
    ```

7. Restart the Neutron and Open vSwitch Agent on the controller and network node of our setup using the following commands:

    ```
    openstack@controller:~$ sudo service neutron-server restart

    openstack@controller:~$ sudo service openvswitch-switch restart

    openstack@controller:~$ sudo service neutron-plugin-openvswitch-
    agent restart
    ```

8. Repeat the first six steps for the compute node.

9. Restart the Neutron OVS L2 agent on the compute node:

    ```
    openstack@controller:~$ sudo service neutron-plugin-openvswitch-
    agent restart
    ```

How it works...

In this recipe, we configured the ML2 plugin to create virtual networks with the GRE tunnels.

The Neutron OVS L2 agent runs as a daemon on each Compute and Network node and is responsible for configuring the OVS instance for the GRE-based virtual network on the local Hypervisor.

GRE is a general-purpose encapsulation protocol; in comparison, VXLAN was designed keeping in mind the requirements of virtual networking and multitenancy.

Viewing a virtual interface on the compute node for GRE tunnels

This recipe shows you how to identify the virtual network interface used by a VM for a GRE-based virtual network. Viewing the network interface can be useful to troubleshoot the connectivity problems between the VMs and network services.

Getting ready

For this recipe, you will need the following information:

- The SSH login credentials for the node where the Neutron client packages are installed
- User-level access to OpenStack
- The name of the VM for which you want to identify the virtual interface

How to do it...

1. Log in to a node with access to OpenStack.
2. Import the OpenStack RC file to set up the user-level access credentials.
3. Use the `nova list` commands to identify the VM instance, virtual network, and IP associated with it. In this case, the VM is `vm1` with an IP of `20.20.20.2` on the `Chapter4_GRE` virtual network:

```
openstack@controller:~$ nova list
+--------------------------------------+------+--------+------------+-------------+-------------------------+
| ID                                   | Name | Status | Task State | Power State | Networks                |
+--------------------------------------+------+--------+------------+-------------+-------------------------+
| 225861c2-992f-4e52-93a3-cb53f593feea | vm1  | ACTIVE | -          | Running     | Chapter4_GRE=20.20.20.2 |
+--------------------------------------+------+--------+------------+-------------+-------------------------+
```

4. Next, we will use the `neutron port-list` command to find the port ID for the virtual interface that is associated with this VM, based on the VM IP that we determined in the previous step:

```
openstack@controller:~$ neutron port-list |grep 20.20.20.2| cut -f2 -d" "
d0edf043-5928-4a99-aaba-c24248238aed
```

5. We will now log in to the compute node and check out the OVS configuration.

6. We can use the `ovs-vsctl show` command to look at the ports created on the OVS instance. The OVS instance has two bridges, `br-int` to communicate with the VMs on this Hypervisor and `br-tun` to send the tunnel traffic to the other Hypervisors. In the following listing, `qvod0edf043-59` is the port corresponding to our virtual interface ID of `d0edf043-5928-4a99-aaba-c24248238aed` and is configured with `tag: 1` in order to mark all the packets entering this interface with VLAN 1:

```
openstack@compute1:~/devstack$ sudo ovs-vsctl show
0f159554-44fe-4003-b2d1-e6f0281edbdc
    Bridge br-tun
        Port "gre-0a000001"
            Interface "gre-0a000001"
                type: gre
                options: {df_default="true", in_key=
        Port br-tun
            Interface br-tun
                type: internal
        Port patch-int
            Interface patch-int
                type: patch
                options: {peer=patch-tun}
    Bridge br-int
        fail_mode: secure
        Port br-int
            Interface br-int
                type: internal
        Port patch-tun
            Interface patch-tun
                type: patch
                options: {peer=patch-int}
        Port "qvod0edf043-59"
            tag: 1
            Interface "qvod0edf043-59"
    ovs version: "2.0.2 "
```

7. Next, we will look at the flow configuration on OVS on the `br-tun` bridge, which sends the packets to the other Hypervisors through the VXLAN tunnels using the `ovs-ofctl dump-flow br-tun` command:

```
openstack@compute1:~/devstack$ sudo ovs-ofctl dump-flows br-tun
NXST_FLOW reply (xid=0x4):
 cookie=0x0, duration=125.858s, table=0, n_packets=5, n_bytes=964,
idle_age=32, priority=1,in_port=3 actions=resubmit(,3)
 cookie=0x0, duration=127.13s, table=0, n_packets=48, n_bytes=3627,
idle_age=0, priority=1,in_port=2 actions=resubmit(,2)
 cookie=0x0, duration=127.054s, table=0, n_packets=0, n_bytes=0,
idle_age=127, priority=0 actions=drop
 cookie=0x0, duration=126.983s, table=2, n_packets=0, n_bytes=0,
idle_age=126, priority=0,dl_dst=00:00:00:00:00:00/01:00:00:00:00:00
actions=resubmit(,20)
 cookie=0x0, duration=126.911s, table=2, n_packets=48, n_bytes=3627,
idle_age=0, priority=0,dl_dst=01:00:00:00:00:00/01:00:00:00:00:00
actions=resubmit(,22)
 cookie=0x0, duration=90.614s, table=3, n_packets=4, n_bytes=874,
idle_age=32, priority=1,tun_id=0x1 actions=mod_vlan_vid:1,resubmit(,10)
 cookie=0x0, duration=126.838s, table=3, n_packets=1, n_bytes=90,
idle_age=91, priority=0 actions=drop
 cookie=0x0, duration=126.765s, table=4, n_packets=0, n_bytes=0,
idle_age=126, priority=0 actions=drop
 cookie=0x0, duration=126.693s, table=10, n_packets=4, n_bytes=874,
idle_age=32, priority=1 actions=learn
(table=20,hard_timeout=300,priority=1,NXM_OF_VLAN_TCI
[0..11],NXM_OF_ETH_DST[]=NXM_OF_ETH_SRC[],load:0->NXM_OF_VLAN_TCI
[],load:NXM_NX_TUN_ID[]->NXM_NX_TUN_ID[],output:NXM_OF_IN_PORT
[]),output:2
 cookie=0x0, duration=88.613s, table=20, n_packets=0, n_bytes=0,
hard_timeout=300, idle_age=88, hard_age=32,
priority=1,vlan_tci=0x0001/0x0fff,dl_dst=fa:16:3e:fe:cc:d3
actions=load:0->NXM_OF_VLAN_TCI[],load:0x1->NXM_NX_TUN_ID[],output:3
 cookie=0x0, duration=126.62s, table=20, n_packets=0, n_bytes=0,
idle_age=126, priority=0 actions=resubmit(,22)
 cookie=0x0, duration=90.686s, table=22, n_packets=35, n_bytes=2308,
idle_age=0, dl_vlan=1 actions=strip_vlan,set_tunnel:0x1,output:3
 cookie=0x0, duration=126.549s, table=22, n_packets=13, n_bytes=1319,
idle_age=90, priority=0 actions=drop
```

8. In the highlighted section of the output, we can see that the configuration strips the local VLAN 1 from the packets going out of the compute node and adds a tunnel key, 0x1. The GRE tunnel key 1 was allocated by Neutron for the Chapter4_GRE network.

How it works...

The OVS configuration for the GRE-based virtual network is similar to those for the VXLAN networks. The OVS instance on the Hypervisor has two bridges, `br-int` for communication in the Hypervisor and `br-tun`, which is used to communicate with the other Hypervisors.

The OVS bridge, `br-int`, uses VLANs to segregate the traffic in the Hypervisors. These VLANs are locally significant to the Hypervisor.

OVS connects to the other Hypervisors using `br-tun` using GRE tunnels. It replaces the VLAN for any packet destined to a different Hypervisor with a GRE header, which contains a unique tunnel key that is allocated by the Neutron server for each virtual network.

5
Managing IP Addresses in Neutron

We have seen that Subnet is a part of the core functionality in OpenStack Networking. The Subnet entity drives the IP address assignment and DHCP servers for the virtual machine instances. In this chapter, we will share the following recipes that will cover the IP address management capabilities in Neutron:

- ▶ Creating an instance with a specific IP address
- ▶ Configuring multiple IP addresses for a virtual interface
- ▶ Creating a redundant DHCP server per OpenStack Network
- ▶ Starting the DHCP server on a specific network node
- ▶ Increasing the number of IP addresses in a Network using the Horizon dashboard

Introduction

The DHCP servers and IP address management go hand in hand. The DHCP servers run on the network nodes in OpenStack. In order to implement the recipes, you will need an OpenStack setup, as shown here:

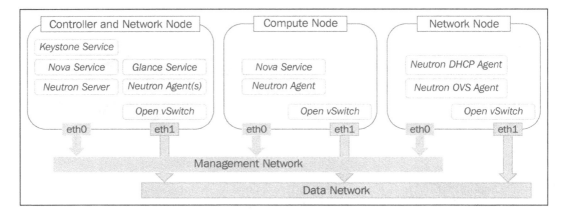

This setup has one **Compute Node**, one dedicated **Network Node**, and one node for the controller and networking services. Some of the recipes require redundant network nodes in order to run redundant DHCP services. Therefore, a single all-in-one setup will not be sufficient.

As mentioned earlier, a Subnet is part of the core services in the OpenStack Neutron. All the recipes of this chapter assume that ML2 is the core plugin in the Neutron configuration file. The recipes also assume that OVS is configured as the mechanism driver and VLAN is configured as the type driver as a part of the ML2 configuration.

Creating an instance with a specific IP address

The VM instances are typically used to host IT applications. Some applications require that a particular VM server should have a specific, fixed IP address. When DHCP is enabled, the virtual machine gets an IP address dynamically. This recipe shows you how we can assign a specific IP address to an instance.

Getting ready

A VM with a specific IP address can only be created using the OpenStack CLI. It involves a Port creation followed by an instance creation. As a prerequisite, ensure that a Network is created with the following attributes:

- Network name: **Cookbook-Network-5**
- Subnet name: **Cookbook-Subnet-5**
- Subnet IP address range: **20.20.20.0/28**

How to do it...

The following steps will show you how to create a VM instance with a specific IP address:

1. Using the appropriate credentials, SSH into the OpenStack node where the Neutron client software packages are installed.

2. Source the shell RC file to initialize the environment variables required for the CLI commands.

3. The command to create a Port is `neutron port-create`, as follows:

   ```
   openstack@controller:~$ neutron port-create \
   --name PortWithSpecificIP \
   --fixed-ip subnet_id=f03d74b1-fc69-49c1-bda798c53ecbd183,ip_
   address=20.20.20.5 Cookbook-Network-5
   ```

4. In the preceding command, we used the UUID of the Subnet and assigned `20.20.20.5` as the IP address for the Port. You can confirm that this port uses the specific IP address using the `neutron port-list` command:

```
openstack@controller:~$ neutron port-list -F id -F name -F fixed_ips
+--------------------------------------+--------------------+-----------------------------------------------------------------------------------------+
| id                                   | name               | fixed_ips                                                                               |
+--------------------------------------+--------------------+-----------------------------------------------------------------------------------------+
| 8a4656ba-8b21-4f62-a741-80bc0137fd18 |                    | {"subnet_id": "f03d74b1-fc69-49c1-bda7-98c53ecbd183", "ip_address": "20.20.20.2"} |
| 9badd396-e95b-4c80-b6d2-c0140c186f91 | PortWithSpecificIP | {"subnet_id": "f03d74b1-fc69-49c1-bda7-98c53ecbd183", "ip_address": "20.20.20.5"} |
+--------------------------------------+--------------------+-----------------------------------------------------------------------------------------+
openstack@controller:~$
```

5. The CLI command to create an instance is `nova boot`. This command supports an argument called `--nic` that allows us to specify a Port ID that we want to associate with the instance:

   ```
   openstack@controller:~$ nova boot --flavor m1.tiny \
   --image cirros-0.3.3-x86_64 \
   --nic port-id=9badd396-e95b-4c80-b6d2-c0140c186f91 CLIPortVM
   ```

6. Once the `nova boot` command is successful, the instance will also be visible in the Horizon dashboard.

7. Log in to the Horizon dashboard and navigate to **Project | Network | Network Topology**. In the **Network Topology**, move the mouse pointer over the icon representing the instance and click on **Open Console**, as shown in the following screenshot:

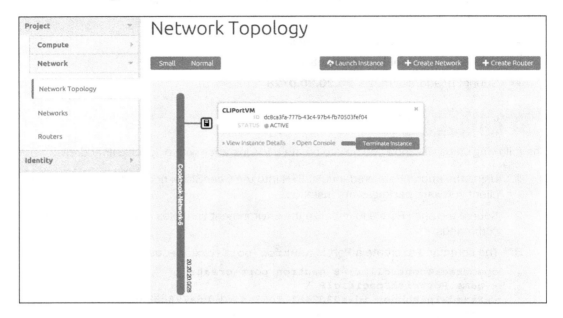

8. In the resulting window, log in to the instance. In our example, we will be using the CirrOS default username and password for the login.

9. At the shell prompt of the instance, type `ifconfig eth0`. This command will show the virtual interface for this instance. You can see that the IP address for this virtual interface (eth0) matches that of the Port that we used in the `nova boot` command:

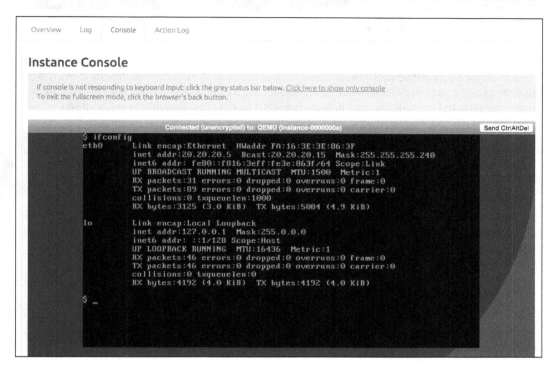

These steps showed you how to create a VM instance with a fixed IP address.

How it works...

When a Network is created, a DHCP port is automatically created. However, the ports associated with the VM instances are created as and when the instances are created using Horizon, but the Neutron CLI allows Ports to be created independent of an instance. The CLI also allows users to boot an instance using an existing port. In this recipe, we first created a Port and specified the IP address that it will use. This IP address must be in the range of the Subnet and must be unassigned. Once the Port is successfully created, we use the Port ID to boot an instance using the Nova CLI. This step ensures that the instance uses the specific IP address for the virtual interface.

Configuring multiple IP addresses for a virtual interface

IP aliasing is a concept where multiple IP addresses are assigned to the same physical network interface. IP aliasing is useful in several scenarios. When multiple small applications running on different servers need to be consolidated into a single large server, the individual IP address for each application needs to be mapped to the same physical interface. As the physical servers get virtualized, there is a need to support IP aliasing for the virtual machine instances also. In Linux, IP aliasing is accomplished by creating subinterfaces on a real interface.

In this recipe, we will see how multiple IP addresses can be allotted to a single virtual interface.

Getting ready

The different IP addresses for the same virtual interface can be a part of the same Subnet or two different Subnets. However, OpenStack does not allow a virtual interface to be associated with two different networks. Therefore, the different Subnets should be a part of the same OpenStack Network.

How to do it...

The following steps will show you how to configure multiple IP addresses for a single virtual interface:

1. Follow the steps mentioned in the recipe titled *Creating a Subnet and Network using Horizon* in *Chapter 1, Getting Started with OpenStack Networking*. Use `Cookbook-Network-5` as the Network name, `Cookbook-Subnet-1` as the Subnet name, and `20.20.20.0/28` as the Network address range:

2. Open the drop-down menu under the **Actions** column and click on **Add Subnet**:

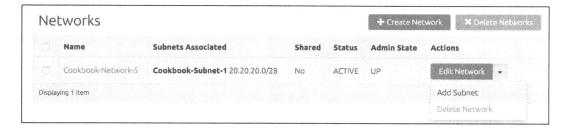

3. Using a Subnet name as `Cookbook-Subnet-2` and a Network address range of `30.30.30.0/28`, create the second Subnet on the same network:

4. Using the appropriate credentials, SSH into the OpenStack node where the Neutron client software packages are installed.

5. Source the shell RC file to initialize the environment variables required for the CLI commands.

6. Create a Port using the `neutron port-create` CLI, as follows:

```
openstack@controller:~$ neutron port-create --name PortWithTwoIP --fixed-ip subnet_id=f7cd93e1-9870-4e1b-b02e-41d9742535d0,
ip_address=20.20.20.8 --fixed-ip subnet_id=e1270169-0063-4603-956b-38e5276ff9cc,ip_address=30.30.30.8 Cookbook-Network-5
Created a new port:
+-----------------------+--------------------------------------------------------------------------------+
| Field                 | Value                                                                          |
+-----------------------+--------------------------------------------------------------------------------+
| admin_state_up        | True                                                                           |
| allowed_address_pairs |                                                                                |
| binding:vnic_type     | normal                                                                         |
| device_id             |                                                                                |
| device_owner          |                                                                                |
| fixed_ips             | {"subnet_id": "f7cd93e1-9870-4e1b-b02e-41d9742535d0", "ip_address": "20.20.20.8"} |
|                       | {"subnet_id": "e1270169-0063-4603-956b-38e5276ff9cc", "ip_address": "30.30.30.8"} |
| id                    | 9b24a25b-1bb1-4909-8a13-9a829944649e                                           |
| mac_address           | fa:16:3e:51:00:de                                                              |
| name                  | PortWithTwoIP                                                                  |
| network_id            | 4ca7fcf1-1706-4cfa-84fd-a71125587fd2                                           |
| security_groups       | f74fd3c6-7465-420e-94cd-0074ce79110e                                           |
| status                | DOWN                                                                           |
| tenant_id             | 3f1171f34ba64dfc950572141aaf96e5                                               |
+-----------------------+--------------------------------------------------------------------------------+
openstack@controller:~$
```

7. In the preceding command, we specified two fixed IP addresses for the same port (hence, the same virtual interface). Also note that the `neutron port-create` command takes only one Network name as the parameter.

8. As shown in the previous recipe, create a VM instance using the `nova boot` command and specify the previous Port, as follows:

```
openstack@controller:~$ nova boot --flavor m1.tiny \
--image cirros-0.3.3-x86_64 \
--nic port-id=9b24a25b-1bb1-4909-8a13-9a829944649e   CLIPortVM
```

9. Once the VM boots up, you will notice that one of the IP addresses is assigned to the virtual interface. This is the limitation when using a DHCP server. The second IP address needs to be manually assigned to a subinterface on the same virtual interface.

How it works...

A single OpenStack Port maps to a single virtual interface in the VM instance. While the Port has multiple IP addresses, when the instance is booted, only one virtual interface is created and Neutron automatically picks one of the IP addresses and assigns it to the virtual interface. The second IP address has to be manually assigned to a subinterface using the `ifconfig` command. The additional benefit of this recipe is that the allocated IP address is stored on the DHCP server and will not be assigned to any other VM instance.

Creating a redundant DHCP server per OpenStack Network

The DHCP server plays a critical role in the IP address management and initial network connectivity for a VM instance. The DHCP server is enabled via an agent on the network node. As it is a critical component, it is a good idea to have a redundant DHCP server per OpenStack Network. This recipe shows you how to configure Neutron to start more than one DHCP agent for each OpenStack Network.

Getting ready

In order to create more than one DHCP agent for each OpenStack Network, we will need to update a setting in the Neutron configuration file.

How to do it...

The following steps will show you how to configure multiple DHCP agents per OpenStack Network:

1. With the appropriate credentials, SSH into the node where the Neutron server is running. In our setup, it will be the Controller and Network node.

2. Open the Neutron configuration file using your desired editor. For example, the command for the vi editor will be as follows:

   openstack@controller:~$ sudo vi /etc/neutron/neutron.conf

3. In the [DEFAULT] section of the file, configure the number of DHCP agents per Network:

   ```
   [ml2]
   . . .
   dhcp_agents_per_network = 2
   ```

4. The previous step configured two DHCP agents per OpenStack network.

How it works...

When the first VM instance is created on a Network, Neutron creates the DHCP agents for the network. The number of the DHCP servers for a Network is based on the configuration file setting. If more than one DHCP agent is required for every Network, then Neutron will create the DHCP agents across the various Network nodes available in the OpenStack setup.

Starting the DHCP server on a specific network node

OpenStack allows multiple Network nodes in a setup. By default, only one DHCP agent (or server) is associated per Network. In case there are multiple Network nodes, the Neutron server automatically schedules a DHCP agent for each Network. However, there could be situations when a particular Network requires a DHCP agent on a specific Network node. For example, for a Network with critical VMs, the user may request for the DHCP server to run on a more responsive Network node.

Getting ready

We will use the Horizon dashboard to show you how to ensure that the DHCP server for a given Network is started on a specific network node. This recipe requires a setup with two Network nodes as shown in the beginning of this chapter.

We will use the Network named `Cookbook-Network-5` for this recipe.

How to do it...

The following steps will show you how to add an additional DHCP agent to an existing Network:

1. Log in to the OpenStack Horizon dashboard using a user ID with an administrative role.

2. Navigate to **Admin** | **System** | **Network** to view the list of Networks:

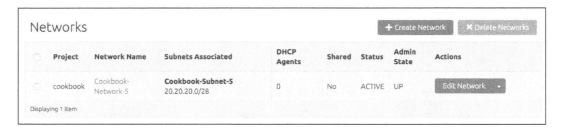

3. As no instances have been created, you will notice that the number of DHCP agents is 0.

4. Click on the name of the Network—**Cookbook-Network-5** in this case.

5. The **Network Detail** page includes information such as **Subnets**, **Ports**, and **DHCP Agents**, as shown in the following screenshot:

6. Click on the **Add DHCP Agent** button and select the Host that will run the DHCP agent. For this recipe, we will choose the **networknode** of our setup in order to run the DHCP agent:

7. Once the DHCP agent is successfully added to the Network, you will notice that a new DHCP port (representing the DHCP server) has now been created for the Network:

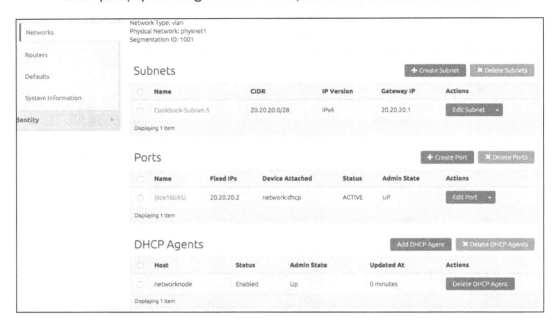

The preceding steps showed you how to start the DHCP agent on a specific network node.

How it works...

The OpenStack Neutron automatically chooses a DHCP agent in order to create a DHCP port. This step happens internally when the first VM instance is created on a Network. The DHCP agent on the first registered network node is selected. The DHCP agent then proceeds to create the DHCP server (dnsmasq) as part of the DHCP Port creation. This recipe shows you how administrative users can force the DHCP agent on a specific network node to be used for a Network.

There's more...

This selection of a specific network node to run the DHCP server can also be performed using the Neutron CLI. The Neutron CLI command, `neutron dhcp-agent-network-add`, can be used for this purpose.

Increasing the number of IP addresses in a Network using the Horizon dashboard

We have seen that, as a part of the Network creation, the user also creates a Subnet, which is essentially an IP address range. Consider a situation where a user creates a Subnet with a set of IP addresses. Once all the IP addresses of this Subnet are assigned to instances, any new instance created will not get an appropriate network connectivity. To increase the IP addresses in the same Network, the user will have to create another Subnet on the same Network. This recipe will show you how to do this.

Getting ready

To create another Subnet, the inputs that you will need are as follows:

- A range of IP addresses
- A name for the Subnet

How to do it...

The following steps will show you how to add another Subnet to a Network:

1. Log in to the OpenStack Horizon dashboard using the appropriate credentials.
2. In the left navigation menu, click on **Project**, then **Network | Networks**.
3. Now, click on the drop-down icon (triangle) next to the **Edit Network** button for the Network to which you want to add another Subnet:

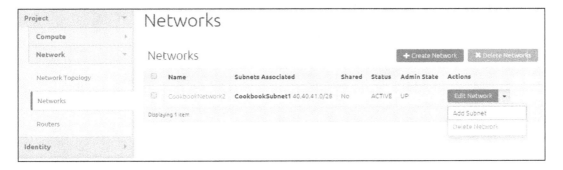

4. Now, clicking on the **Add Subnet** option will show you a window, as follows:

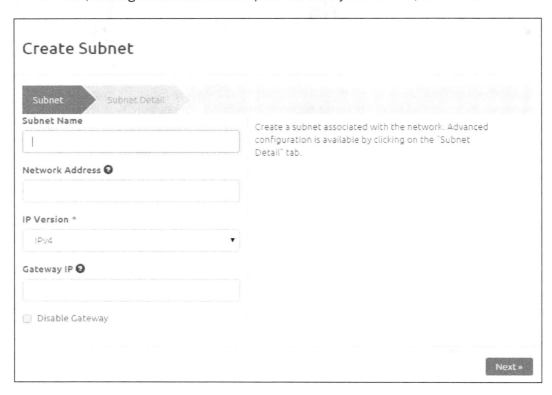

5. Enter the **Subnet Name** and **Network Address** (IP range in a CIDR format) and click on **Next**. Then click on **Create**.

6. You can see that the Network now has a second Subnet (IP range) associated with it.

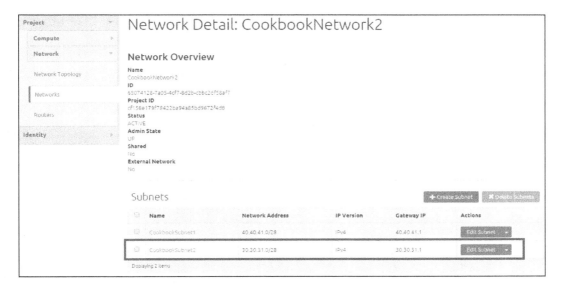

This recipe showed you how to add multiple Subnets to a particular Network. This flexibility to add more IP addresses helps in cases where more VMs are created than initially planned.

How it works...

Neutron supports the multiple Subnets to be associated with each Network but such Subnets cannot have overlapping IP addresses. Using multiple Subnets, more instances can be part of a single Network. However, communication between the instances is limited to the instances that have an IP address in the same Subnet. In order for the instances across a Subnet to communicate, a Neutron router will be required.

Using the Horizon dashboard, users can choose a Network only during the instance creation. Neutron will automatically assign the instance to the first Subnet in the Network. CLI allows users to force an instance onto a particular Subnet.

6
Using Routing Services in Neutron

The first five chapters focused on the OpenStack Networking capabilities available as part of a Network. Now, we will delve deeper into OpenStack Networking and discuss the following recipes related to IP Routing:

- ▶ Configuring Neutron for Routing services
- ▶ Creating a Router using the Horizon dashboard and Neutron CLI
- ▶ Enabling instances on different Networks to communicate
- ▶ Allowing the Virtual Machine instances to access the Internet
- ▶ Providing access to a virtual machine from an external Network or the Internet using Horizon
- ▶ Creating and deleting a floating IP address using the Neutron CLI
- ▶ Associating a floating IP address to a virtual machine using the Neutron CLI

Introduction

We saw that the Network provides tenants with an isolated Layer 2 domain in which virtual machines can communicate with one another. However, in real-life deployment, you will find many scenarios where two or more networks need to communicate with each other. This connectivity between virtual machines across two different Layer 2 Networks is accomplished using a Router. The Router object in OpenStack provides VMs with Layer 3-based IP Routing services.

The OpenStack default Router runs on the Network nodes in OpenStack. In order to implement the recipes, you will need an OpenStack setup as described in the following figure:

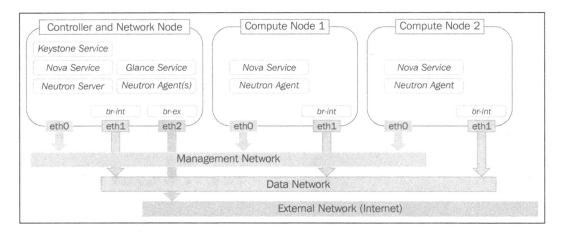

This setup has two compute nodes and one node for the controller and networking services. For this chapter, you can also use a setup with just one compute node. Compared to the earlier chapters, this setup has an additional Network called **External Network**. This Network allows the Network node to carry traffic from the VM instances to an external Network and vice versa.

Configuring Neutron for Routing services

As mentioned earlier, the OpenStack Networking functionalities can be classified as core and service. Routing or L3 networking is part of the service functionality and Neutron needs to be configured in order to support it.

Getting ready

We will configure the Neutron server as well as the Neutron L3 agent in order to enable the Routing functionality in OpenStack. For this chapter, we will assume that the Neutron ML2 plugin has been configured to use VLAN as the type driver and Open vSwitch as the mechanism driver.

How to do it...

The following steps will show you how to configure Neutron to provide Routing services in OpenStack:

1. With the appropriate credentials, SSH into the node where the Neutron server is running. In our setup, it will be the Controller and Network Node.

2. Open the `neutron.conf configuration` file using your desired editor.
    For example, the command for the vi editor will be as follows:

    openstack@controller:~$ sudo vi /etc/neutron/neutron.conf

3. In the `[DEFAULT]` section of the file, configure router as the service plugin
    for Neutron:

    ```
    [DEFAULT]
    ...
    service_plugins = router
    ```

4. Open the `l3_agent.ini` file using your desired editor. For example, the command
    for the vi editor will be as follows:

    openstack@controller:~$ sudo vi /etc/neutron/l3_agent.ini

5. As we are using Open vSwitch as the mechanism driver, in the `[DEFAULT]` section
    of the file, we will configure `interface_driver` accordingly:

    ```
    [DEFAULT]
    ...
    interface_driver =
        neutron.agent.linux.interface.OVSInterfaceDriver
    ```

6. The final step is to configure `external_network_bridge` in the `l3_agent.ini`
    file:

    ```
    [DEFAULT]
    ...
    external_network_bridge = br-ex
    ```

How it works...

Once router is added to the list of service plugins in the Neutron configuration file, the support
for Router is enabled in OpenStack. You will see that the Horizon dashboard now has an
option called **Router** when you navigate to **Project | Network**.

The external Network bridge name is important when using the Open vSwitch mechanism
driver. For a Linux bridge, the corresponding bridge is created automatically. This bridge
is bound to the Ethernet interface that allows the traffic to be routed to networks that are
external to OpenStack.

Creating a Router using the Horizon dashboard and Neutron CLI

Once OpenStack is configured in order to support the Routing services, the next step is to create a Router. Similar to a Network, Subnet, and Port, a Router is a logical entity that is used by Neutron to provide connectivity between two different OpenStack Networks or Subnets.

In this recipe, we will see how to create a Router using the Horizon dashboard and Neutron CLI.

Getting ready

The only information required to create a Router is the name of the Router.

How to do it...

The following steps will show you how to create a Router in OpenStack:

1. Log in to the OpenStack Horizon dashboard using the appropriate credentials.
2. In the left navigation menu, navigate to **Projects** | **Network** | **Router**.

3. Now click on **+ Create Router**. In the resulting screen, enter the **Router Name** and click on the **Create Router** button:

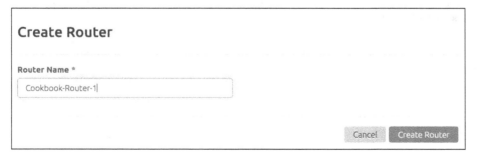

4. The newly created Router should now appear in the **Routers** table:

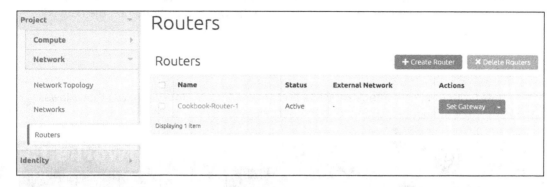

5. We will now create another Router named `Cookbook-Router-2` using the Neutron CLI. The command to create a Router using CLI is `neutron router-create`. If the command was successful, it should show you the following output:

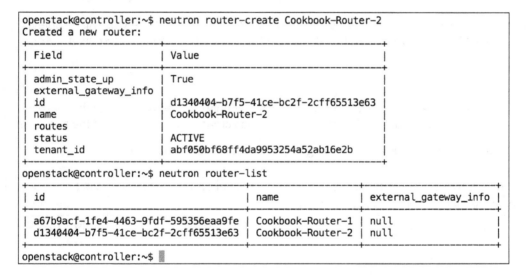

```
openstack@controller:~$ neutron router-create Cookbook-Router-2
Created a new router:
+---------------------+--------------------------------------+
| Field               | Value                                |
+---------------------+--------------------------------------+
| admin_state_up      | True                                 |
| external_gateway_info |                                    |
| id                  | d1340404-b7f5-41ce-bc2f-2cff65513e63 |
| name                | Cookbook-Router-2                    |
| routes              |                                      |
| status              | ACTIVE                               |
| tenant_id           | abf050bf68ff4da9953254a52ab16e2b     |
+---------------------+--------------------------------------+
openstack@controller:~$ neutron router-list
+--------------------------------------+-------------------+----------------------+
| id                                   | name              | external_gateway_info |
+--------------------------------------+-------------------+----------------------+
| a67b9acf-1fe4-4463-9fdf-595356eaa9fe | Cookbook-Router-1 | null                 |
| d1340404-b7f5-41ce-bc2f-2cff65513e63 | Cookbook-Router-2 | null                 |
+--------------------------------------+-------------------+----------------------+
openstack@controller:~$ 
```

6. You can delete this Router using the `neutron router-delete` command by specifying the Router name.

How it works...

As mentioned earlier, an OpenStack Router is the entity that represents Layer 3 IP Routing in OpenStack. A Router needs to be associated with subnetworks in order to provide a Routing functionality between these subnetworks.

OpenStack supports IP Routing using the Linux namespaces and iptables on the network node. This is a centralized model for Routing where the VM traffic that needs to go out of a Network is first sent to the network node and then the OpenStack Router on the network node routes it further.

There's more...

In the newer releases, OpenStack supports **Distributed Virtual Routing** (**DVR**) that allows each Hypervisor to support routing for a better scale and performance.

Enabling instances on different Networks to communicate

In order to make use of the OpenStack IP Routing capabilities, a Router needs to be associated with the desired subnetworks. Once this step is completed, the data traffic from one VM in a Subnet will be able to communicate with another VM in another Subnet.

This recipe shows you how to associate subnetworks to a Router. While VMs will be able to communicate with one another, the VMs will not yet have access to the Internet.

Getting ready

First, we will create two Networks and a Router and then we will associate the two Networks (or the corresponding Subnet) to the Router. We will also create one VM in each of the Networks.

For this recipe, we will use the following information to create the Networks:

Network Name	Subnet Name	Network Address Range	VM Instance
Cookbook-Network-1	Cookbook-Subnet-1	20.20.20.0/28	Network-1-VM
Cookbook-Network-2	Cookbook-Subnet-2	30.30.30.0/28	Network-2-VM

How to do it...

The following steps will show you how to create two Networks and one Router and then associate them together:

1. Follow the steps mentioned in the recipe titled *Creating a Subnet and Network using the Horizon* in *Chapter 1, Getting Started with OpenStack Networking*. Use the Network Name, Subnet Name, and Network Address from the preceding table for `Cookbook-Network-1`.

2. Repeat the previous steps for `Cookbook-Network-2`. Once again, use the information in the table. You should see a list of Networks as follows:

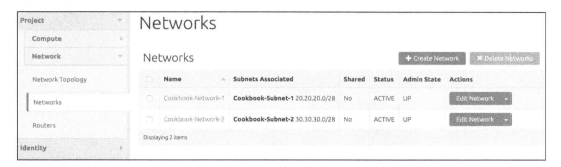

3. Create an instance called `Network-1-VM` by following the steps of the recipe titled *Associating a Network to an instance using Horizon* in *Chapter 1, Getting Started with OpenStack Networking*. Ensure that **Cookbook-Network-1** is chosen in the Selected networks field.

4. Create an instance called `Network-2-VM` by following the steps of the recipe titled *Associating a Network to an instance using Horizon* in *Chapter 1, Getting Started with OpenStack Networking*. Ensure that **Cookbook-Network-2** is chosen in the Selected networks field.

5. At this stage, you should see a list of instances, as follows:

6. Note that the two instances cannot ping each other as yet.

7. The next step is to create a Router called `Cookbook-Router-1`. Follow the steps mentioned in the recipe titled *Creating a Router using the Horizon dashboard and Neutron CLI* earlier in this chapter.

8. Click on the name of the Router to view the details of the Router:

9. To associate the Networks to the Router, click on **+ Add Interface**:

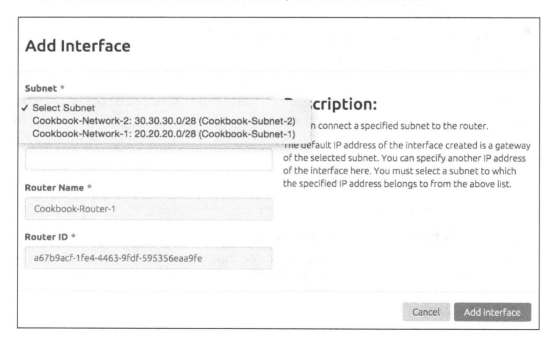

10. Select **Cookbook-Network-1** (and its associated Subnet) and then click on **Add Interface**.

11. Repeat this step to add **Cookbook-Network-2** as the second interface in the Router.

12. Navigate to **Project | Networks | Network Topology**. Here, you will see that the two Networks are now connected via the Router:

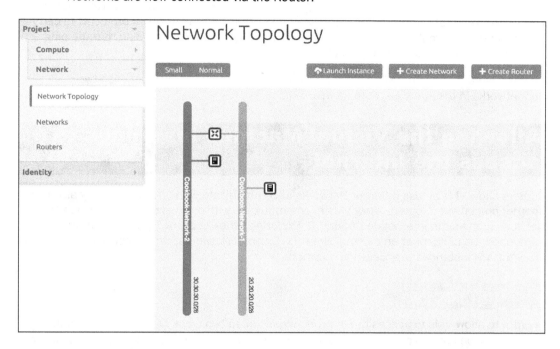

13. At this stage, both the Networks are connected to each other via the Router. You can now execute the `ping` command from one VM to another. You will notice that the `ping` command succeeds. Note that you may have to check the security group settings in order to ensure that ICMP (ping) traffic is allowed.

How it works...

When a VM is created on a Network, we know that OpenStack creates a namespace with a prefix of `qdhcp`. Similarly, when the first interface is added to the Router, Neutron (using the L3 agent) creates a namespace with a prefix of `qrouter`. You can view these namespaces using the `ip netns` command on the Network node.

The `qrouter` namespace represents the OpenStack Router. You can run the `ifconfig` command in the namespace and see that the Router has one interface on each of the Networks. The IP address assigned to these Router interfaces will be added as the default gateway on the respective VMs. This is how the Router provides an IP Routing service between the two Networks.

There's more...

In case you use VXLAN as the overlay Network technology, then ensure that the TCP Maximum Transmission Unit (MTU) settings are configured appropriately on the DHCP server (dnsmasq). This will ensure that the VM instances have enough space for the Network protocols to carry all the header information. Without a proper MTU configuration, you may find that the ping commands between the VMs might fail.

Another useful thing to note is that Routers can be used to route traffic between two Subnetworks in the same Network as well.

Allowing the Virtual Machine instances to access the Internet

Routers allow VMs across different Networks to communicate with each other. They also play another crucial role. Routers allow VMs to communicate with entities outside the OpenStack Network such as the Internet. In *Chapter 3, Exploring Other Network Types in Neutron*, we introduced the concept of an external Network. External Networks, when used with a Router, allow the VM instances to access the Internet.

Getting ready

In order to allow VMs to access the Internet, we will need two types of Networks. A tenant Network will be used to create an instance and associate it to a Router. Next, the Router needs to be connected to an External Network that has access to the Internet. Note that an OpenStack user with the administrator's privilege can create the External Network.

This recipe assumes that the OpenStack administrator has followed the steps mentioned in the recipe titled *Creating an External Networks using Horizon* in *Chapter 3, Exploring Other Network Types in Neutron* and created an External Network called `External-Network`.

How to do it...

The following steps will show you how to allow VMs to access the Internet:

1. Follow the steps mentioned in the recipe titled *Creating a Subnet and Network using the Horizon* in *Chapter 1, Getting Started with OpenStack Networking* to create a Network named `Cookbook-Network-1` and a Subnet IP range of `20.20.20.0/24`:

2. Create an instance called `Network-1-VM` by following the steps of the recipe titled *Associating a Network to an instance using Horizon* in *Chapter 1, Getting Started with OpenStack Networking*. Ensure that **Cookbook-Network-1** is chosen in the Selected networks field.

3. The next step is to create a Router called `Cookbook-Router-1`. Follow the steps mentioned in the recipe titled *Creating a Router using the Horizon dashboard and Neutron CLI* earlier in this chapter.

4. As shown in the recipe titled *Enabling instances on different Networks to communicate* in this chapter, add `Cookbook-Network-1` as an interface to `Cookbook-Router-1`.

5. Navigate to **Project | Network | Routers**. Click on **Set Gateway** under the actions column for the Router named `Cookbook-Router-1`:

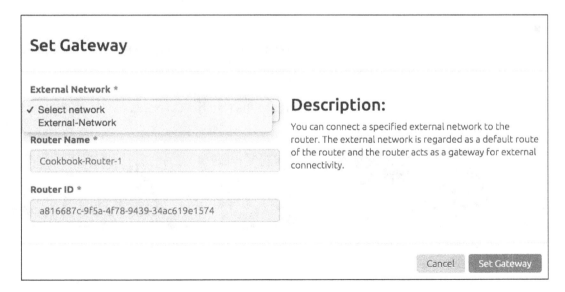

6. In the **Set Gateway** window, select the external Network that the administrator has created for you. Click on the **Set Gateway** button.

7. At this stage, the VM instance, **Network-1-VM**, should be able to communicate with the IP addresses on the external Network Subnet.

How it works...

As discussed in *Chapter 3*, *Exploring Other Network Types in Neutron*, the external network is critical in order to provide you with Internet access. In the External Network, the Subnet IP range plays a crucial role.

We know that a Router connects two Networks. When a Network is added as an interface to a Router, a Router port is created. The gateway IP addresses from the Network are then assigned to this Router port. Similarly, for the second Network, another Router port is created and associated with the gateway IP address of that Network. The OpenStack Router is implemented using the Linux namespaces.

In the case of Internet access, a Router port is created using the External Network and is assigned an IP address from the corresponding Subnet. Neutron uses iptables to configure the SNAT rules for all the traffic trying to access the external network. The Router is then able to provide IP Routing between a VM on a tenant Network to a port on the external Network. This ensures that the VM traffic can reach the Internet while the VMs are not directly accessible from the Internet.

There's more...

This recipe showed you how to perform a Set Gateway operation using the Horizon dashboard. The same can also be accomplished using the OpenStack Neutron CLI. The command to set the gateway using an external Network is `neutron router-gateway-set`.

A user can also clear the gateway using Horizon and the Neutron CLI (`neutron router-gateway-clear`).

Providing access to a Virtual Machine from an external Network or the Internet using Horizon

As mentioned in the previous recipe, Routers along with an external network can be used to provide VMs with access to the Internet. With the External Network set as a gateway on the Router, the VMs can access the Internet from their private IP address. However, the VM cannot be reached from the Internet using the private IP address.

What happens if you are running a web server in your VM? It may be important to allow the users to access the web server from the Internet. OpenStack extends the concept of the Router and external Network and supports the floating IP addresses that can be used to connect to a VM from the Internet.

Getting ready

Similar to the previous recipe, we will need two Networks and a Router to enable Internet access to the VM. This recipe also assumes that the OpenStack administrator has followed the steps mentioned in the recipe titled *Creating an External Networks using Horizon* in *Chapter 3, Exploring Other Network Types in Neutron* and created an External Network called External-Network.

How to do it...

The following steps will show you how to allow a VM to be accessible from the Internet:

1. Follow the steps mentioned in the recipe titled *Creating a Subnet and Network using Horizon* in *Chapter 1, Getting Started with OpenStack Networking* to create a Network named `Cookbook-Network-1` and a Subnet IP range of `20.20.20.0/24`:

2. The next step is to create a Router called `Cookbook-Router-1`. Follow the steps mentioned in the recipe titled *Creating a Router using the Horizon dashboard and Neutron CLI* earlier in this chapter.

3. As shown in the recipe titled *Enabling instances on different Networks to communicate* in this chapter, add `Cookbook-Network-1` as an interface to `Cookbook-Router-1`.

4. As shown in the previous recipe, set the gateway on `Cookbook-Router-1` using the External-Network.

5. Create an instance called `Network-1-VM` by following the steps of the recipe titled *Associating a Network to an instance using Horizon* in *Chapter 1, Getting Started with OpenStack Networking*. Ensure that `Cookbook-Network-1` is chosen in the Selected networks field.

6. In the **Actions** column for the instance, select the **Associate Floating IP** action, as shown in the following screenshot:

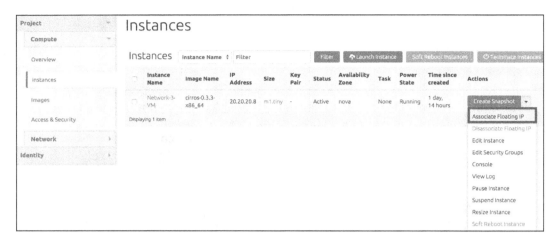

7. In the resulting window, you will need to select a floating **IP Address**. If you did not allocate any floating IP address earlier, the window will say **No floating IP addresses allocated**. Click on the **+** symbol, as follows:

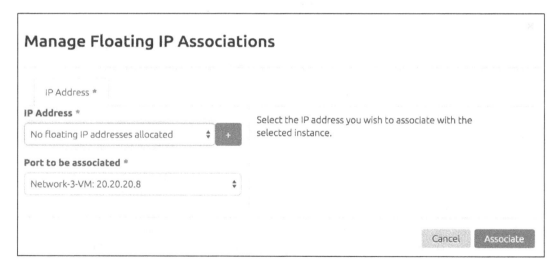

8. Once you click on the **+** symbol, the **Allocate Floating IP** screen will be displayed. This screen will let you choose the appropriate external Network. Select **Pool** and click on **Allocate IP**:

9. You will be taken back to the **Manage Floating IP Associations** screen once again. This time, an IP address will have been selected for the instance. Click on the **Associate** button to complete the assignment of the floating IP to an instance:

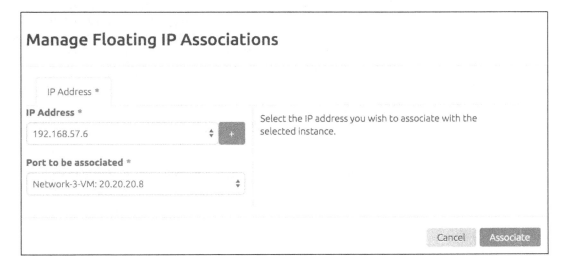

Note that if your instance has multiple virtual network interfaces, you will be able to choose a floating IP address for each virtual interface.

How it works...

We have seen that access to the Internet requires an external network. The Router uses an IP address from the Subnet of the external Network in order to provide an instance with Internet access.

In the same fashion, when we need to access a VM from the Internet, we need an IP address from the External Network Subnet. This mechanism is referred to as assigning a floating IP address to the VM. The **Manage Floating IP Associations** screen shown in this recipe results in an additional IP address being assigned to the VM. Using this additional IP address, we can access the VM from the Internet.

Creating and deleting a floating IP address using the Neutron CLI

As seen in the previous recipe, we first selected an instance in order to create and associate a floating IP. For better planning, it may be required to create a set of floating IP addresses even if instances have not yet been created. We will now show you how a floating IP address can be created and deleted using the Neutron CLI.

Getting ready

As we have seen, floating IP addresses are chosen automatically from the specified external Network. Therefore, you will need the following information to create a Network using CLI:

▶ The name of the external Network—in our case, it will be `External-Network`

▶ The login credentials for SSH to a node where the Neutron client packages are installed

▶ A shell RC file that initializes the environment variables for CLI

How to do it...

1. Using the appropriate credentials, SSH into the OpenStack node where the Neutron client software packages are installed.

2. Source the shell RC file to initialize the environment variables required for the CLI commands, as follows:

   ```
   openstack@controller:~$ source author_openrc.sh
   ```

3. The command to create a floating IP address is `neutron floatingip-create`, as shown here:

```
openstack@controller:~$ neutron floatingip-create External-Network
Created a new floatingip:
+---------------------+--------------------------------------+
| Field               | Value                                |
+---------------------+--------------------------------------+
| fixed_ip_address    |                                      |
| floating_ip_address | 192.168.57.8                         |
| floating_network_id | 22050ae9-4f3e-4ca4-8769-cb59c90be95f |
| id                  | 60abf7ee-8043-484a-924b-bf2073726cab |
| port_id             |                                      |
| router_id           |                                      |
| status              | DOWN                                 |
| tenant_id           | 86f0760ab47945ceae255c5c3842f3cf     |
+---------------------+--------------------------------------+
openstack@controller:~$
```

4. As you can see, the floating IP address of `192.168.57.8` was automatically selected by Neutron.

5. You can view all the floating IP addresses currently in the system by using the `neutron floatingip-list` command:

```
openstack@controller:~$ neutron floatingip-list
+--------------------------------------+------------------+---------------------+---------+
| id                                   | fixed_ip_address | floating_ip_address | port_id |
+--------------------------------------+------------------+---------------------+---------+
| 60abf7ee-8043-484a-924b-bf2073726cab |                  | 192.168.57.8        |         |
| dda3e041-4ac7-4c1d-a322-f57a34a6037c |                  | 192.168.57.6        |         |
+--------------------------------------+------------------+---------------------+---------+
openstack@controller:~$
```

6. You can delete a floating IP address using the `neutron floatingip-delete` command by specifying the ID of the floating IP, as follows:

```
openstack@controller:~$ neutron floatingip-delete 60abf7ee-8043-484a-924b-bf2073726cab
Deleted floatingip: 60abf7ee-8043-484a-924b-bf2073726cab
openstack@controller:~$ neutron floatingip-list
+--------------------------------------+------------------+---------------------+---------+
| id                                   | fixed_ip_address | floating_ip_address | port_id |
+--------------------------------------+------------------+---------------------+---------+
| dda3e041-4ac7-4c1d-a322-f57a34a6037c |                  | 192.168.57.6        |         |
+--------------------------------------+------------------+---------------------+---------+
openstack@controller:~$
```

We have now seen the different CLI commands related to the floating IP addresses.

How it works...

When the `neutron floatingip-create` command is executed, Neutron takes the Subnet information of the specified External Network and automatically selects an IP address to be used as a floating IP address for an instance.

This IP address can then be associated with an instance using the Horizon dashboard as shown in the previous recipe. This IP address can also be used with the Neutron CLI.

There's more...

Users can also create independent floating IP addresses using the Horizon GUI. This is done by selecting **Project** | **Access & Security** | **Floating IPs** on the GUI.

Associating a floating IP address to a virtual machine using the Neutron CLI

We have seen that the Neutron CLI allows users to create a floating IP address independent of the existence of an instance. We will now show you how to associate a floating IP address to an instance using CLI.

Getting ready

For this recipe, you will need to know the virtual interface or the Port of the instance to which you need to bind the floating IP address. You will also need the following information:

 ▶ The login credentials for SSH to a node where the Neutron client packages are installed
 ▶ A shell RC file that initializes the environment variables for CLI

How to do it...

1. Using the appropriate credentials, SSH into the OpenStack node where the Neutron client software packages are installed.
2. Source the shell RC file to initialize the environment variables required for the CLI commands.

3. We will first execute the `neutron port-list` command to identify the ID of the virtual interface port to which the floating IP will be assigned. In our case, we will need to look for a port with an IP address of 20.20.20.9 (which is an internal IP address):

```
openstack@controller:~$ neutron port-list -c id -c fixed_ips
+--------------------------------------+-----------------------------------------------------------------------------------+
| id                                   | fixed_ips                                                                         |
+--------------------------------------+-----------------------------------------------------------------------------------+
| 6871ff7e-6c52-4999-9a03-20dfabf392be | {"subnet_id": "fb5e3a3f-157a-4cba-a9f3-4fbc085e7dd7", "ip_address": "192.168.57.4"} |
| 8d5db5ad-e58b-499a-ae9d-d5d005489344 | {"subnet_id": "f8c7e590-fce5-4307-9af2-6d9b8b11f24f", "ip_address": "20.20.20.9"}  |
| da8f2ea5-5923-4214-905c-133dc89147ca | {"subnet_id": "f8c7e590-fce5-4307-9af2-6d9b8b11f24f", "ip_address": "20.20.20.3"}  |
| ffc23807-791c-4dfd-a143-3cf16b463b34 | {"subnet_id": "f8c7e590-fce5-4307-9af2-6d9b8b11f24f", "ip_address": "20.20.20.1"}  |
+--------------------------------------+-----------------------------------------------------------------------------------+
openstack@controller:~$
```

4. The next step is to identify the ID of the floating IP address. We will use the `neutron floatingip-list` command for this. Note that the selected floating IP does not have any fixed IP address assigned:

```
openstack@controller:~$ neutron floatingip-list
+--------------------------------------+------------------+---------------------+---------+
| id                                   | fixed_ip_address | floating_ip_address | port_id |
+--------------------------------------+------------------+---------------------+---------+
| dda3e041-4ac7-4c1d-a322-f57a34a6037c |                  | 192.168.57.6        |         |
+--------------------------------------+------------------+---------------------+---------+
openstack@controller:~$
```

5. The command to associate a floating IP address to the virtual interface of an instance is `neutron floatingip-associate`, as follows:

```
openstack@controller:~$ neutron floatingip-associate dda3e041-4ac7-4c1d-a322-f57a34a6037c 8d5db5ad-e58b-499a-ae9d-d5d005489344
Associated floating IP dda3e041-4ac7-4c1d-a322-f57a34a6037c
openstack@controller:~$
```

6. Once the command is successful, you can execute the `neutron floatingip-list` command again and verify that the floating IP address has been associated to a fixed (internal) IP address:

```
openstack@controller:~$ neutron floatingip-list
+--------------------------------------+------------------+---------------------+--------------------------------------+
| id                                   | fixed_ip_address | floating_ip_address | port_id                              |
+--------------------------------------+------------------+---------------------+--------------------------------------+
| dda3e041-4ac7-4c1d-a322-f57a34a6037c | 20.20.20.9       | 192.168.57.6        | 8d5db5ad-e58b-499a-ae9d-d5d005489344 |
+--------------------------------------+------------------+---------------------+--------------------------------------+
openstack@controller:~$
```

The preceding steps showed you how to associate a floating IP address to an instance using the Neutron CLI.

How it works...

As discussed earlier, a floating IP address is an IP address from the Subnet of the External Network. A VM instance normally has a fixed (internal) IP address that is a part of the Subnet of the tenant Network. The CLI commands seen in this recipe allow us to associate and disassociate these two IP addresses (fixed and floating) from one another.

There's more...

You can use the `neutron floatingip-disassociate` command to remove the fixed IP to a floating IP mapping.

7
Using Neutron Security and Firewall Services

In this chapter, we will look at the following recipes to create and manage the security rules with Neutron Security Groups and Firewalls:

- ▶ Creating a security group using Horizon
- ▶ Configuring the security group rules using Horizon
- ▶ Creating a security group using CLI
- ▶ Configuring the security group rules using CLI
- ▶ Securing the traffic between instances on the same Network
- ▶ Creating the security group rules to allow web traffic
- ▶ Configuring Neutron for the Firewall service
- ▶ Creating the Firewall rules
- ▶ Creating the Firewall policies
- ▶ Creating a Firewall
- ▶ Viewing and verifying the Firewall rules on the network node

Introduction

The OpenStack Neutron provides a comprehensive set of features to secure access to the network resources. Neutron provides two levels of security restrictions. Security groups control the traffic flow between two ports in a Network by applying security rules on the ports. Firewalls secure the traffic flowing across the Networks by applying security rules on the Router.

To implement these recipes, we will use an OpenStack setup as described in the following image:

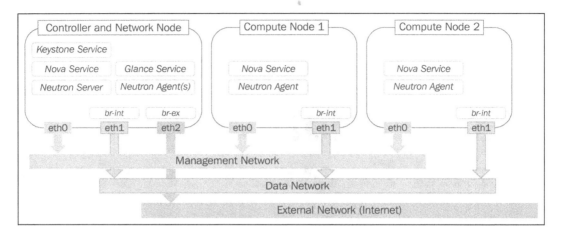

This setup has two compute nodes and one node for the controller and networking services.

Creating a security group using Horizon

Security groups provide you with ways to control the Network traffic between ports in an OpenStack Network. Security group rules are applied at a Network port level. To apply port level security, we will start by creating a security group and then adding security rules to this group. The security groups are attached to the instances when they are launched.

Getting ready

For creating a security group, you will need the following information:

  ▸ The security group name
  ▸ A description for the security group

How to do it...

The following recipe will show you how to create a security group using Horizon:

1. Log in to Horizon with the appropriate credentials.
2. In the left navigation menu, navigate to **Project** | **Compute** | **Access & Security**:

3. In the **Security Groups** tab, click on **+ Create Security Group**.

4. Fill in an appropriate security group **Name** and **Description**:

5. Click the **Create Security Group** button. Once the security group has been created successfully, it should be listed in the table, as shown in the following screenshot:

In the subsequent recipes, we will see how rules can be added to the security group in order to allow traffic.

How it works...

In this recipe, we created a security group. The security group bundles a set of rules, which can be associated to a Network port, and by default denies all access to the associated ports.

Configuring the security group rules using Horizon

Once a security group has been created, access to all the ports associated with the security group is denied. Security rules are then added to the group in order to allow only certain type of traffic, thereby securing the Network. The rules are defined using Network traffic attributes such as protocol (TCP, UDP, or ICMP), the direction of traffic flow, for example, entering the port (ingress) or exiting the port (egress), and the application port, that is, the UDP or TCP socket ports.

Getting ready

For this recipe, you will need the following information:

- ▸ The name of the security group to which the rules will be added
- ▸ The type of protocol to be allowed
- ▸ The direction of the traffic, that is, originating from the port (egress) or destined to the port (ingress)
- ▸ The protocol port or port range that should be allowed

How to do it...

The following steps will show you how to create the security group rules using Horizon:

1. Log in to Horizon with the appropriate credentials.
2. In the left navigation menu, navigate to **Project | Compute | Access & Security**.
3. Select the entry in the security group table, and in the **Actions** column, select **Manage Rules**. For this example, we will use the default security group.
4. This will open the screen to manage the rules for a selected security group:

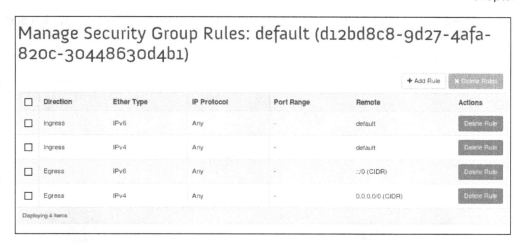

5. Add a new security rule by clicking **+Add Rule**.

6. Security rules can be added using the predefined templates by choosing application names in the **Rule** drop-down menu (for example, HTTP or SSH) or providing a custom port, protocol, and remote address combination:

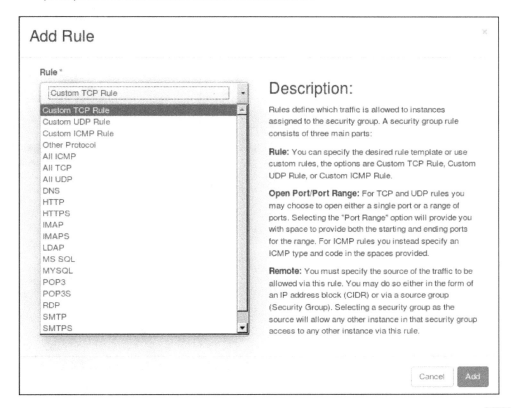

7. Select the rule type from the drop-down menu titled **Rule**. For this recipe, we will add a **Custom TCP Rule**.

8. Select the direction of the traffic flow in the menu, **Direction**:

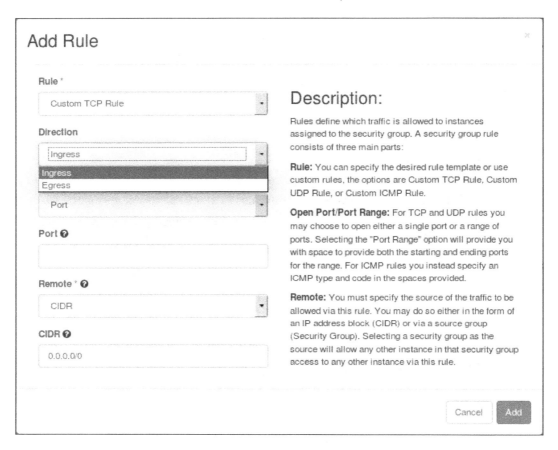

Add Rule

Rule *

Custom TCP Rule

Direction

Ingress

Ingress
Egress

Port

Port ❓

Remote * ❓

CIDR

CIDR ❓

0.0.0.0/0

Description:

Rules define which traffic is allowed to instances assigned to the security group. A security group rule consists of three main parts:

Rule: You can specify the desired rule template or use custom rules, the options are Custom TCP Rule, Custom UDP Rule, or Custom ICMP Rule.

Open Port/Port Range: For TCP and UDP rules you may choose to open either a single port or a range of ports. Selecting the "Port Range" option will provide you with space to provide both the starting and ending ports for the range. For ICMP rules you instead specify an ICMP type and code in the spaces provided.

Remote: You must specify the source of the traffic to be allowed via this rule. You may do so either in the form of an IP address block (CIDR) or via a source group (Security Group). Selecting a security group as the source will allow any other instance in that security group access to any other instance via this rule.

Cancel   Add

9. Next, select whether you want to open a single port or multiple ports using the **Open Port** menu. In this example, we will open a single port:

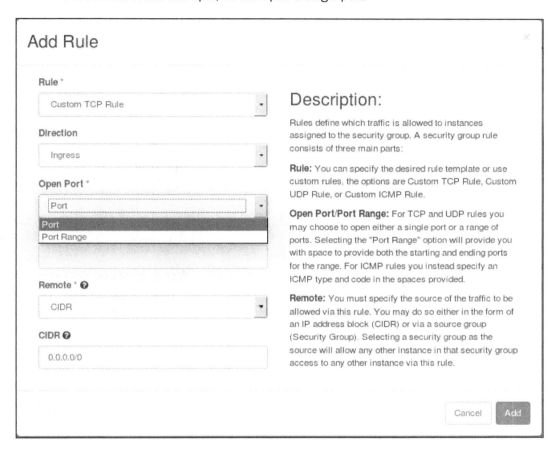

10. In the **Port** textbox, enter the protocol port number to open it. For this example, we will use port 22.

11. In the **Remote** menu, choose a method of identifying the remote address; it can be either a CIDR type network address or the name of another security group. We will use **CIDR** for this example.

12. In the **CIDR** menu, mention the Network address with a mask from which to allow traffic:

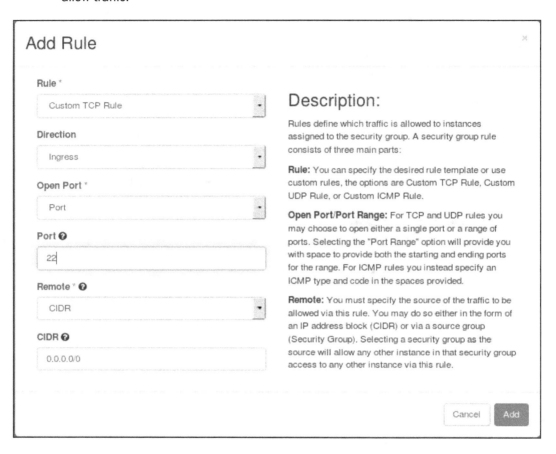

13. Click **Add** to create the security group rule:

	Direction	Ether Type	IP Protocol	Port Range	Remote	Actions
☐	Ingress	IPv6	Any	-	default	Delete Rule
☐	Ingress	IPv4	Any	-	default	Delete Rule
☐	Egress	IPv6	Any	-	::/0 (CIDR)	Delete Rule
☐	Egress	IPv4	Any	-	0.0.0.0/0 (CIDR)	Delete Rule
☐	Ingress	IPv4	TCP	22 (SSH)	0.0.0.0/0 (CIDR)	Delete Rule

Manage Security Group Rules: default (d12bd8c8-9d27-4afa-820c-30448630d4b1)

+ Add Rule   ✕ Delete Rules

Displaying 5 items

The new rule is now a part of the security group. In this example, we added a rule to allow access to port 22, which is used for SSH from any remote IP.

How it works...

A security group by default blocks all the traffic to and from the Network port that is associated with it. The user can then define the rules to open up the port for specific types of traffic.

Each security group rule opens up a certain type of traffic on the Network port. In this recipe, we created a Custom rule to open a TCP port for the incoming (ingress) traffic.

The rule can allow traffic based on its origin. The origin can be either a **Classless Inter-Domain Routing** (**CIDR**) Network or another security group. The IP address, 0.0.0.0/0, matches any source address.

The reference implementation of security groups in OpenStack is provided using the iptables.

In case a security group name is used as the origin, the packet trying to reach the associated port will be matched against both the security groups one after another. Either of these security groups may explicitly allow the packet. If the packet does not match any of the rules, it will be dropped.

Creating a security group using CLI

We have seen how to create a security group using Horizon; this recipe shows you how to create a security group using the CLI.

Getting ready

For this recipe, you will need the following information:

▸ The SSH login credentials for a node where the Neutron client packages are installed

▸ A shell RC file that initializes the environment variables for CLI

▸ The name and description of the security group

How to do it...

The following steps will show you how to create a security group using the Neutron CLI:

1. Using the appropriate credentials, SSH into the OpenStack node installed with the Neutron client packages.

2. Source the shell RC file to initialize the environment variables required for the CLI commands.

3. Execute the `neutron security-group-create` command to create a security group with the desired name and description:

```
openstack@controller:~$ neutron security-group-create Chapter7_SecurityGroup2 \
--description "Security Group 2 for Chapter7 recipe"
```

4. To list the security groups defined for the tenant, use the `security-group-list` command:

```
openstack@controller:~$ neutron security-group-list
+--------------------------------------+-------------------------+-------------------------------------+
| id                                   | name                    | description                         |
+--------------------------------------+-------------------------+-------------------------------------+
| 149b6027-e8ed-4cd5-9d54-dec3ece54331 | Chapter7_SecurityGroup2 | Security Group 2 for Chapter7 recipe |
| d12bd8c8-9d27-4afa-820c-30448630d4b1 | default                 | Default security group              |
| f162e97b-486c-45c4-91ed-18a03003397d | Chapter7_SecurityGroup1 | Security Group for Chapter7 recipe  |
+--------------------------------------+-------------------------+-------------------------------------+
```

5. To see the details of the security group that has been created, use the `security-group-show` command with the name or ID of the security group:

```
openstack@controller:~$ neutron security-group-show Chapter7_SecurityGroup2 -c name -c id -c description -c tenant_id
+-------------+-------------------------------------+
| Field       | Value                               |
+-------------+-------------------------------------+
| description | Security Group 2 for Chapter7 recipe |
| id          | 149b6027-e8ed-4cd5-9d54-dec3ece54331 |
| name        | Chapter7_SecurityGroup2             |
| tenant_id   | 588dcd43ec014863875de133ca0e3c25    |
+-------------+-------------------------------------+
```

The security group rules can also be deleted using the Neutron CLI command `security-group-delete`.

How it works...

In this recipe, we created a security group using the Neutron CLI. We can also list and view the newly created security group using the CLI commands. In case multiple security groups with the same name are present, use the security group ID with the `delete` or `show` commands.

In the following recipes, we will learn about populating this security group with rules in order to allow specific traffic packets using the CLI commands.

Configuring the security group rules using CLI

In the previous section, we saw the creation of a security group using the Neutron CLI. In this recipe, we will see how to create the security group rules using the Neutron CLI.

Getting ready

For this recipe, you will need the following information:

- ▶ The SSH login credentials for a node where the Neutron client packages are installed
- ▶ A shell RC file that initializes the environment variables for CLI
- ▶ The name of the security group, protocol, direction of the traffic flow, protocol port, and a remote CIDR network

How to do it...

The following steps will show you how to create a security group rule using the Neutron CLI:

1. Using the appropriate credentials, SSH into the OpenStack node installed with the Neutron client packages.

2. Source the shell RC file to initialize the environment variables required for the CLI commands.

3. To create a security group rule, use `neutron security-group-rule-create`, as follows:

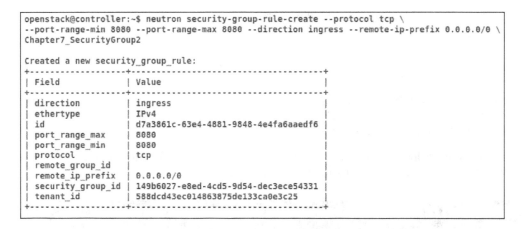

```
openstack@controller:~$ neutron security-group-rule-create --protocol tcp \
--port-range-min 8080 --port-range-max 8080 --direction ingress --remote-ip-prefix 0.0.0.0/0 \
Chapter7_SecurityGroup2

Created a new security_group_rule:
+--------------------+--------------------------------------+
| Field              | Value                                |
+--------------------+--------------------------------------+
| direction          | ingress                              |
| ethertype          | IPv4                                 |
| id                 | d7a3861c-63e4-4881-9848-4e4fa6aaedf6 |
| port_range_max     | 8080                                 |
| port_range_min     | 8080                                 |
| protocol           | tcp                                  |
| remote_group_id    |                                      |
| remote_ip_prefix   | 0.0.0.0/0                            |
| security_group_id  | 149b6027-e8ed-4cd5-9d54-dec3ece54331 |
| tenant_id          | 588dcd43ec014863875de133ca0e3c25     |
+--------------------+--------------------------------------+
```

The Neutron CLI commands can also be used to list, view, and delete the security group rules.

How it works...

The security group rules open the associated port for certain type of traffic packets. To specify the type of traffic, we can provide parameters such as protocol, application port, direction of the traffic flow, source of traffic, and so on. When a packet arrives at the port that is associated with the security group, its parameters are matched against each security group rule. If the packet matches the traffic pattern defined in any of the rules, it is allowed to pass through the port. If none of the rules match the packet, the security group drops the packet.

Securing the traffic between instances on the same Network

In this recipe, we will see how to use security groups to secure the instances on the same Network. We will create a Network and launch two instances connected to the Network. We will then use security groups in order to restrict the traffic between VMs.

Getting ready

For this recipe, you will need the following information:

- ▶ The name for the Network
- ▶ The name for the security group

How to do it...

1. Log in to Horizon with the appropriate credentials.

2. Follow the recipe titled *Creating a Subnet and Network using Horizon* in *Chapter 1, Getting Started with OpenStack Networking* to create a Network and its Subnet. For this recipe, we will create a Network called `Chapter7_Network1` with a Subnet IP range of `70.70.70.0/24`:

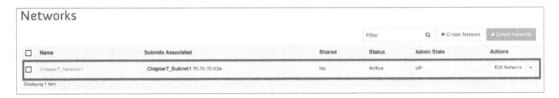

3. Next, we will launch two VM instances named `Chapter7_VM1` and `Chapter7_VM2` on the Network, `Chapter7_Network1`, and associate them with the security group, `Chapter7_SecurityGroup1`, that was created in the previous recipe:

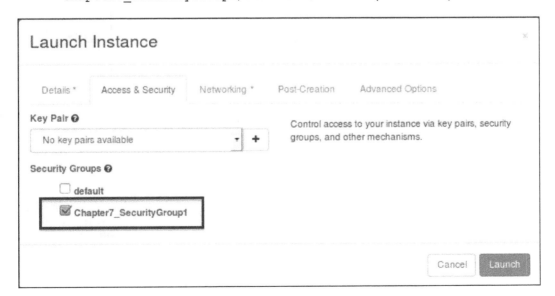

4. Once the VMs are active, verify the security group and Network associated with them by selecting the VM from the Network list by clicking on the instance name such as `Chapter7_VM1` and looking in the **Overview** tab:

5. We will now log in to one of the VMs and try to ping the IP of the second VM:

```
$ ifconfig
eth0      Link encap:Ethernet  HWaddr FA:16:3E:D0:9B:D8
          inet addr:70.70.70.5  Bcast:70.70.70.255  Mask:255.255.255.0
          inet6 addr: fe80::f816:3eff:fed0:9bd8/64 Scope:Link
          UP BROADCAST RUNNING MULTICAST  MTU:1500  Metric:1
          RX packets:85 errors:0 dropped:0 overruns:0 frame:0
          TX packets:99 errors:0 dropped:0 overruns:0 carrier:0
          collisions:0 txqueuelen:1000
          RX bytes:5374 (5.2 KiB)  TX bytes:5863 (5.7 KiB)

lo        Link encap:Local Loopback
          inet addr:127.0.0.1  Mask:255.0.0.0
          inet6 addr: ::1/128 Scope:Host
          UP LOOPBACK RUNNING  MTU:65536  Metric:1
          RX packets:46 errors:0 dropped:0 overruns:0 frame:0
          TX packets:46 errors:0 dropped:0 overruns:0 carrier:0
          collisions:0 txqueuelen:0
          RX bytes:4192 (4.0 KiB)  TX bytes:4192 (4.0 KiB)

$
$ ping 70.70.70.4
PING 70.70.70.4 (70.70.70.4): 56 data bytes

--- 70.70.70.4 ping statistics ---
11 packets transmitted, 0 packets received, 100% packet loss
```

6. As discussed earlier, specific security group rules are required in order to allow specific types of traffic. As we have not created any rule for ping (ICMP) traffic, pinging between the VMs fail.

7. Now, we will add rules to the security group in order to allow pings from any source. To do this, we will navigate to the security group list and click on **Manage Rules** for the security group, `Chapter7_SecurityGroup1`:

8. We will then add a rule to allow all incoming ICMP traffic to the port from any source CIDR network:

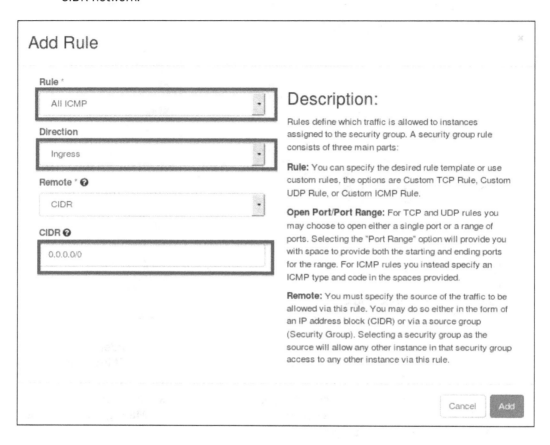

Add Rule

Rule *

All ICMP

Direction

Ingress

Remote * ❓

CIDR

CIDR ❓

0.0.0.0/0

Description:

Rules define which traffic is allowed to instances assigned to the security group. A security group rule consists of three main parts:

Rule: You can specify the desired rule template or use custom rules, the options are Custom TCP Rule, Custom UDP Rule, or Custom ICMP Rule.

Open Port/Port Range: For TCP and UDP rules you may choose to open either a single port or a range of ports. Selecting the "Port Range" option will provide you with space to provide both the starting and ending ports for the range. For ICMP rules you instead specify an ICMP type and code in the spaces provided.

Remote: You must specify the source of the traffic to be allowed via this rule. You may do so either in the form of an IP address block (CIDR) or via a source group (Security Group). Selecting a security group as the source will allow any other instance in that security group access to any other instance via this rule.

Cancel   Add

9. We can now repeat the following test to verify that pinging from one VM to another will work:

```
$ ping 70.70.70.4
PING 70.70.70.4 (70.70.70.4): 56 data bytes
64 bytes from 70.70.70.4: seq=0 ttl=64 time=0.177 ms
64 bytes from 70.70.70.4: seq=1 ttl=64 time=0.159 ms
64 bytes from 70.70.70.4: seq=2 ttl=64 time=0.133 ms
64 bytes from 70.70.70.4: seq=3 ttl=64 time=0.123 ms
64 bytes from 70.70.70.4: seq=4 ttl=64 time=0.161 ms

--- 70.70.70.4 ping statistics ---
5 packets transmitted, 5 packets received, 0% packet loss
round-trip min/avg/max = 0.123/0.150/0.177 ms
```

With the security group rule in place, pinging from one VM to another is now allowed.

How it works...

The security group drops all the packets by default. In this case, ping (ICPM) traffic between the instances was blocked initially as there was no explicit rule to allow the traffic. Once rules were added to allow all the ICMP packets, pinging between the VMs was allowed. Note that rules can also be defined with specific criteria such as the source address of the packet in order to provide more security.

Creating the security group rules to allow web traffic

In this recipe, you will learn how to allow web traffic. We will create rules to allow the traffic destined only to a web server running in a VM. Web traffic is associated with TCP ports 80 for HTTP and 443 for HTTPS.

Getting ready

For this recipe, you will need the following information:

- ▸ The name of the Network
- ▸ The name for the security group

For this recipe, we will use the `Chapter7_Network1` Network and the `Chapter7_SecurityGroup1` security group that we created in the previous recipe.

How to do it...

The following steps will show you how to open specific application-related protocol ports in a security group:

1. Log in to Horizon with the appropriate credentials.
2. Navigate to **Project | Compute | Access & Security**.

3. Click on **Manage Rules** for the Chapter7_SecurityGroup1 security group to go to the security group management page:

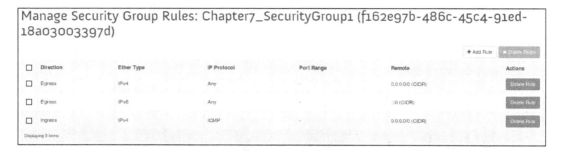

4. Click on **+Add Rule** to add a new rule. We will select the rule type HTTP in the **Rule** menu and **CIDR** as 0.0.0.0/0 to allow HTTP traffic from all remote locations:

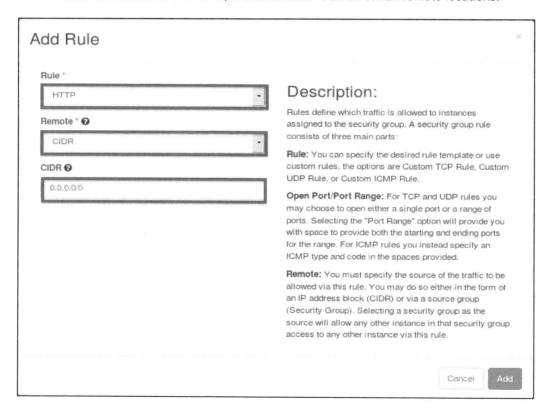

5. We will follow the same process to add a rule for HTTPS traffic:

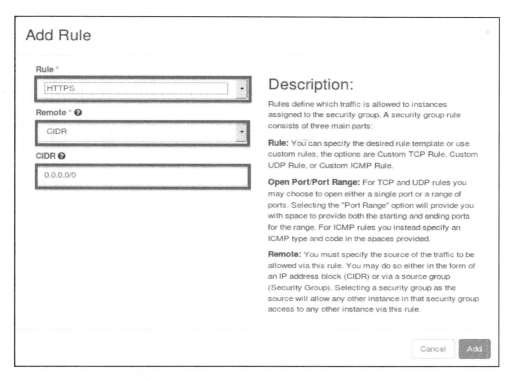

6. On completing these steps, the `Chapter7_SecurityGroup1` security group will show the rules to allow the web traffic of HTTP and HTTPS from all locations:

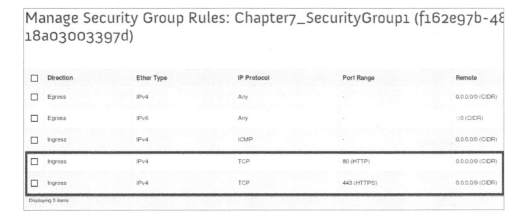

With the preceding security group rules in place, web access on the ports associated with the `Chapter7_SecurityGroup1` security group is allowed from any source.

How it works...

In this recipe, we saw the creation of security group rules to allow web access on the associated port. The associated port can be a VM, which is running a web application. To allow the traffic to reach the web server, we will need to open TCP port 80 and 443, which are the well-known ports for HTTP and HTTPS protocol, respectively. With this rule added, all the ports associated to the Chapter7_SecurityGroup1 security group will allow the passing of the web access traffic.

Configuring Neutron for the Firewall service

The OpenStack Networking functionalities can be classified as core and service. Firewall is part of the service functionality and Neutron needs to be configured in order to support it.

In this recipe, we will configure the Neutron server as well as the Neutron FWaaS agent in order to enable the Firewall functionality in OpenStack.

Getting ready

For this recipe, we will assume that the Neutron ML2 plugin has been configured to use VLAN as the type driver and Open vSwitch as the mechanism driver.

How to do it...

The following steps will show you how to configure Neutron to provide a Firewall service in OpenStack:

1. With the appropriate credentials, SSH into the node where the Neutron server is running. In our setup, it will be the Controller and Network node.

2. Open the neutron.conf configuration file using your desired editor. For example, the command for the vi editor will be as follows:

   ```
   openstack@controller:~$ sudo vi /etc/neutron/neutron.conf
   ```

3. In the [DEFAULT] section of the file, configure firewall as the service plugin for Neutron. If service_plugins is already configured, add firewall to the list, separated by a comma:

   ```
   [DEFAULT]
   . . .
   service_plugins = firewall
   ```

4. In the `[service_providers]` section of the file, add `FIREWALL` as a service provider. If `service_provider` is already configured, add `FIREWALL` to the list, separated by a comma:

```
[service_providers]
...
service_provider = FIREWALL:Iptables:neutron.agent.linux.iptables_
firewall.OVSHybridIptablesFirewallDriver:default
```

5. Add a `[fwaas]` section of the file, as shown here:

```
[fwaas]
driver = neutron_fwaas.services.firewall.drivers.linux.iptables_
fwaas.IptablesFwaasDriver
enabled = True
```

6. Open the `l3_agent.ini` file using your desired editor. For example, the command for the vi editor will be as follows:

```
openstack@controller:~$ sudo vi /etc/neutron/l3_agent.ini
```

7. As we are using Open vSwitch as the mechanism driver, in the `[DEFAULT]` section of the file, we will configure `interface_driver` accordingly:

```
[DEFAULT]
...
interface_driver = neutron.agent.linux.interface.
OVSInterfaceDriver
```

8. To configure the Horizon dashboard for Firewall, open the `/usr/share/openstack-dashboard/openstack_dashboard/local/local_settings.py` file and set an `enable_firewall` option in the `OPENSTACK_NEUTRON_NETWORK` setting:

```
'enable_firewall' = True
```

9. Once the changes are done, restart `neutron-server`, `neutron-l3-agent`, and horizon for the changes to take effect.

How it works...

Once Firewall is added to the list of service plugins in the Neutron configuration file and the Horizon dashboard has been configured, the support for Firewall is enabled in OpenStack. You will see that Horizon now has an option called Firewall when you navigate to **Project | Network**. The configuration of Neutron with an iptables-based FWaaS plugin is now complete. In the following recipes, we will use the Firewall service in order to secure the network access.

Creating the Firewall rules

In OpenStack Neutron, Firewall provides security by configuring the access control at the Network Router, in contrast to the security group, which provided the access control at the Network port. The Firewall policies provide you with the access control over the traffic crossing the Network boundary.

In Neutron, a Firewall service is composed of a Firewall policy, which in turn is composed of many Firewall rules. We will start exploring Firewall as a service by first looking at the Firewall rules. We will then create a Firewall policy by grouping these rules. Finally, we will define a Firewall that will use the Firewall policy that we created.

Getting ready

In this recipe, we will go through the process of creating a Firewall rule using Horizon. For this recipe, you will need the following information:

- ▶ The Firewall rule name
- ▶ The rule description
- ▶ The protocol to define the type of traffic, for example, TCP, UDP, or ICMP
- ▶ The type of action that the rule will add, for example, allow or deny a traffic type
- ▶ The source and destination of the traffic and their port or port-range

How to do it...

The following steps will show you how to create a Firewall from Horizon:

1. Log in to Horizon with the appropriate credentials.
2. Navigate to **Project | Network | Firewall** and click on the **Firewall Rules** tab:

3. Click on **Add Rules** to open the menu.

4. In the **Add Rule** menu, provide the rule **Name**, **Description**, **Protocol**, **Action**, **Source**, **Destination IP**, and **Port** or **Port Range**:

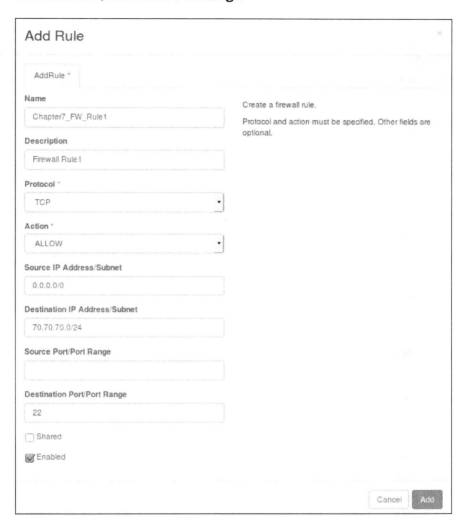

5. Click **Add** to create the Firewall rule:

The Firewall rules can also be created using the CLI commands, as follows:

1. Using the appropriate credentials, SSH into the OpenStack node installed with the Neutron client packages.

2. Source the shell RC file to initialize the environment variables required for the CLI commands.

3. To create a Firewall rule, use the `neutron firewall-rule-create` command:

```
openstack@controller:~/devstack$ neutron firewall-rule-create --name Chapter7_FW_Rule3\
--description "Chapter7 Firewall Rule 3" --source-ip-address 0.0.0.0/0\
--destination-ip-address 70.70.70.0/24 --destination-port 22 --protocol tcp\
--action allow
Created a new firewall_rule:
+-------------------------+--------------------------------------+
| Field                   | Value                                |
+-------------------------+--------------------------------------+
| action                  | allow                                |
| description             | Chapter7 Firewall Rule 3             |
| destination_ip_address  | 70.70.70.0/24                        |
| destination_port        | 22                                   |
| enabled                 | True                                 |
| firewall_policy_id      |                                      |
| id                      | 8a911621-a6d0-43f9-998c-db22f675385b |
| ip_version              | 4                                    |
| name                    | Chapter7_FW_Rule3                    |
| position                |                                      |
| protocol                | tcp                                  |
| shared                  | False                                |
| source_ip_address       | 0.0.0.0/0                            |
| source_port             |                                      |
| tenant_id               | 7b9c44c4b2ab40b48c688ab33419be7b     |
+-------------------------+--------------------------------------+
```

Once the rule has been created, the rule details are displayed.

How it works...

The Firewall rule consists of two parts. The first part is the match condition. When a packet arrives at the Network, the Firewall uses the match condition to select a packet for an action. The second part in the rule is the action to take when a packet matches the condition. In this recipe, we created a rule to allow the matching traffic on port 22 for a destination network with the `70.70.70.0/24` address, and once this condition matches, the rule defines the action to allow the packet.

Creating the Firewall policies

A Firewall policy is a grouping of the Firewall rules. We will now create a Firewall policy and add the Firewall rules that we created earlier. The order of the rules in a Firewall policy is important and a different ordering may give you a different result.

A Firewall policy may also be shared between tenants.

Getting ready

We will create the Firewall policy using Horizon. For this recipe, we will need the following information:

- The Firewall policy name
- The Firewall policy description
- Names of the Firewall rules to be added to the policy

How to do it...

The following steps will show you how to create a Firewall policy and add the Firewall rules to it:

1. Log in to Horizon with the appropriate credentials.
2. Navigate to **Project | Network | Firewalls** and click on **Firewall Policies**.
3. In the **Add Policy** menu, provide Policy **Name** and **Description**:

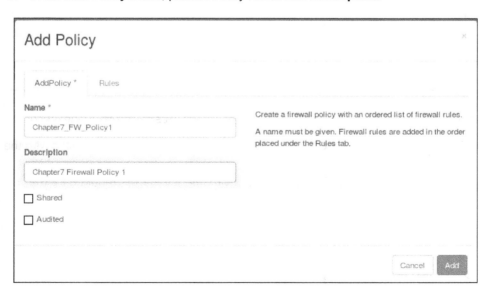

4. In the **Rules** tab in the **Add Policy** menu, choose and add the Firewall rules in **Available Rules** to **Selected Rules**. Dragging them up or down can reorder the rules:

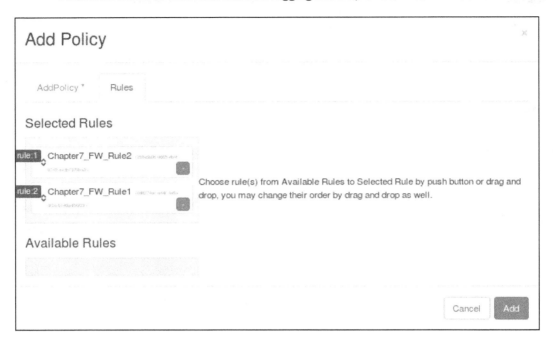

5. Click **Add** to create the Firewall policy:

We can also use the Neutron CLI to create the Firewall policy using the following steps:

1. Using the appropriate credentials, SSH into the OpenStack node installed with the Neutron client packages.

2. Source the shell RC file to initialize the environment variables required for the CLI commands.

3. To create a Firewall policy, use the `neutron firewall-policy-create` command:

```
openstack@controller:~/devstack$ neutron firewall-policy-create --firewall-rules \
"Chapter7_FW_Rule4 Chapter7_FW_Rule3" --description "Chapter7 Firewall Policy 2" \
Chapter7_FW_Policy2
Created a new firewall_policy:
+----------------+------------------------------------------+
| Field          | Value                                    |
+----------------+------------------------------------------+
| audited        | False                                    |
| description    | Chapter7 Firewall Policy 2               |
| firewall_rules | 9788a775-84cb-437e-a246-728a2961cdb2     |
|                | 8a911621-a6d0-43f9-998c-db22f675385b     |
| id             | 0d64800f-c1b9-4930-a647-907303b9ae28     |
| name           | Chapter7_FW_Policy2                      |
| shared         | False                                    |
| tenant_id      | 7b9c44c4b2ab40b48c688ab33419be7b         |
+----------------+------------------------------------------+
```

In the preceding command, the Firewall rules should be provided as an ordered list. The ordering of the rules in the list determines the order in which the Network packets will be matched.

How it works...

A Firewall policy is composed of rules, which match a traffic packet based on parameters such as the protocol, application port, and so on. The rules can either allow or deny the traffic that matches the rule. This makes the ordering of the rules in a policy significant. For example, if a rule that allows SSH traffic from any location is placed before a rule that denies any traffic from CIDR 20.20.20.0/24, an attempt to connect to a VM using SSH from CIDR 20.20.20.0/24 will still be allowed.

Creating a Firewall

A Firewall is associated with a Firewall policy. In the previous two recipes, you learned how to create Firewall rules and a policy. We will now create a Firewall and associate it with the policy that we created in the previous section.

Getting ready

We will create the Firewall using Horizon. For this recipe, we will need the following information:

- ► The Firewall policy name
- ► The Firewall name
- ► The Firewall description

How to do it...

The following steps will show you how to create a firewall using Horizon:

1. Log in to Horizon with the appropriate credentials.

2. Navigate to **Project | Network | Firewalls** and click on the **Firewalls** tab and click on **Create Firewalls**.

3. In the **Add Firewall** menu, provide **Name** and **Description** and choose the **Policy** of the Firewall from the drop-down menu:

4. Click **Add** to create the Firewall:

We can also create the Firewall with the Neutron CLI using the following steps:

1. Using the appropriate credentials, SSH into the OpenStack node installed with the Neutron client packages.

2. Source the shell RC file to initialize the environment variables required for the CLI commands.

3. To create a Firewall, use the `neutron firewall-create` command and provide the Firewall policy that should be associated with this Firewall:

```
openstack@controller:~/devstack$ neutron firewall-create --name Chapter7_FW2 \
--description "Chapter7 Firewall 2" Chapter7_FW_Policy2
Created a new firewall:
+--------------------+--------------------------------------+
| Field              | Value                                |
+--------------------+--------------------------------------+
| admin_state_up     | True                                 |
| description        | Chapter7 Firewall 2                  |
| firewall_policy_id | 0d64800f-c1b9-4930-a647-907303b9ae28 |
| id                 | 6bfb1d38-b966-45db-a850-6eae23608564 |
| name               | Chapter7_FW2                         |
| router_ids         | 7dff588c-942d-407a-a325-3afca137bc24 |
| status             | PENDING_CREATE                       |
| tenant_id          | 7b9c44c4b2ab40b48c688ab33419be7b     |
+--------------------+--------------------------------------+
```

How it works...

Once a Firewall has been created using a predefined policy, all the Firewall policy rules are automatically applied to the Routers that already exist or those that will be created later. The reference implementation of FWaaS applies the Firewall rules as an iptables configuration in the Router's namespace. The Firewall policy of a tenant is applied to all the Routers that the tenant owns. This behavior will change in the future version of Neutron and allow the user to associate the Firewall policy to the chosen Routers.

In the next recipe, we will explore the iptables configuration in detail.

Viewing and verifying the Firewall rules on the Network node

We created a Firewall and its policies and rules in the previous recipes. The Neutron reference implementation uses iptables to provide FWaaS. As discussed earlier, FWaaS policies are implemented at the Routers. Neutron uses the Network's namespace to implement the Routers. In this recipe, we will fnd out how the Firewall policies and rules are converted to the iptables configuration by Neutron.

Getting ready

For this recipe, you will need the following information:

- ▶ An administrative user access to OpenStack
- ▶ A root or equivalent sudo access to the Network node

How to do it...

The following steps will show you how to view the Firewall rules on the Network node:

1. Using the appropriate credentials, SSH into the OpenStack node installed with the Neutron client packages.

2. Source the shell RC file to initialize the environment variables required for the CLI commands.

3. Use the CLI commands to list the Firewall, Firewall policy, Firewall rule, and Routers. Note the Router ID in the following image. We will use this ID to find the namespace corresponding to this Router on the Network node:

```
openstack@controller:~$ neutron firewall-rule-list
+------------------------------------------+-----------------+------------------------------------------+--------------------------------+---------+
| id                                       | name            | firewall_policy_id                       | summary                        | enabled |
+------------------------------------------+-----------------+------------------------------------------+--------------------------------+---------+
| 8a911621-a6d0-43f9-998c-db22f675385b     | Chapter7_FW_Rule3 | 0d64800f-c1b9-4930-a647-907303b9ae28   | TCP,                           | True    |
|                                          |                 |                                          |   source: 0.0.0.0/0(none),     |         |
|                                          |                 |                                          |   dest: 70.70.70.70/24(22),    |         |
|                                          |                 |                                          |   allow                        |         |
| 9788a775-84cb-437e-a246-728a2961cdb2     | Chapter7_FW_Rule4 | 0d64800f-c1b9-4930-a647-907303b9ae28   | TCP,                           | True    |
|                                          |                 |                                          |   source: 0.0.0.0/0(none),     |         |
|                                          |                 |                                          |   dest: 70.70.70.70/24(80),    |         |
|                                          |                 |                                          |   allow                        |         |
+------------------------------------------+-----------------+------------------------------------------+--------------------------------+---------+
openstack@controller:~$ neutron firewall-policy-list
+------------------------------------------+-----------------+------------------------------------------+
| id                                       | name            | firewall_rules                           |
+------------------------------------------+-----------------+------------------------------------------+
| 0d64800f-c1b9-4930-a647-907303b9ae28     | Chapter7_FW_Policy2 | [9788a775-84cb-437e-a246-728a2961cdb2, |
|                                          |                 |  8a911621-a6d0-43f9-998c-db22f675385b]   |
| 7ac444ed-adde-4bf0-a67d-38ecf7e90234     | Chapter7_FW_Policy1 | [259e5b06-0665-4b4f-9742-e4db7370ba2f, |
|                                          |                 |  8d8274ac-e44f-4e5a-9f2e-b143a4fb002f]   |
+------------------------------------------+-----------------+------------------------------------------+
openstack@controller:~$ neutron firewall-list
+------------------------------------------+-----------------+------------------------------------------+
| id                                       | name            | firewall_policy_id                       |
+------------------------------------------+-----------------+------------------------------------------+
| 6bfb1d38-b966-45db-a850-6eae23608564     | Chapter7_FW2    | 0d64800f-c1b9-4930-a647-907303b9ae28     |
+------------------------------------------+-----------------+------------------------------------------+
openstack@controller:~$ neutron router-list -c id -c name
+------------------------------------------+---------+
| id                                       | name    |
+------------------------------------------+---------+
| 7dff588c-942d-407a-a325-3afca137bc24     | router1 |
+------------------------------------------+---------+
```

4. Log in to the network node as the root user (or an equivalent sudo user) account using SSH.

5. Use the `ip netns` command to locate the namespace for the Router. Neutron creates the Router's namespace using a `qrouter` prefix with the Router ID.

6. Start a shell in the Router's namespace using the `ip netns exec` command:

```
openstack@controller:~$ sudo ip netns
qrouter-7dff588c-942d-407a-a325-3afca137bc24
qdhcp-20fdfb74-524d-45e7-97c9-64b0176ef15a

openstack@controller:~$ sudo ip netns exec qrouter-7dff588c-942d-407a-a325-3afca137bc24 bash
```

7. List the iptables rules in this namespace using `iptables -L -n -v`, as follows:

```
Chain FORWARD (policy ACCEPT)
target          prot opt source             destination
neutron-filter-top  all  --  0.0.0.0/0          0.0.0.0/0
neutron-l3-agent-FORWARD  all  --  0.0.0.0/0        0.0.0.0/0

Chain OUTPUT (policy ACCEPT)
target          prot opt source             destination
neutron-filter-top  all  --  0.0.0.0/0          0.0.0.0/0
neutron-l3-agent-OUTPUT  all  --  0.0.0.0/0         0.0.0.0/0

Chain neutron-filter-top (2 references)
target          prot opt source             destination
neutron-l3-agent-local  all  --  0.0.0.0/0          0.0.0.0/0

Chain neutron-l3-agent-FORWARD (1 references)
target          prot opt source             destination
neutron-l3-agent-iv46bfb1d38  all  --  0.0.0.0/0        0.0.0.0/0
neutron-l3-agent-ov46bfb1d38  all  --  0.0.0.0/0        0.0.0.0/0
neutron-l3-agent-fwaas-defau  all  --  0.0.0.0/0        0.0.0.0/0
neutron-l3-agent-fwaas-defau  all  --  0.0.0.0/0        0.0.0.0/0

Chain neutron-l3-agent-INPUT (1 references)
target          prot opt source             destination
ACCEPT          all  --  0.0.0.0/0          0.0.0.0/0          mark match 0x1
DROP            tcp  --  0.0.0.0/0          0.0.0.0/0          tcp dpt:9697

Chain neutron-l3-agent-OUTPUT (1 references)
target          prot opt source             destination

Chain neutron-l3-agent-fwaas-defau (2 references)
target          prot opt source             destination
DROP            all  --  0.0.0.0/0          0.0.0.0/0

Chain neutron-l3-agent-iv46bfb1d38 (1 references)
target          prot opt source             destination
DROP            all  --  0.0.0.0/0          0.0.0.0/0          state INVALID
ACCEPT          all  --  0.0.0.0/0          0.0.0.0/0          state RELATED,ESTABLISHED
ACCEPT          tcp  --  70.70.70.0/24      0.0.0.0/0          tcp dpt:80
ACCEPT          tcp  --  70.70.70.0/24      0.0.0.0/0          tcp dpt:22

Chain neutron-l3-agent-local (1 references)
target          prot opt source             destination

Chain neutron-l3-agent-ov46bfb1d38 (1 references)
target          prot opt source             destination
DROP            all  --  0.0.0.0/0          0.0.0.0/0          state INVALID
ACCEPT          all  --  0.0.0.0/0          0.0.0.0/0          state RELATED,ESTABLISHED
ACCEPT          tcp  --  70.70.70.0/24      0.0.0.0/0          tcp dpt:80
ACCEPT          tcp  --  70.70.70.0/24      0.0.0.0/0          tcp dpt:22
```

You can see that the Firewall rules have been converted to the iptables configuration and applied in the Router's namespace.

How it works...

Linux network namespace is used by Neutron to implement a Router. When the Firewall rules are created, Neutron configures iptables in the Router's namespace to implement the Firewall rules. In this example, we can see that the Router ID, `7dff588c-942d-407a-a325-3afca137bc24`, is used to create the `qrouter-7dff588c-942d-407a-a325-3afca137bc24` namespace.

Neutron then creates the iptables configuration in this namespace in order to implement the Firewall rules. For every Firewall that is created by the tenant, Neutron creates a pair of the iptables chains and names them using a prefix of the Firewall's ID. In this example, the chains are named as `neutron-l3-agent-iv46bfb1d38` and `neutron-l3-agent-ov46bfb1d38` and represent the ingress (input) and egress (output) direction of the match, respectively. In the chains, the individual rule configuration matches the Firewall rules created by the user.

8
Using HAProxy
for Load Balancing

OpenStack Neutron provides Load Balancer as a Service to distribute traffic to your application that is running on the virtual machines. In this chapter, we will explore the Neutron load balancer service plugin with the following recipes:

- ► Installing and configuring the Neutron load balancer service plugin
- ► Creating a load balancer pool using Horizon
- ► Creating a load balancer pool using CLI
- ► Adding a load balancer member using Horizon
- ► Adding a load balancer member using CLI
- ► Adding a load balancer health monitor using Horizon
- ► Adding a load balancer health monitor using CLI
- ► Creating a Virtual IP using Horizon
- ► Creating a Virtual IP using CLI
- ► Making the load balancer accessible to the Internet
- ► Testing the load balancer
- ► Viewing the load balancer on the network node

Introduction

Critical applications and services need to be resilient to failures and capable of handling high network traffic. One of the strategies to achieve the scale and high availability is using a load balancer. A load balancer distributes an incoming service request to a pool of servers, which process the request, thus providing a higher throughput. If one of the servers in the pool fails, the load balancer removes it from the pool and the subsequent service requests are distributed among the remaining servers. The load balancer acts as a frontend to a cluster of worker nodes, which provide the actual service.

To implement these recipes, we will use an OpenStack setup, as described in the following image:

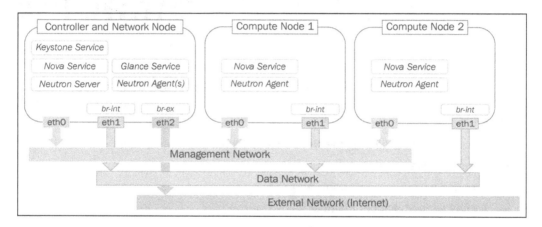

This setup has two compute nodes and one node for the controller and networking services.

Installing and configuring the Neutron load balancer service plugin

This recipe shows you how to install and configure the **Load Balancer as a Service** (**LBaaS**) plugin in Neutron.

The reference implementation of LBaaS in Neutron uses HAProxy along with the network namespace.

Getting ready

For this recipe, you will need the following information:

> ▸ The login credentials to the Controller and Network node

How to do it...

The following steps will show you how to install the load balancer service with Neutron:

1. With the appropriate credentials, SSH into the node where the Neutron server is running. In our setup, it will be the Controller and Network node.

2. Install the packages required to provide the load balancer services using a package manager such as `yum` or `apt` on the Network node, as follows:

   ```
   openstack@controller:~$ sudo apt-get install python-neutron-lbaas
   neutron-lbaas-agent haproxy
   ```

3. Open the `neutron.conf` configuration file using your desired editor. For example, the command for the vi editor will be as follows:

   ```
   openstack@controller:~$ sudo vi /etc/neutron/neutron.conf
   ```

4. In the `[DEFAULT]` section of the file, configure load balancer as the service plugin for Neutron. If `service_plugins` is already configured, add the load balancer configuration to the list, separated by a comma:

   ```
   [DEFAULT]
   ...
   service_plugins = lbaas
   ```

5. In the `[service_providers]` section of the file, add `LOADBALANCER` as a service provider. If `service_provider` is already configured, add `LOADBALANCER` to the list, separated by a comma:

   ```
   [service_providers]
   ...
   service_provider = LOADBALANCER:Haproxy:neutron.services.
   loadbalancer.drivers.haproxy.plugin_driver.HaproxyOnHostPluginDriv
   er:default
   ```

6. Open the `/etc/neutron/lbaas_agent.ini` configuration file and update the `device_driver` and `interface_driver` settings:

   ```
   interface_driver = neutron.agent.linux.interface.
   OVSInterfaceDriver

   device_driver = neutron.services.loadbalancer.drivers.haproxy.
   namespace_driver.HaproxyNSDriver
   ```

7. To configure Horizon for the load balancer, open the `/usr/share/openstack-dashboard/openstack_dashboard/local/local_settings.py` file and set an `enable_lb` option in the `OPENSTACK_NEUTRON_NETWORK` setting:

   ```
   'enable_lb' = True
   ```

8. Restart neutron-server, neutron-lbaas-agent, and apache2 or the httpd server for the changes to take effect.

How it works...

The load balancer service in Neutron is supported using a service plugin. The reference implementation of the load balancer uses HAProxy as the service provider. The plugin spawns the instances of HAProxy in a Linux network namespace on the network node in order to act as a load balancer node.

Creating a load balancer pool using Horizon

A typical load balancer installation consists of a pool of servers called members, each of which will run an instance of the application. All the clients will connect to the service using a Virtual IP that is configured on the load balancer node, as shown in the following image:

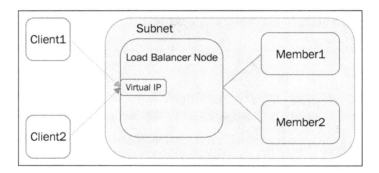

The load balancer node then forwards the traffic transparently to the member servers. To accomplish this, it can adopt various strategies in order to distribute the traffic load to member servers such as round robin, least connected, and so on.

To configure the load balancer, we would need some member servers connected to a virtual network. For this recipe, we will host a web server on each member server. These servers will be connected to a virtual network on the same subnet.

We will then use Neutron to configure the load balancer to distribute traffic to the member servers.

Follow the *Creating Network and Subnet using Horizon* recipe in *Chapter 1, Getting Started with OpenStack Networking* to create a LoadBalancer_Net1 Network and its Subnet with a network address of 20.20.20.0/24.

The following table shows you the VM details:

Virtual Machine name	Role	IP address
Chapter8_vm1	A load balancer member	20.20.20.3
Chapter8_vm2	A load balancer member	20.20.20.4

Getting ready

In this recipe, we will use Horizon to create a load balancer pool. A load balancer pool defines a group of servers on a Subnet to be used to process the service requests. The pool also defines the strategy of distributing the load among the member servers.

To create a load balancer pool, you will need the following information:

- ▶ The name of the load balancer pool
- ▶ The description of the pool
- ▶ The Subnet associated with the pool
- ▶ An application protocol for the load balancer
- ▶ The method used to spread the load to the pool members

How to do it...

The following steps will show you how to create a load balancer pool using Horizon:

1. Log in to Horizon with the appropriate credentials.
2. In the left navigation menu, navigate to **Project | Network | Load Balancers**:

3. Click on **+Add Pool**.
4. In the **Add Pool** screen, provide a **Name** for this pool.

5. Add a **Description** for the pool.

6. Select **haproxy** as **Provider** for this pool.

7. Select **Subnet** for this load balancer pool. For our example, we will use the **20.20.20.0/24** Subnet on `LoadBalancer_Net1` as the CIDR.

8. Select the application **Protocol** for this pool. For our example, we will use **HTTP** as the protocol:

9. Select **Method** used by the load balancer in order to select a server for the new request traffic. We will use the **ROUND_ROBIN** method:

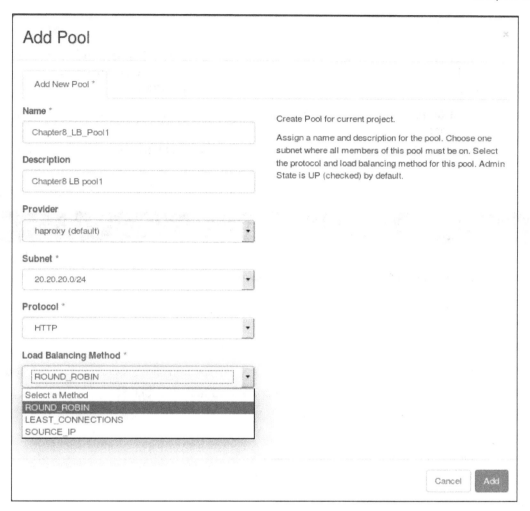

10. Click on **Add** to create the pool:

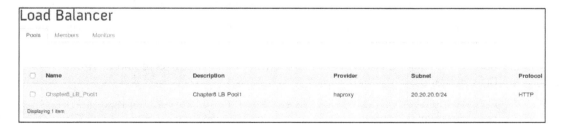

The load balancer pool that you created should now be listed in the Pools table.

How it works...

The load balancer pool in Neutron defines the attributes of the load balancer such as the Subnet and load distribution method. The pool is associated with a protocol such as HTTP, HTTPS, or TCP. The following load distribution methods are supported:

- **Least Connection**: This forwards a request to the member having the least number of client requests
- **Round Robin**: This evenly distributes the service request between the members but does not take into account the current load on a member
- **Source IP**: This always forwards the requests from a client to a certain member

Creating a load balancer pool using CLI

In the previous recipe, we saw how to create a load balancer pool using Horizon. In this recipe, we will use the Neutron CLI to create a load balancer pool.

Getting ready

For this recipe, you will need the following information:

- The SSH login credentials for a node where the Neutron client packages are installed
- A shell RC file that initializes the environment variables for CLI
- The name of the load balancer pool
- The Subnet ID for the load balancer
- The method to use for the load balancing
- The protocol that needs to be load balanced

How to do it...

The following steps will show you how to create a load balancer pool using the Neutron CLI:

1. Using the appropriate credentials, SSH into the OpenStack node installed with the Neutron client packages.

2. Source the shell RC file to initialize the environment variables required for the CLI commands.

3. Execute the `neutron lb-pool-create` command to create the load balancer pool:

```
openstack@controller:~$ neutron lb-pool-create --name Chapter8_LB_Pool2\
--protocol HTTP --subnet-id 7c070ec9-7222-4954-b1f4-015432e9ca95\
--provider haproxy --lb-method ROUND_ROBIN
Created a new pool:
+--------------------------+------------------------------------------+
| Field                    | Value                                    |
+--------------------------+------------------------------------------+
| admin_state_up           | True                                     |
| description              |                                          |
| health_monitors          |                                          |
| health_monitors_status   |                                          |
| id                       | 88c35213-d6b4-4018-a8d2-ad3f09eec5f8     |
| lb_method                | ROUND_ROBIN                              |
| members                  |                                          |
| name                     | Chapter8_LB_Pool2                        |
| protocol                 | HTTP                                     |
| provider                 | haproxy                                  |
| status                   | PENDING_CREATE                           |
| status_description       |                                          |
| subnet_id                | 7c070ec9-7222-4954-b1f4-015432e9ca95     |
| tenant_id                | 6d39c84e59a84425bedbcebdf674e2c9         |
| vip_id                   |                                          |
+--------------------------+------------------------------------------+
```

4. Once created, Neutron will display the details of the load balancer pool.

How it works...

The load balancer pool defines the protocol, Subnet, and method used to distribute the requests among the load balancer members.

Adding a load balancer member using Horizon

When a load balancer receives a service request from the client, it forwards the request to one of the load balancer members running the application and the application does the actual request processing.

In this recipe, we will use Horizon to add members to the load balancer pool that we created earlier.

Getting ready

To add a member to a load balancer pool, you will need the following information:

► The name of the load balancer pool
► The VM name or IP to add as the pool member

- ▶ The weight associated with the pool member
- ▶ The port on the VM to which the traffic would be redirected by the load balancer

How to do it...

The following steps will show you how to add a load balancer pool member using Horizon:

1. Log in to Horizon with the appropriate credentials.
2. In the left navigation menu, navigate to **Project | Network | Load Balancers**.
3. Select the **Members** tab.
4. Click on **+Add Member**.
5. In the **Add Member** screen, select the name of the load balancer pool in the **Pool** field:

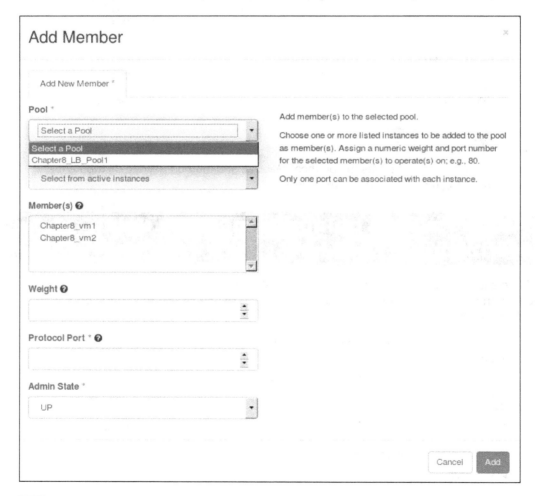

6. Set **Member Source** as **Select from active instances**. It is also possible to add a member based on the IP address. The IP address of the member must be in the Subnet that is associated with the pool.

7. In the **Member(s)** field, select the VM instance to be added:

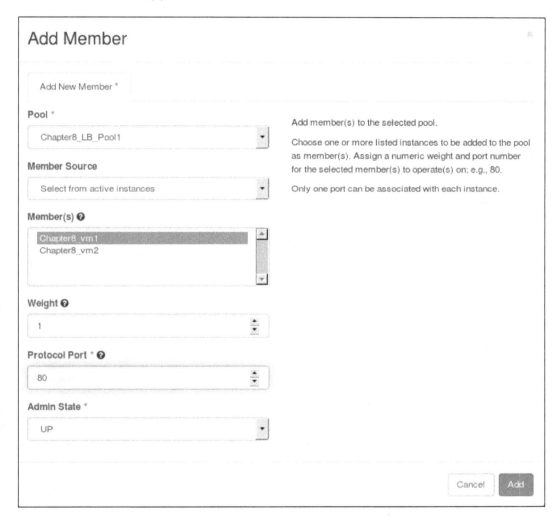

8. In the **Weight** text box, provide the member's weight. This is an indicator of the relative load handling capacity of the member with respect to the other members in the pool. A higher weight of a member indicates a higher request handling capability.

9. In **Protocol Port**, provide the port on the VM to which the traffic should be redirected:

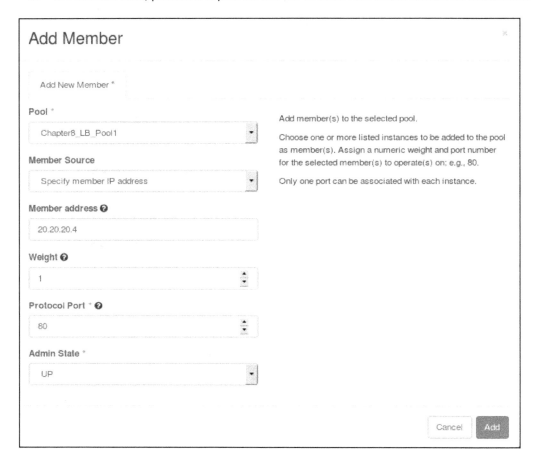

10. Click **Add** to create the member:

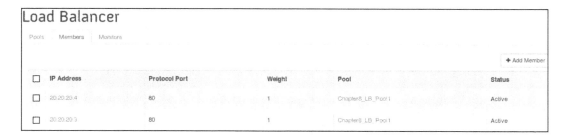

The newly added member is now displayed in the **Members** tab.

How it works...

The load balancer member runs the application that processes the client requests. In this recipe, we added two members to the load balancer pool. The load balancer distributes the client request to these two member servers, which do the actual request processing.

Adding a load balancer member using CLI

In this recipe, we will add a load balancer member using the Neutron CLI.

Getting ready

For this recipe, you will need the following information:

- The SSH login credentials for a node where the Neutron client packages are installed
- A shell RC file that initializes the environment variables for CLI
- The IP address of the member
- The protocol port of the application running in the member
- The name of the load balancer pool where this member will be added

How to do it...

The following steps will show you how to add a load balancer member using the Neutron CLI:

1. Using the appropriate credentials, SSH into the OpenStack node installed with the Neutron client packages.
2. Source the shell RC file to initialize the environment variables required for the CLI commands.
3. Execute the `neutron lb-member-create` command to add the member to the load balancer pool. Optionally, you can also provide a weight for this member:

```
openstack@controller:~$ neutron lb-member-create --address 20.20.20.6\
--protocol-port 80 --weight 1 Chapter8_LB_Pool2
Created a new member:
+--------------------+--------------------------------------+
| Field              | Value                                |
+--------------------+--------------------------------------+
| address            | 20.20.20.6                           |
| admin_state_up     | True                                 |
| id                 | 2fa7c388-9e38-4704-b98e-301bf89bd89e |
| pool_id            | 88c35213-d6b4-4018-a8d2-ad3f09eec5f8 |
| protocol_port      | 80                                   |
| status             | PENDING_CREATE                       |
| status_description |                                      |
| tenant_id          | 6d39c84e59a84425bedbcebdf674e2c9     |
| weight             | 1                                    |
+--------------------+--------------------------------------+
```

How it works...

The weight of the member is a relative value that decides the ratio of requests that can be handled by a member. If one of the members in the pool is a more powerful machine, it can be given a higher weight. The load balancer will distribute a bigger percentage of the requests to the member with the higher weight.

Adding a load balancer health monitor using Horizon

In this recipe, you will learn how to create a heath monitor for the load balancer that monitors the health of the applications that are running on the member servers.

Getting ready

To create a health monitor for our load balancer, we will need the following information:

- ▶ The type of monitor
- ▶ The time interval between consecutive health check request sent by the monitor
- ▶ The amount of time to wait for a reply from the application
- ▶ The number of times the monitor will try to get a reply from the application

How to do it...

The following steps will show you how to add a heath monitor for the load balancer:

1. Log in to Horizon with the appropriate credentials.
2. In the left navigation menu, navigate to **Project | Network | Load Balancers**.
3. Select the **Monitors** tab and click on **Add New Monitor**.
4. In the monitor screen, add the monitor **Type**. For our example, we will use **HTTP** as the monitor type.
5. In the **Delay** field, provide the time interval between consecutive health check request sent by the monitor.
6. In the **Timeout** field, enter the amount of time to wait for a reply from the application.
7. In the **Max Retries** field, enter the number of times that the monitor will try to get a reply from the application.

8. In case you selected an HTTP or HTTPS type monitor, you should provide the type of **HTTP Method** that the monitor should invoke in order to check the health of the application. For our example, we will use the **GET** method.

9. For an HTTP/HTTPS type monitor, you should also provide a URL for the application and **Expected HTTP Status Code** for a healthy application. We will use the **URL /** and a status code of **200**:

10. Click on **Add** to create the monitor.

11. Click on the **Pool** tab to go back to the load balancer pool list.

12. In the **Actions** column, click on the drop-down menu and select **Associate Monitor**:

13. In the **Associate Monitor** screen, select the monitor that you want to associate with the load balancer pool and click on **Associate**:

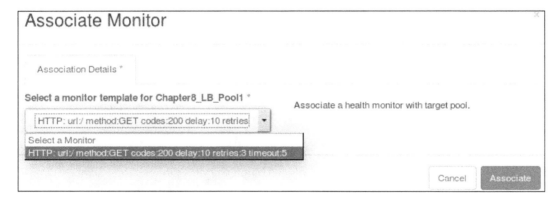

Now the health monitor is associated with the load balancer pool.

How it works...

The load balancer needs to keep a track of the health of the application that is running on its member servers. The health monitor associated with the load balancer is responsible for monitoring the application on the member servers and making sure that in case the application on a member fails, it is excluded from the pool and no further client requests are forwarded to that failed member.

Adding a load balancer health monitor using CLI

In this recipe, we will create a health monitor to watch the health of the application that is running on the load balancer members using the Neutron CLI.

Getting ready

For this recipe, you will need the following information:

- ▶ The SSH login credentials for a node where the Neutron client packages are installed
- ▶ A shell RC file that initializes the environment variables for CLI
- ▶ The type of monitor
- ▶ The time interval between consecutive health check request sent by the monitor
- ▶ The amount of time to wait for a reply from the application
- ▶ The number of times the monitor will try to get a reply from the application

How to do it...

The following steps will show you how to create and associate a health monitor with a load balancer pool:

1. Using the appropriate credentials, SSH into the OpenStack node installed with the Neutron client packages.
2. Source the shell RC file to initialize the environment variables required for the CLI commands.
3. Execute the `neutron lb-healthmonitor-create` command to create a load balancer health monitor:

```
openstack@controller:~$ neutron lb-healthmonitor-create --type HTTP\
--delay 10 --timeout 5 --max-retries 3 --http-method GET --url-path /
Created a new health_monitor:
+-----------------+--------------------------------------+
| Field           | Value                                |
+-----------------+--------------------------------------+
| admin_state_up  | True                                 |
| delay           | 10                                   |
| expected_codes  | 200                                  |
| http_method     | GET                                  |
| id              | bee54dad-aa90-46a5-bb87-bf3ed8132320 |
| max_retries     | 3                                    |
| pools           |                                      |
| tenant_id       | 6d39c84e59a84425bedbcebdf674e2c9     |
| timeout         | 5                                    |
| type            | HTTP                                 |
| url_path        | /                                    |
+-----------------+--------------------------------------+
```

4. Execute the `neutron lb-healthmonitor-associate` command to associate the health monitor that we created in the previous step with the load balancer pool:

```
openstack@controller:~$ neutron lb-healthmonitor-associate bee54dad-aa90-46a5-bb87-bf3ed8132320 Chapter8_LB_Pool2
Associated health monitor bee54dad-aa90-46a5-bb87-bf3ed8132320

stack@controller:~$ neutron lb-healthmonitor-show bee54dad-aa90-46a5-bb87-bf3ed8132320
+----------------+------------------------------------------------------------------------------------------------+
| Field          | Value                                                                                          |
+----------------+------------------------------------------------------------------------------------------------+
| admin_state_up | True                                                                                           |
| delay          | 10                                                                                             |
| expected_codes | 200                                                                                            |
| http_method    | GET                                                                                            |
| id             | bee54dad-aa90-46a5-bb87-bf3ed8132320                                                           |
| max_retries    | 3                                                                                              |
| pools          | {"status": "ACTIVE", "status_description": null, "pool_id": "88c35213-d6b4-4018-a8d2-ad3f09eec5f8"} |
| tenant_id      | 6d39c84e59a84425bedbcebdf674e2c9                                                               |
| timeout        | 5                                                                                              |
| type           | HTTP                                                                                           |
| url_path       | /                                                                                              |
+----------------+------------------------------------------------------------------------------------------------+
```

How it works...

The Neutron CLI can be used to create a load balancer health monitor. The health monitor continuously checks the health of the member instances. The health monitor consists of a method to test the application health and an expected result. If the health test fails for a member, the load balancer excludes this member from the pool. If a previously failed member becomes healthy, it is added again to the load balancer pool.

Creating a Virtual IP using Horizon

The final step in the creation of the load balancer is to provide it with a Virtual IP address (VIP). The clients connect to the load balanced application using the VIP. In this recipe, we will associate a VIP to the load balancer pool using Horizon.

Getting ready

To create a VIP, you will need the following information:

- ▸ A name to identify the VIP
- ▸ The name of the load balancer pool
- ▸ The Subnet CIDR associated with this pool
- ▸ A free IP address in the Subnet for the VIP configuration
- ▸ The protocol port on which the load balancer will listen for the client request
- ▸ The protocol type
- ▸ The method of session persistence
- ▸ The connection limit for the load balancer

How to do it...

The following steps will show you how to attach a VIP to a load balancer:

1. Log in to Horizon with the appropriate credentials.

2. In the left navigation menu, navigate to **Project | Network | Load Balancers**.

3. Click on the **Actions** drop-down menu for a specific load balancer pool and select **Add VIP**:

4. In the **Add VIP** screen, provide **Name** for the VIP.

5. Add **Description** for the VIP.

6. Select the Subnet for the VIP; this should be the same Subnet that was used by the VM instance running the application that will use the load balancer.

7. Next, provide a free IP address in the Subnet that will be used at the VIP address by the load balancer. The clients connecting to the application will use this IP address.

8. Specify the port in the **Protocol Port** field. For our example, we will use port 80.

9. Specify the protocol in the Protocol list. We will use HTTP for our example.

10. Next, in **Session Persistence**, choose the method used to maintain the client sessions while balancing a service request. We will use **SOURCE_IP** to persist the session.

11. In the **Connection Limit** field, provide the maximum number of clients that the load balancer can handle. We will use `-1` so that no limit is set for the number of client connections:

12. Click **Add** to create the VIP:

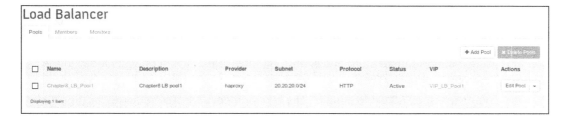

The VIP is then displayed in the corresponding column of the Pools table.

How it works...

The clients connect to the VIP in order to access the application running on the load balancer members. For the client, it appears as though the application is running on a port on the VIP. The client is unaware of the existence of a load balancer and the two member servers.

The VIP creation also defines the session persistence method in order to determine how the client session is maintained. Sessions can be maintained using the source IP, which uses the source IP of the request to determine the member that handles a service request. Session persistence can also be based on HTTP or application cookies.

It is also possible to limit the number of connections that the load balancer will handle using the connection limit setting.

Creating a Virtual IP using CLI

In this recipe, we will use the Neutron CLI to create and associate a VIP with a load balancer pool.

Getting ready

For this recipe, you will need the following information:

▶ The SSH login credentials for a node where the Neutron client packages are installed
▶ A shell RC file that initializes the environment variables for CLI
▶ The name of the VIP
▶ The name of the load balancer pool
▶ The Subnet CIDR associated with this pool
▶ A free IP address in the Subnet for the VIP configuration
▶ The protocol port
▶ The protocol type

How to do it...

The following steps will show you how to create a VIP and associate it with a load balancer pool using the Neutron CLI:

1. Using the appropriate credentials, SSH into the OpenStack node installed with the Neutron client packages.

2. Source the shell RC file to initialize the environment variables required for the CLI commands.

3. Execute the `neutron lb-vip-create` command to create a VIP for the load balancer pool:

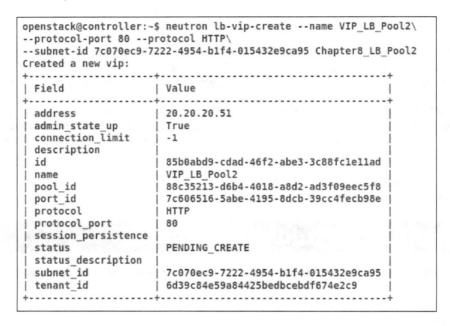

```
openstack@controller:~$ neutron lb-vip-create --name VIP_LB_Pool2\
--protocol-port 80 --protocol HTTP\
--subnet-id 7c070ec9-7222-4954-b1f4-015432e9ca95 Chapter8_LB_Pool2
Created a new vip:
+---------------------+---------------------------------------+
| Field               | Value                                 |
+---------------------+---------------------------------------+
| address             | 20.20.20.51                           |
| admin_state_up      | True                                  |
| connection_limit    | -1                                    |
| description         |                                       |
| id                  | 85b0abd9-cdad-46f2-abe3-3c88fc1e11ad  |
| name                | VIP_LB_Pool2                          |
| pool_id             | 88c35213-d6b4-4018-a8d2-ad3f09eec5f8  |
| port_id             | 7c606516-5abe-4195-8dcb-39cc4fecb98e  |
| protocol            | HTTP                                  |
| protocol_port       | 80                                    |
| session_persistence |                                       |
| status              | PENDING_CREATE                        |
| status_description  |                                       |
| subnet_id           | 7c070ec9-7222-4954-b1f4-015432e9ca95  |
| tenant_id           | 6d39c84e59a84425bedbcebdf674e2c9      |
+---------------------+---------------------------------------+
```

How it works...

To create the VIP, the Neutron CLI creates a Port on the associated Subnet. The IP address of this Port is used as the VIP for the load balancer pool. The load balancer will distribute any request that it receives on the VIP and configured protocol port to the pool members to be processed.

Making the load balancer accessible to the Internet

In this recipe, we will make our load balancer accessible to the Internet.

Getting ready

In the previous recipe, we created a VIP for our load balancer. The clients will access the service available behind the load balancer using this VIP. To make the service accessible through the Internet, the VIP must be reachable from the external Networks.

In this recipe, we will associate a floating IP to the VIP of the load balancer. We will need the Neutron port ID of the load balancer's VIP. Use the `neutron port-list` command to look for the port associated with the address of the VIP.

For this recipe, you will need the following information:

- The SSH login credentials for a node where the Neutron client packages are installed
- A shell RC file that initializes the environment variables for CLI
- The Neutron port ID for the load balancer's VIP

How to do it...

The following steps will show you how to create a VIP and associate it with a load balancer pool using the Neutron CLI:

1. Using the appropriate credentials, SSH into the OpenStack node installed with the Neutron client packages.
2. Source the shell RC file to initialize the environment variables required for the CLI commands.
3. Execute the `neutron floatingip-create` command to make the VIP for the load balancer pool accessible from the external world:

```
openstack@controller:~$ neutron floatingip-create \
--port-id 7c606516-5abe-4195-8dcb-39cc4fecb98e public
Created a new floatingip:
+---------------------+--------------------------------------+
| Field               | Value                                |
+---------------------+--------------------------------------+
| fixed_ip_address    | 20.20.20.51                          |
| floating_ip_address | 192.168.0.3                          |
| floating_network_id | 5507d585-cb44-45c5-a53c-385069e2b5b1 |
| id                  | de3f4923-2f6e-4271-b23a-98815ea4f324 |
| port_id             | 7c606516-5abe-4195-8dcb-39cc4fecb98e |
| router_id           | 1994ec2b-9f74-4407-a515-2c2c6464de87 |
| status              | ACTIVE                               |
| tenant_id           | bfd02b5c180f4765b6ff2a4ba3636413     |
+---------------------+--------------------------------------+
```

With the floating IP associated with the load balancer's VIP, the clients can now access the application behind the load balancer over the Internet.

How it works...

The load balancer uses the VIP address to redirect the service requests to the member nodes. To make the services that are running on the member node available to the external world, the VIP address must be reachable from the Internet. This can be achieved by associating a floating IP with the VIP of the load balancer.

Testing the load balancer

We added two servers as the load balancer members. We also created a health monitor in order to keep a track of the health of the application that is running on the member servers and also associated a VIP with the load balancer.

The following table summarizes our example setup:

Virtual Machine name	Role	IP address
Chapter8_vm1	A load balancer member	20.20.20.3
Chapter8_vm2	A load balancer member	20.20.20.4

The load balancer configuration is as follows:

Resource	IP address
Subnet CIDR	20.20.20.0/24
Network name	LoadBalancer_net1
Virtual IP	20.20.20.50
Application port	80

In this recipe, we will test the load balancer setup by connecting to its VIP and sending a request to the application.

Getting ready

For this recipe, you will need the following information:

- ▶ The VIP of the load balancer
- ▶ The protocol port of the load balancer

How to do it...

The following steps will show you how to test the load balancer:

1. Log in to Horizon with the appropriate credentials.

2. Launch a VM on the `LoadBalancer_net1` Network. This instance will act as the client machine to test the load balancer. We already added the load balancer member VMs in the previous recipe.

3. In the left navigation menu, navigate to **Project | Network | Load Balancers** and click on the **Members** tab:

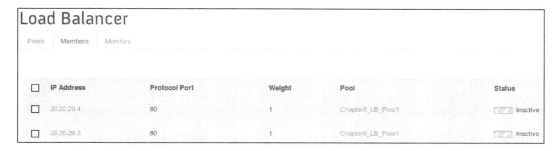

4. The monitor associated with the load balancer has put the members in an inactive state as the application health test is failing currently.

5. Log in to each member VM and start a web server. For our test, we will use the following simple script to simulate a web server. Update the `echo` statement with the correct hostname when launching the script:

```
while true; do echo -e 'HTTP/1.0 200 OK\r\n\r\nChapter8_vm1' |
sudo nc -l -p 80 ; done
```

6. Once the scripts are running on both the members, the health monitor will update the status of the members to active:

7. Log in to the client VM on `LoadBalancer_net1` and use the `curl` command to send an HTTP request to the VIP address:

```
$ ifconfig
eth0      Link encap:Ethernet   HWaddr FA:16:3E:20:30:B4
          inet addr:20.20.20.5  Bcast:20.20.20.255  Mask:255.255.255.0
          inet6 addr: fe80::f816:3eff:fe20:30b4/64 Scope:Link
          UP BROADCAST RUNNING MULTICAST  MTU:1500  Metric:1
          RX packets:76 errors:0 dropped:0 overruns:0 frame:0
          TX packets:157 errors:0 dropped:0 overruns:0 carrier:0
          collisions:0 txqueuelen:1000
          RX bytes:6386 (6.2 KiB)  TX bytes:11484 (11.2 KiB)

lo        Link encap:Local Loopback
          inet addr:127.0.0.1  Mask:255.0.0.0
          inet6 addr: ::1/128 Scope:Host
          UP LOOPBACK RUNNING  MTU:65536  Metric:1
          RX packets:46 errors:0 dropped:0 overruns:0 frame:0
          TX packets:46 errors:0 dropped:0 overruns:0 carrier:0
          collisions:0 txqueuelen:0
          RX bytes:4192 (4.0 KiB)  TX bytes:4192 (4.0 KiB)
$ curl http://20.20.20.50
Chapter8_vm1
$ curl http://20.20.20.50
Chapter8_vm2
$ curl http://20.20.20.50
Chapter8_vm1
$ curl http://20.20.20.50
Chapter8_vm2
```

For the purpose of this example, we updated the VIP configuration in order to disable the session persistence. Due to this, the client requests are distributed in a Round-Robin fashion among the load balancer members.

How it works...

In this recipe, we saw the load balancer in action. The health monitor checks the status of the application running on the member nodes continuously and distributes the client requests to only the active members in the pool. In case a failed member becomes healthy, its status changes to active and it starts processing the client requests.

Viewing the load balancer on the network node

In the earlier recipes of this chapter, we configured the load balancer using both Horizon and the Neutron CLI. In this recipe, we will learn how Neutron implements the load balancer on the Network node.

Getting ready

For this recipe, you need the following information:

- ▶ An administrative user access to OpenStack
- ▶ A root or equivalent sudo access to the Network node

How to do it...

The following steps will show you how to view the load balancer on the Network node:

1. Using the appropriate credentials, SSH into the OpenStack node installed with the Neutron client packages.

2. Source the shell RC file to initialize the environment variables required for the CLI commands.

3. Use the Neutron CLI commands to list the load balancer. Note the load balancer ID.

4. Next, use the `ip netns` command and find the network namespace that matches the pool ID. The load balancer plugin has configured this namespace as the load balancer node:

```
openstack@controller:~$ neutron lb-pool-list
+--------------------------------------+----------------+----------+-----------+----------+----------------+--------+
| id                                   | name           | provider | lb_method | protocol | admin_state_up | status |
+--------------------------------------+----------------+----------+-----------+----------+----------------+--------+
| a711d27b-285d-4b05-b090-4fa72ab22059 | Chapter8_LB_Pool1 | haproxy | ROUND_ROBIN | HTTP   | True           | ACTIVE |
+--------------------------------------+----------------+----------+-----------+----------+----------------+--------+

openstack@controller:~$ ip netns|grep a711d27b-285d-4b05-b090-4fa72ab22059
qlbaas-a711d27b-285d-4b05-b090-4fa72ab22059
```

5. Next, we will find the VIP that has been associated with the load balancer pool. Note the VIP assigned with the load balancer:

```
openstack@controller:~$ neutron lb-vip-show VIP_LB_Pool1
+---------------------+--------------------------------------+
| Field               | Value                                |
+---------------------+--------------------------------------+
| address             | 20.20.20.50                          |
| admin_state_up      | True                                 |
| connection_limit    | -1                                   |
| description         | VIP for LB_Pool1                     |
| id                  | 649d8559-1eb1-4d74-a7d7-7a5bfeb9bfdd |
| name                | VIP_LB_Pool1                         |
| pool_id             | a711d27b-285d-4b05-b090-4fa72ab22059 |
| port_id             | 50941290-fa35-42e5-9e7a-f601447d5048 |
| protocol            | HTTP                                 |
| protocol_port       | 80                                   |
| session_persistence |                                      |
| status              | ACTIVE                               |
| status_description  |                                      |
| subnet_id           | 7c070ec9-7222-4954-b1f4-015432e9ca95 |
| tenant_id           | 1bdec15637584058875b0e302d00cc83     |
+---------------------+--------------------------------------+
```

6. Use the `ip netns` command to verify that the VIP is configured in the namespace acting as the load balancer node:

```
openstack@controller:~$ sudo ip netns exec qlbaas-a711d27b-285d-4b05-b090-4fa72ab22059 ifconfig
lo        Link encap:Local Loopback
          inet addr:127.0.0.1  Mask:255.0.0.0
          inet6 addr: ::1/128 Scope:Host
          UP LOOPBACK RUNNING  MTU:65536  Metric:1
          RX packets:0 errors:0 dropped:0 overruns:0 frame:0
          TX packets:0 errors:0 dropped:0 overruns:0 carrier:0
          collisions:0 txqueuelen:0
          RX bytes:0 (0.0 B)  TX bytes:0 (0.0 B)

tap50941290-fa Link encap:Ethernet  HWaddr fa:16:3e:96:2e:3a
          inet addr:20.20.20.50  Bcast:20.20.20.255  Mask:255.255.255.0
          inet6 addr: fe80::f816:3eff:fe96:2e3a/64 Scope:Link
          UP BROADCAST RUNNING  MTU:1500  Metric:1
          RX packets:192798 errors:0 dropped:0 overruns:0 frame:0
          TX packets:198014 errors:0 dropped:0 overruns:0 carrier:0
          collisions:0 txqueuelen:0
          RX bytes:11525832 (11.5 MB)  TX bytes:13154322 (13.1 MB)
```

7. Next, use the `ip netns` command to verify that the HAProxy process is bound to the VIP and is listening for traffic on the application port:

```
openstack@controller:~$ sudo ip netns exec qlbaas-a711d27b-285d-4b05-b090-4fa72ab22059 netstat -tan
Active Internet connections (servers and established)
Proto Recv-Q Send-Q Local Address           Foreign Address         State
tcp        0      0 20.20.20.50:80          0.0.0.0:*               LISTEN
```

How it works...

Neutron uses the Linux network namespace as the load balancer node. The namespace is named using a prefix of `qlbaas`, the ID of the load balancer pool `a711d27b-285d-4b05-b090-4fa72ab22059`. The namespace is configured with the load balancer's VIP. In our example, the VIP address of `20.20.20.50` is used. The load balancer plugin starts a HAProxy process in this namespace that binds the VIP on the protocol port, 80, receives the client requests, and distributes them to the pool members.

9
Monitoring OpenStack Networks

The recipes in this chapter will explore the various means to monitor the network resource utilization using Ceilometer. We will cover the following topics:

- Monitoring the Virtual Machine bandwidth
- Monitoring the L3 bandwidth
- Monitoring the load balancer connection statistics
- Monitoring the per project and per user bandwidth
- Monitoring the host Network bandwidth

Introduction

Due to the dynamic nature of virtual infrastructure and multiple users sharing the same cloud platform, the OpenStack administrator needs to track how the tenants use the resources. In this chapter, we will look at ways to monitor the usage of virtual and physical networking resources. The resource utilization data can be used to bill the users of a public cloud and to debug infrastructure-related problems. The data can also help in capacity planning by giving an estimate of the capacity of the physical devices and trends of resource usage.

OpenStack Ceilometer project provides you with telemetry service. It can measure the usage of resources by collecting statistics across the various OpenStack components. The resource utilization data is collected over the message bus or by polling the various components. OpenStack Neutron provides Ceilometer with the statistics that are related to the virtual networks.

The following figure shows you how Ceilometer interacts with the Neutron and Nova services:

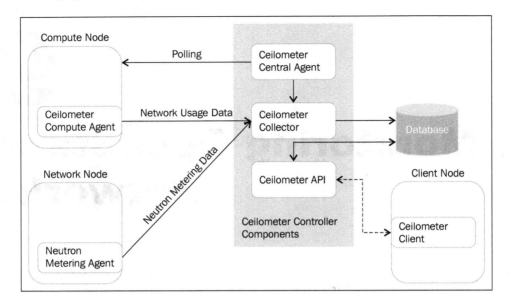

To implement these recipes, we will use an OpenStack setup as described in the following image:

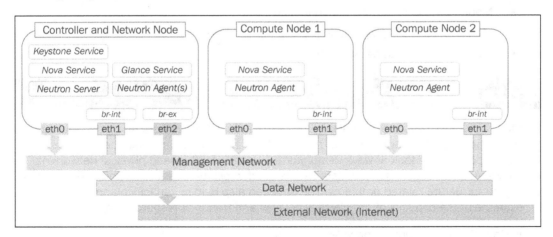

This setup has two compute nodes and one node for the controller and networking services.

Monitoring the Virtual Machine bandwidth

OpenStack Ceilometer collects the resource utilization of the VMs by running a Ceilometer compute agent on all the compute nodes. These agents collect the various metrics that are related to each VM running on the compute node. The data that is collected is periodically sent to the Ceilometer collector over the message bus.

In this recipe, we will learn how to use the Ceilometer client to check the bandwidth utilization by a VM.

Getting ready

For this recipe, you will need the following information:

- The SSH login credentials for a node where the OpenStack client packages are installed
- A shell RC file that initializes the environment variables for CLI

How to do it...

The following steps will show you how to determine the bandwidth utilization of a VM:

1. Using the appropriate credentials, SSH into the OpenStack node installed with the OpenStack client packages.

2. Source the shell RC file to initialize the environment variables required for the CLI commands.

3. Use the `nova list` command to find the ID of the VM instance that you want to monitor:

```
openstack@controller:~$ nova list
+--------------------------------------+------+--------+------------+-------------+------------------+
| ID                                   | Name | Status | Task State | Power State | Networks         |
+--------------------------------------+------+--------+------------+-------------+------------------+
| d6010e17-d3c1-4be1-b71a-9946f79e96ce | vm1  | ACTIVE | -          | Running     | private=10.10.10.3 |
+--------------------------------------+------+--------+------------+-------------+------------------+
```

4. Use the `ceilometer resource-list|grep <virtual-machine-id>` command to find the resource ID of the network port associated with the VM. Note down the resource ID for the virtual port associated to the VM for use in the later commands. The virtual port resource ID is a combination of the VM ID and name of the tap interface for the virtual port, which is named `instance-<virtual-machine-id>-<tap-interface-name>`:

```
openstack@controller:~$ ceilometer resource-list|grep d6010e17-d3c1-4be1-b71a-9946f79e96ce
| d6010e17-d3c1-4be1-b71a-9946f79e96ce                          | openstack | 9520da0d064a40e894c978f4b16858ad | f5d27b0a42d74459bb1cbd86115ad8ff |
| instance-00000002-d6010e17-d3c1-4be1-b71a-9946f79e96ce-tap9a5b4358-1c | openstack | 9520da0d064a40e894c978f4b16858ad | f5d27b0a42d74459bb1cbd86115ad8ff |
```

5. Use `ceilometer meter-list -q resource=<virtual-port-resource-id>` to find the meters associated with the network port on the VM:

```
openstack@controller:~$ ceilometer meter-list -q resource=instance-00000002-d6010e17-d3c1-4be1-b71a-9946f79e96ce-tap9a5b4358-1c
+------------------------------+------------+----------+------------------------------------------------------------------------+
| Name                         | Type       | Unit     | Resource ID                                                            |
+------------------------------+------------+----------+------------------------------------------------------------------------+
| network.incoming.bytes       | cumulative | B        | instance-00000002-d6010e17-d3c1-4be1-b71a-9946f79e96ce-tap9a5b4358-1c   |
| network.incoming.bytes.rate  | gauge      | B/s      | instance-00000002-d6010e17-d3c1-4be1-b71a-9946f79e96ce-tap9a5b4358-1c   |
| network.incoming.packets     | cumulative | packet   | instance-00000002-d6010e17-d3c1-4be1-b71a-9946f79e96ce-tap9a5b4358-1c   |
| network.incoming.packets.rate| gauge      | packet/s | instance-00000002-d6010e17-d3c1-4be1-b71a-9946f79e96ce-tap9a5b4358-1c   |
| network.outgoing.bytes       | cumulative | B        | instance-00000002-d6010e17-d3c1-4be1-b71a-9946f79e96ce-tap9a5b4358-1c   |
| network.outgoing.bytes.rate  | gauge      | B/s      | instance-00000002-d6010e17-d3c1-4be1-b71a-9946f79e96ce-tap9a5b4358-1c   |
| network.outgoing.packets     | cumulative | packet   | instance-00000002-d6010e17-d3c1-4be1-b71a-9946f79e96ce-tap9a5b4358-1c   |
| network.outgoing.packets.rate| gauge      | packet/s | instance-00000002-d6010e17-d3c1-4be1-b71a-9946f79e96ce-tap9a5b4358-1c   |
+------------------------------+------------+----------+------------------------------------------------------------------------+
```

6. Next, use `ceilometer statistics -m <meter-name> -q resource=<virtual-port-resource-id>` to view the network usage statistics. Use the meters that we discovered in the previous step in order to view the associated data:

```
openstack@controller:~$ ceilometer statistics -m network.incoming.bytes -q resource=instance-00000002-d6010e17-d3c1-4be1-b71a-9946f79e96ce-tap9a5b4358-1c
+--------+---------------------+---------------------+---------+---------+--------------+-----------+-------+----------+---------------------+------------+
| Period | Period Start        | Period End          | Max     | Min     | Avg          | Sum       | Count | Duration | Duration Start      | Duration En|
+--------+---------------------+---------------------+---------+---------+--------------+-----------+-------+----------+---------------------+------------+
| 0      | 2015-07-03T06:04:24 | 2015-07-04T08:14:25 | 10957.0 | 10139.0 | 10397.8607595| 1642862.0 | 158   | 94201.0  | 2015-07-03T06:04:24 | 2015-07-04T|
+--------+---------------------+---------------------+---------+---------+--------------+-----------+-------+----------+---------------------+------------+
openstack@controller:~$ ceilometer statistics -m network.outgoing.bytes -q resource=instance-00000002-d6010e17-d3c1-4be1-b71a-9946f79e96ce-tap9a5b4358-1c
+--------+---------------------+---------------------+---------+---------+--------------+-----------+-------+----------+---------------------+------------+
| Period | Period Start        | Period End          | Max     | Min     | Avg          | Sum       | Count | Duration | Duration Start      | Duration En|
+--------+---------------------+---------------------+---------+---------+--------------+-----------+-------+----------+---------------------+------------+
| 0      | 2015-07-03T06:04:24 | 2015-07-04T08:14:25 | 13423.0 | 12693.0 | 12924.0126582| 2041994.0 | 158   | 94201.0  | 2015-07-03T06:04:24 | 2015-07-04T|
+--------+---------------------+---------------------+---------+---------+--------------+-----------+-------+----------+---------------------+------------+
```

Ceilometer stores the port bandwidth data for the incoming and outgoing packets and the bytes and their rates.

How it works...

The OpenStack Ceilometer compute agent collects the statistics related to the network port connected to the VMs and posts them on the message bus. These statistics are collected by the Ceilometer collector daemon. Ceilometer client can be used to query a meter and filter the statistical data based on the resource ID.

Monitoring the L3 bandwidth

The OpenStack Neutron provides you with metering commands in order to enable the monitoring of the **Layer 3** (**L3**) traffic. The metering commands create a label that can hold a list of the packet matching rules. Neutron counts and associates any L3 packet that matches these rules with the metering label. In this recipe, we will learn how to use the L3 traffic monitoring commands of Neutron to enable packet counting.

Getting ready

For this recipe, we will use a VM connected to a network that in turn is connected to a router. The following figure describes the topology:

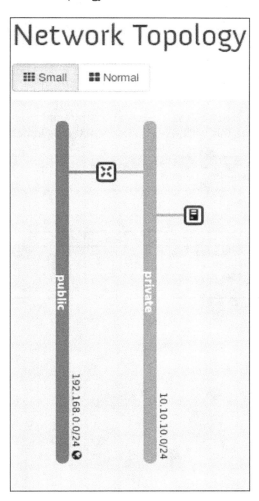

We will use a network called private with a CIDR of **10.10.10.0/24**.

For this recipe, you will need the following information:

- ▶ The SSH login credentials for a node where the OpenStack client packages are installed
- ▶ A shell RC file that initializes the environment variables for CLI
- ▶ The name of the L3 metering label
- ▶ The CIDR for which the traffic needs to be measured

How to do it...

The following steps will show you how to enable the monitoring of the traffic to or from any L3 network:

1. Using the appropriate credentials, SSH into the OpenStack node installed with the OpenStack client packages.

2. Source the shell RC file to initialize the environment variables required for the CLI commands.

3. Use the `neutron meter-label-create` command to create a metering label. Note the label ID as this will be used later with the Ceilometer commands:

```
openstack@controller:~$ neutron meter-label-create Chapter9-label1
Created a new metering_label:
+--------------+--------------------------------------+
| Field        | Value                                |
+--------------+--------------------------------------+
| description  |                                      |
| id           | 9f8a2d88-d7db-43fe-8050-5c195b25bed1 |
| name         | Chapter9-label1                      |
| shared       | False                                |
| tenant_id    | f5d27b0a42d74459bb1cbd86115ad8ff     |
+--------------+--------------------------------------+
```

4. Use the `neutron meter-label-rule-create` command to create a rule that associates a network address to the label that we created in the previous step. In our case, we will count any packet that reaches the gateway from the CIDR 10.10.10.0/24 network to which the VM is connected:

```
openstack@controller:~$ neutron meter-label-rule-create Chapter9-label1  10.10.10.0/24 --direction egress
Created a new metering_label_rule:
+------------------+--------------------------------------+
| Field            | Value                                |
+------------------+--------------------------------------+
| direction        | egress                               |
| excluded         | False                                |
| id               | e3228350-778b-4183-8be8-e7f9172bf1e9 |
| metering_label_id | 9f8a2d88-d7db-43fe-8050-5c195b25bed1 |
| remote_ip_prefix | 10.10.10.0/24                        |
+------------------+--------------------------------------+
```

5. Use the `ceilometer meter-list` command with a resource filter in order to find the meters associated with the label resource:

```
openstack@controller:~$ ceilometer meter-list -q resource=9f8a2d88-d7db-43fe-8050-5c195b25bed1
+-----------+-------+------+--------------------------------------+---------+----------------------------------+
| Name      | Type  | Unit | Resource ID                          | User ID | Project ID                       |
+-----------+-------+------+--------------------------------------+---------+----------------------------------+
| bandwidth | delta | B    | 9f8a2d88-d7db-43fe-8050-5c195b25bed1 | None    | f5d27b0a42d74459bb1cbd86115ad8ff |
+-----------+-------+------+--------------------------------------+---------+----------------------------------+
```

6. Use the `ceilometer statistics` command to view the number of packets matching the metering label:

```
openstack@controller:~$ ceilometer statistics -m bandwidth  -q resource=9f8a2d88-d7db-43fe-8050-5c195b25bed1
+--------+----------------------------+----------------------------+--------+-----+-------+--------+-------+------------+
| Period | Period Start               | Period End                 | Max    | Min | Avg   | Sum    | Count | Duration   |
+--------+----------------------------+----------------------------+--------+-----+-------+--------+-------+------------+
| 0      | 2015-07-04T08:51:48.208668 | 2015-07-04T09:14:48.229038 | 5040.0 | 0.0 | 374.5 | 8988.0 | 24    | 1380.02037 |
+--------+----------------------------+----------------------------+--------+-----+-------+--------+-------+------------+
```

The packet counting has now been enabled and the bandwidth statistics can be viewed using Ceilometer.

How it works...

The Neutron monitoring agent implements the packet counting meter in the L3 router. It uses iptables to implement a packet counter. The Neutron L3 agent collects the counter statistics periodically and posts on the message bus, which is collected by the Ceilometer collector daemon.

Monitoring the load balancer connection statistics

We have seen earlier that the OpenStack Neutron provides a load balancer as a service. The load balancer service provides you with the statistics of the utilization for each instance created in the load balancer cluster. In this recipe, we will view the load balancer-related usage data collected by OpenStack Ceilometer.

Getting ready

For this recipe, we will need to create a load balancer setup. Use the recipes described in *Chapter 8, Using HAProxy for Load Balancing* to create a load balancer with two members in the pool. We will also create a virtual IP and health monitor as described in the chapter. The following table describes our load balancer setup:

Virtual Machine	Role	IP address
vm1	Member	20.20.20.3
vm2	Member	20.20.20.4
Virtual IP	Virtual IP	20.20.20.50
Client-1	Client	20.20.20.51

For this recipe, you will need the following information:

▶ The SSH login credentials for a node where the OpenStack client packages are installed

▶ A shell RC file that initializes the environment variables for CLI

How to do it...

The following steps will show you how to view the statistics available for a load balancer instance:

1. Using the appropriate credentials, SSH into the OpenStack node installed with the OpenStack client packages.

2. Source the shell RC file to initialize the environment variables required for the CLI commands.

3. Use the `ceilometer statistics` command to find the number of load balancer members and pools. The meters associated with the load balancer instances use the prefix, `network.services.lb`:

```
openstack@controller:~$ ceilometer statistics -m network.services.lb.member
+--------+-----------------------------+-----------------------------+-----+-----+-----+-----+-------+-----------+
| Period | Period Start                | Period End                  | Max | Min | Avg | Sum | Count | Duration  |
+--------+-----------------------------+-----------------------------+-----+-----+-----+-----+-------+-----------+
| 0      | 2015-07-04T10:42:52.312525  | 2015-07-04T10:46:54.242365  | 1.0 | 0.0 | 0.5 | 2.0 | 4     | 241.92984 |
+--------+-----------------------------+-----------------------------+-----+-----+-----+-----+-------+-----------+

openstack@controller:~$ ceilometer statistics -m network.services.lb.pool
+--------+-----------------------------+-----------------------------+-----+-----+-----+-----+-------+-----------+
| Period | Period Start                | Period End                  | Max | Min | Avg | Sum | Count | Duration  |
+--------+-----------------------------+-----------------------------+-----+-----+-----+-----+-------+-----------+
| 0      | 2015-07-04T10:39:08.003635  | 2015-07-04T10:46:54.279411  | 1.0 | 1.0 | 1.0 | 2.0 | 2     | 466.275776|
+--------+-----------------------------+-----------------------------+-----+-----+-----+-----+-------+-----------+
```

4. Next, use the `ceilometer statistics` command with the `network.services.lb.total.connections` meter in order to find the number of total connections served by the load balancer. Use the pool ID to query the connection per load balancer instance:

```
openstack@controller:~$ ceilometer statistics -m network.services.lb.total.connections -q resource=a7f7429b-9276-41c2-a007-30e7ff12d131
+--------+---------------------+---------------------+-------+-----+------+-------+-------+----------+---------------------+---------------------+
| Period | Period Start        | Period End          | Max   | Min | Avg  | Sum   | Count | Duration | Duration Start      | Duration End        |
+--------+---------------------+---------------------+-------+-----+------+-------+-------+----------+---------------------+---------------------+
| 0      | 2015-07-04T10:46:54 | 2015-07-04T11:06:54 | 291.0 | 0.0 | 97.0 | 291.0 | 3     | 1200.0   | 2015-07-04T10:46:54 | 2015-07-04T11:06:54 |
+--------+---------------------+---------------------+-------+-----+------+-------+-------+----------+---------------------+---------------------+
```

5. Use the `ceilometer statistic` command with the `network.services.lb.incoming.bytes` meter to find the number of bytes received by the load balancer:

```
openstack@controller:~$ ceilometer statistics -m network.services.lb.incoming.bytes
+--------+---------------------+---------------------+--------+-----+--------+----------+-------+----------+---------------------+---------------------+
| Period | Period Start        | Period End          | Max    | Min | Avg    | Sum      | Count | Duration | Duration Start      | Duration End        |
+--------+---------------------+---------------------+--------+-----+--------+----------+-------+----------+---------------------+---------------------+
| 0      | 2015-07-04T10:46:54 | 2015-07-04T12:16:54 | 202760.0| 0.0| 114552.0| 1145520.0| 10   | 5400.0   | 2015-07-04T10:46:54 | 2015-07-04T12:16:54 |
+--------+---------------------+---------------------+--------+-----+--------+----------+-------+----------+---------------------+---------------------+
```

You can use the `ceilometer meter-list` command to find out the other metering data available for the load balancer.

How it works...

The Neutron load balancer agent collects the statistics for each instance of the load balancer that is created; the usage data is periodically reported to Ceilometer. The Ceilometer client can then be used to track the various metrics associated with the load balancer instances.

Monitoring the per project and per user bandwidth

In the first recipe, we looked at the monitoring of resource utilization for a VM. In a cloud shared by multiple tenants and users, it is important to gather information about the utilization of the resources by a user or by the whole project. In this recipe, you will learn how to use the Ceilometer client to monitor the network bandwidth utilization by a tenant or project and an individual user of OpenStack.

Getting ready

For this recipe, you will need the following information:

▶ The SSH login credentials for a node where the OpenStack client packages are installed

▶ A shell RC file that initializes the environment variables for CLI

▶ The ID of the OpenStack tenant and user

How to do it...

The following steps will show you how to determine the bandwidth utilization of a VM:

1. Using the appropriate credentials, SSH into the OpenStack node installed with the OpenStack client packages.

2. Source the shell RC file to initialize the environment variables required for the CLI commands.

3. Use `ceilometer statistics` with the network meters to view the network resource utilization. Use `user=<user-id>` and `project=<tenant-id>` to filter the utilization by the user ID and tenant ID, respectively. The tenant and project IDs are the same:

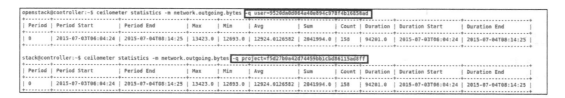

The other meters can also be queried in a similar manner in order to find the resources used by a user or project.

How it works...

All the usage data stored by Ceilometer is associated with a user and project. So, it is possible to retrieve the monitoring data for a given user or tenant (project).

Monitoring the host Network bandwidth

In the previous recipes, we looked at monitoring the virtual infrastructure resources. For the cloud administrator, it is also very important to know about the utilization of the physical resources. In this recipe, you will learn about monitoring the Network utilization statistics for a compute or network node.

Ceilometer can collect the physical network statistics for the compute or network node using a central agent and SNMP. The Ceilometer central agent must be configured in order to collect the physical resource utilization data from the compute and network nodes. On the Compute and Network nodes, the SNMP daemon must be configured to provide the physical resource utilization data that is queried by the Ceilometer central agent.

In this recipe, you will learn how to use the Ceilometer commands in order to view the physical network statistics of the Compute and Network nodes. For this recipe, we will view the statistics collected for the Compute node, `compute1`.

Getting ready

For this recipe, you will need the following information:

 ▸ The SSH login credentials for a node where the OpenStack client packages are installed
 ▸ A shell RC file that initializes the environment variables for CLI

How to do it...

The following steps will show you how to view the physical network utilization data for a Compute or Network Node:

1. Using the appropriate credentials, SSH into the OpenStack node installed with the OpenStack client packages.
2. Source the shell RC file to initialize the environment variables required for the CLI commands.

3. Use the `ceilometer meter-list` command to query all the meters associated with the OpenStack node. For our example, we will use the node, `compute1`:

```
openstack@controller:~$ ceilometer meter-list -q resource=compute1
+-------------------------------------------+------------+-----------+-------------+---------+------------+
| Name                                      | Type       | Unit      | Resource ID | User ID | Project ID |
+-------------------------------------------+------------+-----------+-------------+---------+------------+
| hardware.cpu.load.15min                   | gauge      | process   | compute1    | None    | None       |
| hardware.cpu.load.1min                    | gauge      | process   | compute1    | None    | None       |
| hardware.cpu.load.5min                    | gauge      | process   | compute1    | None    | None       |
| hardware.disk.size.total                  | gauge      | B         | compute1    | None    | None       |
| hardware.disk.size.used                   | gauge      | B         | compute1    | None    | None       |
| hardware.memory.swap.avail                | gauge      | B         | compute1    | None    | None       |
| hardware.memory.swap.total                | gauge      | B         | compute1    | None    | None       |
| hardware.memory.total                     | gauge      | B         | compute1    | None    | None       |
| hardware.memory.used                      | gauge      | B         | compute1    | None    | None       |
| hardware.network.ip.incoming.datagrams    | cumulative | datagrams | compute1    | None    | None       |
| hardware.network.ip.outgoing.datagrams    | cumulative | datagrams | compute1    | None    | None       |
| hardware.system_stats.cpu.idle            | gauge      | %         | compute1    | None    | None       |
| hardware.system_stats.io.incoming.blocks  | cumulative | blocks    | compute1    | None    | None       |
| hardware.system_stats.io.outgoing.blocks  | cumulative | blocks    | compute1    | None    | None       |
+-------------------------------------------+------------+-----------+-------------+---------+------------+
```

4. Next, use the `ceilometer statistics` command to view any of the meters associated with the node. For this example, we will view the incoming network packets, as follows:

```
openstack@controller:~$ ceilometer statistics -m hardware.network.ip.incoming.datagrams -q resource=compute1
+--------+---------------------+---------------------+----------+---------+-------------+-------------+-------+----------+---------------------+---------------------+
| Period | Period Start        | Period End          | Max      | Min     | Avg         | Sum         | Count | Duration | Duration Start      | Duration End        |
+--------+---------------------+---------------------+----------+---------+-------------+-------------+-------+----------+---------------------+---------------------+
| 0      | 2015-07-03T06:44:03 | 2015-07-04T15:46:55 | 611055.0 | 94205.0 | 264648.491468 | 77542008.0 | 293   | 118972.0 | 2015-07-03T06:44:03 | 2015-07-04T15:46:55 |
+--------+---------------------+---------------------+----------+---------+-------------+-------------+-------+----------+---------------------+---------------------+
```

Use the Ceilometer commands with the other hardware meters to view the associated data for the node.

How it works...

The Ceilometer central agent periodically polls the SNMP agent on the OpenStack nodes and collects the hardware-related statistics. The hardware status data is then stored by Ceilometer and can be queried using the client.

10

Writing Your Own Neutron ML2 Mechanism Driver

In this chapter, we will learn how to develop a custom ML2 mechanism driver for Neutron using the following recipes:

- ▶ Creating a basic ML2 mechanism driver
- ▶ Registering your ML2 mechanism driver with the Neutron server
- ▶ Processing API requests for a Network
- ▶ Processing API requests for a Subnet
- ▶ Processing API requests for a Port

Introduction

This chapter is targeted towards developers and we will use DevStack to develop the driver for the ML2 plugin. DevStack is a tool to install an all-in-one OpenStack node. DevStack also provides you with a development environment for OpenStack-related programming. Knowledge of the Python programming language is a prerequisite for this chapter.

Before we dive into the recipes, let's understand how the plugin works.

As discussed in the first chapter, Neutron supports the core networking features using entities such as Network, Subnet, and Port. These entities are implemented using virtual and physical networking technologies. In order to allow multiple networking technologies to interoperate, Neutron uses the concept of plugins. The following image shows the Neutron plugin model:

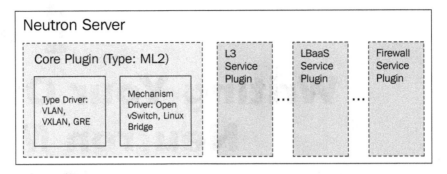

As shown here, Neutron supports one core plugin. The **Modular Layer 2** (**ML2**) is a type of a core plugin that supports multiple drivers so that the plugin functionality can be extended and customized. The ML2 plugin comprises of type drivers and mechanism drivers.

Type drivers represent different types of networking technologies that provide the segmentation of Networks, for example, VLAN or VXLAN-based segmentation. The mechanism drivers on the other hand are software and hardware solutions that implement one or more of the Network type.

In this chapter, we will see how to write a custom ML2 mechanism driver from scratch. We will implement a simple driver that logs the key Neutron API calls in a log file. We will also see how to extract crucial information that has been passed to the Neutron API.

The source code used in this chapter is available on GitHub at `https://github.com/reachsrirams/packt-openstack-networking-cookbook`. You will need all the files from the GitHub repository. The repository also contains a reference `local.conf` file that may be useful in your DevStack installation.

Creating a basic ML2 mechanism driver

The first step in the journey to write an ML2 mechanism driver is to create a basic driver class. This will also help us understand the code structure.

Getting ready

As mentioned earlier, we will use DevStack in order to write and test our plugin. So, ensure that the DevStack environment is up and running successfully.

How to do it...

1. With the appropriate credentials, SSH into your DevStack setup.

2. Ensure that all the driver files from the GitHub repository are copied to `/opt/stack/neutron/neutron/plugins/ml2/drivers`.

3. The `ch10_ml2_mech_driver.py` file will be our main mechanism driver file, as follows:

```python
# Import Neutron Database API
from neutron.db import api as db
from oslo_log import log as logger
from neutron.plugins.ml2 import driver_api as api

driver_logger = logger.getLogger(__name__)


class CookbookMechanismDriver(api.MechanismDriver):

    def initialize(self):
        driver_logger.info("Inside Mech Driver Initialize")
```

4. The `CookbookMechanismDriver` class extends the `MechanismDriver` class of the Neutron API and overrides only the initialize method for now.

5. You can view the `MechanismDriver` class defined in the `/opt/stack/neutron/neutron/plugins/ml2/driver_api.py` file. You will notice that the `MechanismDriver` class supports many methods related to the Network, Subnet, and Port.

How it works...

As ML2 is a core plugin, the driver is intended to support operations on the core objects, namely Network, Subnet, and Port.

As seen in the `MechanismDriver` class, there are Python methods to create, delete, and update these core entities. These operations result in the addition, removal, and updates to the Neutron database.

Registering your ML2 mechanism driver with the Neutron server

Once the driver code is added, the next step is to register the driver with Neutron. In this recipe, we will see how to register the new mechanism driver with Neutron. We will also check whether our mechanism driver has been loaded and initialized successfully as we restart the Neutron server.

Getting ready

The previous recipe is the prerequisite for this recipe. The basic ML2 driver code is required to be placed at the location mentioned in the previous recipe.

How to do it...

1. With the appropriate credentials, SSH into your DevStack setup.

2. Open the `/etc/neutron/plugins/ml2/ml2_conf.ini` configuration file using your desired editor. For example, the command for the vi editor will be as follows:

```
openstack@devstack:~$
openstack@devstack:~$ vi /etc/neutron/plugins/ml2/ml2_conf.ini
```

3. In the `[ml2]` section of the file, configure `mechanism_drivers`, as follows:

```
[ml2]
tenant_network_types = vlan
type_drivers = local,flat,vlan,gre,vxlan
mechanism_drivers = openvswitch,cookbook
# (ListOpt) List of network type driver entrypoints to be loaded from
# the neutron.ml2.type_drivers namespace.
#
```

4. Next, open the `/opt/stack/neutron/neutron.egg-info/entry_points.txt` file using your desired editor. For example, the command for the vi editor will be as follows:

```
openstack@devstack:~$
openstack@devstack:~$ vi /opt/stack/neutron/neutron.egg-info/entry_points.txt
```

5. In the `[neutron.ml2.mechanism_drivers]` section of the file, configure the Python class that needs to be loaded for the mechanism driver named `cookbook`. Note that the mechanism driver name must match the one that is used in the `ml2_conf.ini` file as shown in step 3:

```
[neutron.ml2.mechanism_drivers]
arista = neutron.plugins.ml2.drivers.arista.mechanism_arista:AristaDriver
bigswitch = neutron.plugins.ml2.drivers.mech_bigswitch.driver:BigSwitchMechanismDriver
brocade = networking_brocade.vdx.ml2driver.mechanism_brocade:BrocadeMechanism
brocade_fi_ni = neutron.plugins.ml2.drivers.brocade.fi_ni.mechanism_brocade_fi_ni:BrocadeFiNiMechanism
cisco_apic = neutron.plugins.ml2.drivers.cisco.apic.mechanism_apic:APICMechanismDriver
cisco_n1kv = neutron.plugins.ml2.drivers.cisco.n1kv.mech_cisco_n1kv:N1KVMechanismDriver
cisco_ncs = neutron.plugins.ml2.drivers.cisco.ncs.driver:NCSMechanismDriver
cisco_nexus = neutron.plugins.ml2.drivers.cisco.nexus.mech_cisco_nexus:CiscoNexusMechanismDriver
cisco_ucsm = neutron.plugins.ml2.drivers.cisco.ucsm.mech_cisco_ucsm:CiscoUcsmMechanismDriver
fake_agent = neutron.tests.unit.plugins.ml2.drivers.mech_fake_agent:FakeAgentMechanismDriver
fslsdn = neutron.plugins.ml2.drivers.freescale.mechanism_fslsdn:FslsdnMechanismDriver
hyperv = neutron.plugins.ml2.drivers.hyperv.mech_hyperv:HypervMechanismDriver
l2population = neutron.plugins.ml2.drivers.l2pop.mech_driver:L2populationMechanismDriver
linuxbridge = neutron.plugins.ml2.drivers.mech_linuxbridge:LinuxbridgeMechanismDriver
logger = neutron.tests.unit.plugins.ml2.drivers.mechanism_logger:LoggerMechanismDriver
mlnx = neutron.plugins.ml2.drivers.mlnx.mech_mlnx:MlnxMechanismDriver
ncs = neutron.plugins.ml2.drivers.cisco.ncs.driver:NCSMechanismDriver
nuage = neutron.plugins.ml2.drivers.mech_nuage.driver:NuageMechanismDriver
ofagent = neutron.plugins.ml2.drivers.ofagent.driver:OfagentMechanismDriver
opendaylight = neutron.plugins.ml2.drivers.opendaylight.driver:OpenDaylightMechanismDriver
openvswitch = neutron.plugins.ml2.drivers.mech_openvswitch:OpenvswitchMechanismDriver
ovsvapp = neutron.plugins.ml2.drivers.ovsvapp.mech_driver:OVSvAppAgentMechanismDriver
sdnve = neutron.plugins.ml2.drivers.ibm.mechanism_sdnve:SdnveMechanismDriver
sriovnicswitch = neutron.plugins.ml2.drivers.mech_sriov.mech_driver:SriovNicSwitchMechanismDriver
test = neutron.tests.unit.plugins.ml2.drivers.mechanism_test:TestMechanismDriver
cookbook = neutron.plugins.ml2.drivers.ch10_ml2_mech_driver:CookbookMechanismDriver
```

6. Restart the Neutron services in your DevStack setup. You will have to use the correct screen instance of your DevStack setup to run this operation.

7. Once the Neutron services have been restarted, we will verify that our basic mechanism driver has been loaded and initialized. To do this, open the Neutron server log file in your DevStack setup. In our DevStack setup, the corresponding file is `/opt/stack/logs/q-svc.log`.

8. In this file, search for the words `Inside Mech`. This will show the corresponding record in the Neutron server log file, as shown in the following screenshot:

```
2015-07-26 23:30:10.235 10669 INFO neutron.plugins.ml2.drivers.type_vlan [-] VlanTypeDriver initialization complete
2015-07-26 23:30:10.236 10669 INFO neutron.plugins.ml2.managers [-] Initializing driver for type 'local'
2015-07-26 23:30:10.236 10669 INFO neutron.plugins.ml2.managers [-] Initializing driver for type 'gre'
2015-07-26 23:30:10.238 10669 INFO neutron.plugins.ml2.drivers.type_tunnel [-] gre ID ranges: [(1, 1000)]
2015-07-26 23:30:10.568 10669 INFO neutron.plugins.ml2.managers [-] Initializing driver for type 'vxlan'
2015-07-26 23:30:10.570 10669 INFO neutron.plugins.ml2.drivers.type_tunnel [-] vxlan ID ranges: [(1001, 2000)]
2015-07-26 23:30:10.868 10669 INFO neutron.plugins.ml2.managers [-] Initializing mechanism driver 'openvswitch'
2015-07-26 23:30:10.868 10669 INFO neutron.plugins.ml2.managers [-] Initializing mechanism driver 'cookbook'
2015-07-26 23:30:10.869 10669 INFO neutron.plugins.ml2.drivers.ch10_ml2_mech_driver [-] Inside Mech Driver Initialize
2015-07-26 23:30:10.874 10669 INFO neutron.plugins.ml2.plugin [-] Modular L2 Plugin initialization complete
2015-07-26 23:30:10.874 10669 DEBUG neutron.manager [-] Loading services supported by the core plugin _load_services_from_core_plugin /opt/stack/neutron/neutron/manager.py:147
2015-07-26 23:30:10.875 10669 INFO neutron.extensions.vlantransparent [-] Disabled vlantransparent extension.
2015-07-26 23:30:10.875 10669 DEBUG neutron.manager [-] Loading service plugins: ['neutron.services.l3_router.l3_router_plugin.L3RouterPlugin'] _load_service_plugins /opt/stack/neutron/neutron/manager.py:168
2015-07-26 23:30:10.875 10669 INFO neutron.manager [-] Loading Plugin: neutron.services.l3_router.l3_router_plugin.L3RouterPlugin
2015-07-26 23:30:10.885 10669 DEBUG neutron.callbacks.manager [-] Subscribe: <function _prevent_l3_port_delete_callback at 0x7f77d8e65320> port before_delete subscribe /opt/stack/neutron/neutron/callbacks/manager.py:43
```

The presence of the `Inside Mech Driver Initialize` shows that our minimal mechanism driver was loaded successfully and it was also initialized by invoking the `initialize()` method of the driver.

Downloading the example code

You can download the example code files for all Packt books you have purchased from your account at `http://www.packtpub.com`. If you purchased this book elsewhere, you can visit `http://www.packtpub.com/support` and register to have the files e-mailed directly to you.

How it works...

During the startup, the Neutron server loads the core plugin based on the configuration in the `neutron.conf` file. In our example, we will use the ML2 plugin as the core plugin. The ML2 plugin, in turn, loads the ML2 type and mechanism drivers as specified in the `ml2_conf.ini` file. In this recipe, the ML2 plugin will attempt to load the mechanism drivers named `openvswitch` and `cookbook`. The ML2 plugin uses the `entry_points.txt` file in order to identify and load the Python class corresponding to the driver name specified in the ML2 configuration.

There's more...

As we are using the DevStack setup for the recipes in this chapter, it is better to include `cookbook` as the mechanism driver in the `local.conf` file. This will ensure that `cookbook` is added to the `ml2_conf.ini` file every time DevStack is restarted. You can find a reference `local.conf` file in the GitHub repository.

Processing API requests for a Network

Vendors and third-party application developers write custom ML2 mechanism drivers in order to integrate their products and applications with OpenStack. The main aspect of writing mechanism drivers is the implementation of specific methods related to the Network, Subnet, and Port. In this recipe, we will see how to process API requests specifically for a Network.

Getting ready

In this recipe, we will enhance our basic mechanism driver code and add two new methods in order to process API requests for a Network. Ensure that your DevStack setup is up and running, with `cookbook` as one of the mechanism drivers, as shown in the previous recipe.

How to do it...

1. With the appropriate credentials, SSH into your DevStack setup.

2. Open `/opt/stack/neutron/neutron/plugins/ml2/drivers/ ch10_ml2_mech_driver.py` using an editor.

3. Add a new import statement, as highlighted in the following screenshot:

```
from neutron.plugins.ml2 import driver_api as api

import ch10_ml2_mech_driver_network as cookbook_network_driver

driver_logger = logger.getLogger(__name__)
```

4. Update the class declaration statement, as follows:

```
class CookbookMechanismDriver(cookbook_network_driver.CookbookNetworkMechanismDriver):

    def initialize(self):
        driver_logger.error("Inside Mech Driver Initialize")
```

5. `CookbookMechanismDriver` now extends the `CookbookNetworkMechanismDriver` class and as a result, inherits the following methods:

```
class CookbookNetworkMechanismDriver(api.MechanismDriver):

    def _log_network_information(self, method_name, current_context, prev_context):
        driver_logger.info("**** %s ****" % (method_name))
        # Print the Network Name using the context
        driver_logger.info("Current Network Name: %s" % (current_context['name']))
        # For create operation prev_context will be None.
        if prev_context is not None:
            driver_logger.info("Previous Network Name: %s" % (prev_context['name']))
        # Print the Network Type
        driver_logger.info("Current Network Type: %s" % current_context['provider:network_type'])
        driver_logger.info("**** %s ****" % (method_name))

    def create_network_postcommit(self, context):
        # Extract the current and the previous network context
        current_network_context = context.current
        previous_network_context = context.original
        self._log_network_information("Create Network PostCommit", current_network_context, previous_network_context)

    def update_network_postcommit(self, context):
        # Extract the current and the previous network context
        current_network_context = context.current
        previous_network_context = context.original
        self._log_network_information("Update Network PostCommit", current_network_context, previous_network_context)
```

6. We will implement only `create_network_postcommit` and `update_network_post_commit` in this driver code. As shown in the code, we will log the Network name and Network type values.

7. Restart the Neutron services in your DevStack setup. You will have to use the correct screen instance to run this operation.

8. Once the Neutron services have been restarted, create an OpenStack Network using the `neutron net-create CookbookNetwork1` CLI command where `CookbookNetwork1` is the Network name.

9. To verify that our mechanism driver code was executed, open the DevStack log file for Neutron. In our DevStack setup, the log file was `/opt/stack/log/q-svc.log`.

10. This log file should contain the specific log messages as per the `create_network_postcommit` method in our mechanism driver. Note that the previous Network name is not printed in the logs as of now:

```
2015-07-26 23:51:30.565 INFO neutron.plugins.ml2.drivers.ch10_ml2_mech_driver_network [req-b0c7382f-119a-4967-96c9-44cdb6425a6c admin admin]
 **** Create Network PostCommit ****
2015-07-26 23:51:30.565 INFO neutron.plugins.ml2.drivers.ch10_ml2_mech_driver_network [req-b0c7382f-119a-4967-96c9-44cdb6425a6c admin admin]
 Current Network Name: CookbookNetwork1
2015-07-26 23:51:30.565 INFO neutron.plugins.ml2.drivers.ch10_ml2_mech_driver_network [req-b0c7382f-119a-4967-96c9-44cdb6425a6c admin admin]
 Current Network Type: vlan
2015-07-26 23:51:30.565 INFO neutron.plugins.ml2.drivers.ch10_ml2_mech_driver_network [req-b0c7382f-119a-4967-96c9-44cdb6425a6c admin admin]
 **** Create Network PostCommit ****
```

11. Now, change the Network name using `neutron net-update CookbookNetwork1 --name CookbookNetwork2` where `CookbookNetwork2` is the new name of the Network. This will trigger the `update_network_post_commit` method of our mechanism driver.

12. Once the operation is successful, you will see that the DevStack log file contains a log message for the `update_network_post_commit` method:

```
2015-07-26 23:54:23.211 INFO neutron.plugins.ml2.drivers.ch10_ml2_mech_driver_network [req-f4fa3cd9-134e-4a2e-8e1a-2e57c83bf573 admin admin]
 **** Update Network PostCommit ****
2015-07-26 23:54:23.211 INFO neutron.plugins.ml2.drivers.ch10_ml2_mech_driver_network [req-f4fa3cd9-134e-4a2e-8e1a-2e57c83bf573 admin admin]
 Current Network Name: CookbookNetwork2
2015-07-26 23:54:23.211 INFO neutron.plugins.ml2.drivers.ch10_ml2_mech_driver_network [req-f4fa3cd9-134e-4a2e-8e1a-2e57c83bf573 admin admin]
 Previous Network Name: CookbookNetwork1
2015-07-26 23:54:23.212 INFO neutron.plugins.ml2.drivers.ch10_ml2_mech_driver_network [req-f4fa3cd9-134e-4a2e-8e1a-2e57c83bf573 admin admin]
 Current Network Type: vlan
2015-07-26 23:54:23.212 INFO neutron.plugins.ml2.drivers.ch10_ml2_mech_driver_network [req-f4fa3cd9-134e-4a2e-8e1a-2e57c83bf573 admin admin]
 **** Update Network PostCommit ****
```

As you can see, this time the log message contain the previous and current Network names.

How it works...

In this recipe, we implemented two methods related to a Network. The ML2 mechanism driver API consists of the create, update and delete operations for the OpenStack Network. In addition, the API also supports methods to handle DB commit related triggers. Once the Network object has been committed to the database, the method `xxxxx_network_postcommit` operation is invoked. In this recipe, we extracted and printed the Network name and Network type in the Neutron log file.

Each of these methods can also pass a context parameter. The context parameter is very important as it contains the details of the Network being created or updated. In the case of an update operation, context also contains the Network information prior to the current update.

In this recipe, we saw how to extract the Network name and Network type as a part of handling the API requests. It is possible to fetch additional attributes of a Network such as the Segmentation ID along similar lines.

Processing API requests for a Subnet

The previous recipe showed you how Neutron invokes methods in a mechanism driver for Network-related operations. In this recipe, we will see how to process API requests for Subnets.

Getting ready

In this recipe, we will enhance our driver and implement the methods that will process API requests for a Subnet. Ensure that your DevStack setup is up and running, with cookbook as one of the mechanism drivers, as shown in the earlier recipe.

How to do it...

1. With the appropriate credentials, SSH into your DevStack setup.

2. Open /opt/stack/neutron/neutron/plugins/ml2/drivers/ ch10_ml2_ mech_driver.py using an editor.

3. Add a new import statement, as highlighted in the following image:

```
from neutron.plugins.ml2 import driver_api as api

import ch10_ml2_mech_driver_network as cookbook_network_driver
import ch10_ml2_mech_driver_subnet as cookbook_subnet_driver

driver_logger = logger.getLogger(__name__)
```

4. Update the class declaration statement to include the Subnet driver class, as follows:

```
class CookbookMechanismDriver(cookbook_network_driver.CookbookNetworkMechanismDriver,
                    cookbook_subnet_driver.CookbookSubnetMechanismDriver):

    def initialize(self):
        driver_logger.error("Inside Mech Driver Initialize")
```

5. `CookbookMechanismDriver` now extends the `CookbookSubnetMechanismDriver` and `CookbookNetworkMechanismDriver` classes. Hence, it inherits the following additional methods:

```python
# Import Neutron Database API
from oslo_log import log as logger
from neutron.plugins.ml2 import driver_api as api

# Import ML2 Database API
from neutron.plugins.ml2 import db as ml2_db


driver_logger = logger.getLogger(__name__)


class CookbookSubnetMechanismDriver(api.MechanismDriver):

    def _log_subnet_information(self, method_name, current_context, prev_context, full_context):
        driver_logger.info("**** %s ****" % (method_name))
        driver_logger.info("Current Subnet Name: %s" % (current_context['name']))
        driver_logger.info("Current Subnet CIDR: %s" % (current_context['cidr']))
        # Extract the Network ID from the Subnet Context
        network_id = current_context['network_id']
        # Get the Neutron DB Session Handle
        session = full_context._plugin_context.session
        # Using ML2 DB API, fetch the Network that matches the Network ID
        networks = ml2_db.get_network_segments(session, network_id)
        driver_logger.info("Network associated to the Subnet: %s" % (networks))
        driver_logger.info("**** %s ****" % (method_name))

    def create_subnet_postcommit(self, context):
        # Extract the current and the previous Subnet context
        current_subnet_context = context.current
        previous_subnet_context = context.original
        self._log_subnet_information("Create Subnet PostCommit", current_subnet_context,
                                     previous_subnet_context, context)
```

6. We will implement only `create_subnet_postcommit` method in this driver code. As shown in the code, we will log the Subnet name, its CIDR, and the Network that it belongs to.

7. Restart the Neutron services in your DevStack setup. You will have to use the correct screen instance to run this operation.

8. Once the Neutron services have been restarted, create a Subnet using `neutron subnet-create --name CookbookSubnet2 CookbookNetwork2 10.20.30.0/24`.

9. Here, `CookbookSubnet2` refers to the Subnet name, `CookbookNetwork2` refers to the Network, and `10.20.30.0/24` refers to the CIDR or IP address range.

10. To verify that our mechanism driver code was executed, open the DevStack log file for Neutron. In our DevStack setup, the log file was `/opt/stack/log/q-svc.log`.

11. This log file should contain the specific log messages as per the `create_subnet_postcommit` method in our mechanism driver:

```
2015-07-25 00:47:19.377 INFO neutron.plugins.ml2.drivers.ch10_ml2_mech_driver_subnet [req-f62a9e88-dd97-43d9-8348-36a5d2c60f6f admin admin]
**** Create Subnet PostCommit ****
2015-07-25 00:47:19.377 INFO neutron.plugin.ml2.drivers.ch10_ml2_mech_driver_subnet [req-f62a9e88-dd97-43d9-8348-36a5d2c60f6f admin admin]
Current Subnet Name: CookbookSubnet2
2015-07-25 00:47:19.377 INFO neutron.plugin.ml2.drivers.ch10_ml2_mech_driver_subnet [req-f62a9e88-dd97-43d9-8348-36a5d2c60f6f admin admin]
Current Subnet CIDR: 10.20.30.0/24
2015-07-25 00:47:19.380 INFO neutron.plugin.ml2.drivers.ch10_ml2_mech_driver_subnet [req-f62a9e88-dd97-43d9-8348-36a5d2c60f6f admin admin]
Network associated to the Subnet: [{'segmentation_id': 1029L, 'physical_network': u'physnet1', 'id': u'75a9628c-d6d6-4668-9979-ffe82cdc0b5a'
, 'network_type': u'vlan'}]
2015-07-25 00:47:19.380 INFO neutron.plugin.ml2.drivers.ch10_ml2_mech_driver_subnet [req-f62a9e88-dd97-43d9-8348-36a5d2c60f6f admin admin]
**** Create Subnet PostCommit ****
```

As seen in the log file, the `create_subnet_postcommit` method of our mechanism driver was executed.

How it works...

In this recipe, we implemented a method related to the Subnet entity. Therefore, context that was passed to the driver methods contains information about the Subnet. In this recipe, we first logged the Subnet name and its CIDR. The Subnet entity has only the ID of the Network that it belongs to. We have to query the ML2 plugin database in order to fetch the details of the Network. The code in this recipe shows you how to access the ML2 plugin database and query it for the Network entity.

Processing API requests for a Port

We will conclude this chapter with a recipe that shows you how to process API requests for a Port. In real-world applications, the Port-related operations are used more frequently when compared to a Network or Subnet. As there are different types of Ports, this recipe will show you how to identify the Port type from the API requests.

Getting ready

Ensure that your DevStack setup is up and running, with `cookbook` as one of the mechanism drivers, as shown in the earlier recipe.

How to do it...

1. With the appropriate credentials, SSH into your DevStack setup.

2. Open `/opt/stack/neutron/neutron/plugins/ml2/drivers/ ch10_ml2_mech_driver.py` using an editor.

3. Add a new import statement, as highlighted in the following image:

```
from neutron.plugins.ml2 import driver_api as api

import ch10_ml2_mech_driver_network as cookbook_network_driver
import ch10_ml2_mech_driver_subnet as cookbook_subnet_driver
import ch10_ml2_mech_driver_port as cookbook_port_driver

driver_logger = logger.getLogger(__name__)
```

4. Update the class declaration statement to include the Port mechanism driver class, as follows:

```
driver_logger = logger.getLogger(__name__)


class CookbookMechanismDriver(cookbook_network_driver.CookbookNetworkMechanismDriver,
                    cookbook_subnet_driver.CookbookSubnetMechanismDriver,
                    cookbook_port_driver.CookbookPortMechanismDriver):

    def initialize(self):
        driver_logger.error("Inside Mech Driver Initialize")
```

5. `CookbookMechanismDriver` now extends the `CookbookPortMechanismDriver`, `CookbookSubnetMechanismDriver`, and `CookbookNetworkMechanismDriver` classes. Hence, it inherits the following additional methods:

```
class CookbookPortMechanismDriver(api.MechanismDriver):

    def _log_port_information(self, method_name, context):
        driver_logger.info("**** %s ****" % (method_name))
        # Extract the current Port context
        current_port_context = context.current
        # Extract the associated Network Context
        network_context = context.network
        driver_logger.info("Port Type: %s" % (current_port_context['device_owner']))
        driver_logger.info("IP Address of the Port: %s" % ((current_port_context['fixed_ips'][0])['ip_address']))
        driver_logger.info("Network name for the Port: %s" % (network_context.current['name']))
        driver_logger.info("Network type for the Port: %s" % (network_context.current['provider:network_type']))
        driver_logger.info("Segmentation ID for the Port: %s" % (network_context.current['provider:segmentation_id']))
        driver_logger.info("**** %s ****" % (method_name))

    def create_port_postcommit(self, context):
        self._log_port_information("Create Port PostCommit", context)
```

6. We will implement only `create_port_postcommit` method in this driver code. In this recipe, we will log the Port type, its IP address, and the Network that it belongs to.

7. Restart the Neutron services in your DevStack setup. You will have to use the correct screen instance to run this operation.

8. Once the Neutron services have been restarted, create a Router and add an interface to it using the `neutron router-create` and `neutron router-interface-add` CLI commands:

```
openstack@devstack:~/devstack$ neutron router-create CookbookRouter
Created a new router:
+-----------------------+--------------------------------------+
| Field                 | Value                                |
+-----------------------+--------------------------------------+
| admin_state_up        | True                                 |
| distributed           | False                                |
| external_gateway_info |                                      |
| ha                    | False                                |
| id                    | 23b1ad61-629a-4f0e-b565-07ec5f6bae9b |
| name                  | CookbookRouter                       |
| routes                |                                      |
| status                | ACTIVE                               |
| tenant_id             | 3161941967014dfeab5b15933c3aed02     |
+-----------------------+--------------------------------------+
openstack@devstack:~/devstack$ neutron router-interface-add CookbookRouter CookbookSubnet2
Added interface 3f3ee8c2-3e30-4b35-bf82-4c9978770eb1 to router CookbookRouter.
openstack@devstack:~/devstack$
```

9. To verify that our mechanism driver code was executed, open the DevStack log file for Neutron. In our DevStack setup, the log file was `/opt/stack/log/q-svc.log`.

10. This log file should contain the specific log messages as per the `create_port_postcommit` method in our mechanism driver:

```
2015-07-25 00:58:48.980 INFO neutron.plugins.ml2.drivers.ch10_ml2_mech_driver_port [req-250e37db-a6e3-4672-a7f2-47b21efae57b admin admin]
**** Create Port PostCommit ****
2015-07-25 00:58:48.980 INFO neutron.plugins.ml2.drivers.ch10_ml2_mech_driver_port [req-250e37db-a6e3-4672-a7f2-47b21efae57b admin admin]
Port Type: network:router_interface
2015-07-25 00:58:48.981 INFO neutron.plugins.ml2.drivers.ch10_ml2_mech_driver_port [req-250e37db-a6e3-4672-a7f2-47b21efae57b admin admin]
IP Address of the Port: 10.20.30.1
2015-07-25 00:58:48.981 INFO neutron.plugins.ml2.drivers.ch10_ml2_mech_driver_port [req-250e37db-a6e3-4672-a7f2-47b21efae57b admin admin]
Network name for the Port: CookbookNetwork2
2015-07-25 00:58:48.981 INFO neutron.plugins.ml2.drivers.ch10_ml2_mech_driver_port [req-250e37db-a6e3-4672-a7f2-47b21efae57b admin admin]
Network type for the Port: vlan
2015-07-25 00:58:48.981 INFO neutron.plugins.ml2.drivers.ch10_ml2_mech_driver_port [req-250e37db-a6e3-4672-a7f2-47b21efae57b admin admin]
Segmentation ID for the Port: 1029
2015-07-25 00:58:48.981 INFO neutron.plugins.ml2.drivers.ch10_ml2_mech_driver_port [req-250e37db-a6e3-4672-a7f2-47b21efae57b admin admin]
**** Create Port PostCommit ****
```

When we add an interface to a Router, it triggers a `Create Port` method on the mechanism driver. As we can see from the logs, the Port type is `network:router_interface`. The log also shows the Network-related information for the Port.

How it works...

In this recipe, we implemented a mechanism driver related to the Port entity. Therefore, context that was passed to the driver methods contains information about the Port. However, unlike a Subnet, context also contains the corresponding Network information.

In this recipe, we saw that you can extract the Port type information from the current Port context using the `device_owner` field. The Port type is useful in case different actions are required for the DHCP port, a VM instance port, or a Router Port. We also saw how to extract the IP address assigned to the Port. This is another useful attribute while building applications.

Finally, we saw how to extract the Network information from the Port context. Mechanism drivers from the Network device vendors often use the Network type and Segmentation ID in order to configure the underlying physical network.

11
Troubleshooting Tips for Neutron

In this chapter, we will cover the following recipes:

- ▶ Troubleshooting a VM that does not get a DHCP IP address
- ▶ Troubleshooting a VM that does not get an initial configuration
- ▶ Troubleshooting a VM that does not get External Network access
- ▶ Troubleshooting a VM not reachable from External Networks
- ▶ Checking the status of the Neutron service
- ▶ Checking the MAC address table on a virtual switch

Introduction

OpenStack provides users with lots of configuration options, but at the same time, it is up to the OpenStack administrator to make sure that the correct combination of runtime options has been configured. A large number of deployment options for OpenStack makes it very flexible, but at the same time, it can lead to errors and misconfiguration. In this chapter, we will look at systematic ways to troubleshoot an OpenStack setup for networking-related issues.

We will use the following topology in order to implement various debugging recipes:

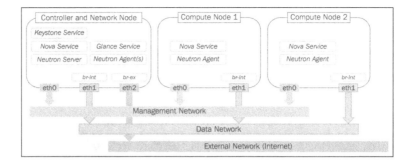

Troubleshooting a VM that does not get a DHCP IP address

In this recipe, we will troubleshoot a scenario where a VM on OpenStack that is connected to a DHCP enabled virtual network is unable to obtain an IP address.

When a tenant attaches the first VM to a DHCP enabled virtual network in OpenStack, Neutron automatically starts a DHCP server for the virtual network. This DHCP server is responsible for providing an IP address to the VM instances created on the virtual network.

Once a VM instance attached to a virtual network boots up, it is assigned an IP address from the DHCP server. In this recipe, we will see some of the possible reasons for a VM instance failing to receive an IP address.

Getting ready

The following information is required for this recipe:

▶ SSH-based login credentials for the Controller and Network node
▶ SSH-based login credentials for the Compute node

How to do it...

The following steps will show you how to troubleshoot your setup when the VM does not get an IP address:

1. With the appropriate credentials, SSH into the node where the Neutron server is running. In our setup, it will be the Controller and Network node.

2. Make sure that the DHCP agent is running on the Network node using the following command:

    ```
    service neutron-dhcp-agent status
    ```

3. Change the DHCP agent configuration in the `/etc/neutron/dhcp_agent.ini` file in order to enable verbose and debug level logging:

```
verbose = True
debug = True
```

The DHCP agent log files are present in the `/var/log/neutron` directory.

4. Restart the DHCP agent with the new configuration changes using the following command:

```
service neutron-dhcp-agent restart
```

5. Verify that the DHCP service process provided by dnsmasq is started on the virtual network. Use the `ps` command along with the Network ID in order to find the DHCP processes and DHCP interface:

```
openstack@controller:~$ ps aux |grep cb766367-b0eb-4552-a202-45ebcc04f1a5
nobody    15405  0.0  0.0  28208  1020 ?        S    08:26   0:00 dnsmasq --no-hosts --no-resolv
--strict-order --bind-interfaces --interface=tap6c77174e-28 --except-interface=lo
--pid-file=/opt/stack/data/neutron/dhcp/cb766367-b0eb-4552-a202-45ebcc04f1a5/pid
--dhcp-hostsfile=/opt/stack/data/neutron/dhcp/cb766367-b0eb-4552-a202-45ebcc04f1a5/host
--addn-hosts=/opt/stack/data/neutron/dhcp/cb766367-b0eb-4552-a202-45ebcc04f1a5/addn_hosts
--dhcp-optsfile=/opt/stack/data/neutron/dhcp/cb766367-b0eb-4552-a202-45ebcc04f1a5/opts
--dhcp-leasefile=/opt/stack/data/neutron/dhcp/cb766367-b0eb-4552-a202-45ebcc04f1a5/leases
--dhcp-range=set:tag0,20.20.21.0,static,86400s --dhcp-lease-max=256 --conf-file= --domain=openstacklocal
```

6. Make sure that the Network node is connected to the data Network. On an Open vSwitch-based setup, use the `ovs-vsctl show` command to view the bridges created. The `br-int` bridge is the integration bridge and all the devices on the network, such as the VMs, DHCP server, Routers, and so on, connect to it. This bridge is connected to the tunnel bridge; `br-tun` in the case of overlay networks or physical networks such as `br-eth1` in the case of VLAN-based networks using a patch port. In case the patch port is not configured, restarting the Open vSwitch agent will create it:

```
service neutron-plugin-openvswitch-agent restart
```

```
openstack@controller:~$ sudo ovs-vsctl show
b81dc65a-aab6-4e85-87a3-9ca7cdeb683f
    Bridge "br-eth1"
        Port "eth1"
            Interface "eth1"
        Port "br-eth1"
            Interface "br-eth1"
                type: internal
        Port "phy-br-eth1"
            Interface "phy-br-eth1"
                type: patch
                options: {peer="int-br-eth1"}
    Bridge br-int
        fail_mode: secure
        Port patch-tun
            Interface patch-tun
                type: patch
                options: {peer=patch-int}
        Port br-int
            Interface br-int
                type: internal
```

7. In case of overlay-based networking such as VXLAN or GRE, make sure that the tunnel endpoints on the hypervisors are configured with the proper IP address and are reachable from the Network node, and the tunnels ports are created on the OVS bridge, `br-tun`.

8. In a VLAN-based setup, make sure that the physical network bridges, such as `br-eth1`, are connected to the actual physical interface, `eth1`, and the physical network interface is up.

9. The preceding steps need to be repeated for the compute node that is hosting the VM instance. As an administrative user, log in to the Horizon dashboard and navigate to **Admin | System | Instances**. View the instances table to identify the compute node that is hosting a VM. Then, follow the same steps mentioned earlier to make sure that the VM has network connectivity through the integration bridge and physical network interface.

10. You can capture the Network packets using the `tcpdump` command on the physical network interface connecting the Network or Compute node in order to verify that the packets from the VM are able to reach the DHCP server. For example, if your tenant network is connected using `eth1`, use the following command to start a packet capture:

```
tcpdump -i eth1 -n -v
```

A packet flowing out of the VM goes through `br-int` and the patch port to `br-ethN` (the bridge connecting to the physical interface, `ethN`) for a VLAN-based Network or to `br-tun` for a tunnel-based Network. Finally, the packet flows to the physical interface used for the tenant Network. You can start a packet trace to troubleshoot the flow using `tcpdump` or `wireshark` at various points on the data path, such as `br-int`, `br-eth1`, or `br-tun`. The following figure shows you the various interfaces where a packet trace can be started for troubleshooting:

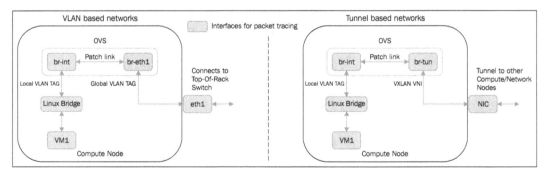

11. DHCP communication happens over the UDP ports 67 and 68 for the DHCP server and client, respectively. Make sure that the security group rules attached to the VM are not preventing the DHCP communication. Please look at *Chapter 7, Using Neutron Security and Firewall Services* to learn about security groups in Neutron.

12. In case the VM gets attached to multiple virtual networks, make sure that the DHCP client is running for all the network cards that you want to configure the DHCP-provided IP address. Most of the cloud images configure the VM for the first network only. You will have to look at the documentation of the operating system to learn about the available DHCP client. On Ubuntu and RHEL-based distributions, you should be able to use the `dhclient` command with the interface name, while the CirrOS image uses udhcpc as a DHCP client.

How it works...

For every virtual network created by the tenant, Neutron starts at least one DHCP server. When the VM boots, it sends a `DHCPDISCOVER` broadcast message to request the DHCP server for its IP address. The DHCP server then allocates an IP address to the VM. In case the VM does not receive the `DHCPOFFER` message, we must make sure that the DHCP server is running, network connectivity between the VM and DHCP server is working, and no security group rule is preventing communication between the VM and DHCP server.

Troubleshooting a VM that does not get an initial configuration

Once the VM boots up, it receives its IP address from the DHCP server. The VM then queries the metadata service in order to get additional configuration data for its initial configuration. During its first boot, the VM tries to receive its configuration by connecting to the metadata server at a well-known IP address of 169.254.169.254 on Port 80. In this recipe, we will learn how to troubleshoot metadata service related problems.

Getting ready

For this recipe, you will need the following information:

▸ SSH-based login credentials for the Controller and Network node
▸ SSH-based login credentials for the Compute node

How to do it...

The following steps will show you how to check the health of the metadata service for a virtual network:

1. With the appropriate credentials, SSH into the Network node. In our setup, it will be the Controller and Network node.

2. Make sure that the metadata agent is running on the Network node using the following command:

   ```
   service neutron-metadata-agent status
   ```

3. Change the metadata agent configuration in the /etc/neutron/metadata_agent.ini file in order to enable verbose and debug level logging. The metadata agent log files are present in the /var/log/neutron directory.

4. Restart the metadata agent with the new configuration changes using the following command:

   ```
   service neutron-metadata-service restart
   ```

5. The metadata service requires the metadata proxy to be started. The proxy service can be started either as a part of the DHCP namespace using neutron-dhcp-agent or as a part of the Router namespace using neutron-l3-agent. Make sure that the metadata proxy option is enabled in one of the configuration files, /etc/neutron/dhcp_agent.ini or /etc/neutron/l3_agent.ini:

   ```
   enable_metadata_proxy = True
   ```

6. For this example, we enabled the metadata proxy as a part of neutron-l3-agent. Connect a shell to the Router namespace using the ip netns exec qrouter-<routers_id> exec bash command. Checking the iptables rules with iptables -t nat -n -L in the Router's namespace should show the configuration that is related to the metadata service, similar to the one shown in the following image:

```
Chain neutron-l3-agent-PREROUTING (1 references)
target     prot opt source               destination
REDIRECT   tcp  --  0.0.0.0/0            169.254.169.254      tcp dpt:80 redir ports 9697
```

The traffic trying to reach the metadata service at the IP address of 169.254.169.254 on Port 80 is redirected to the Router's IP on Port 9697.

How it works...

Once a VM instance gets its IP address, it tries to retrieve further configuration by contacting the metadata service provided by OpenStack. The cloud-enabled VM images are installed with the cloud-init service, which is used to download an additional configuration from the metadata service. The metadata service is available at the well-known IP address of 169.254.169.254.

The Neutron metadata agent is responsible for starting this service. The metadata service provides the VM instance with configuration data, such as the hostname, SSH keys, and so on. The cloud-init service provides a host of other configuration options such as installing extra packages, running custom scripts, and others.

Troubleshooting a VM that does not get external Network access

In this recipe, we will look at some of the reasons where the VM might not get external Network access in OpenStack.

To provide external access to your VM, you must fulfill the following prerequisites:

▸ Your VM must be connected to a Router

▸ The Router must have its external gateway set

Getting ready

The following information is required for this recipe:

▸ OpenStack Horizon access as an administrator

▸ SSH-based login credentials for the Controller and Network node

▸ SSH-based login credentials for the Compute node

How to do it...

The following steps will show you how to troubleshoot the VMs that are unable to access the external Networks:

1. Log in to Horizon and make sure that the VM is connected to a Router through the internal Network. This can be seen by navigating to **Project | Network | Network Topology**.

2. On Horizon, navigate to **Project | Network | Router** and make sure that the Router has its gateway set. Note the ID for this Router on the Router details screen; it will be used in the subsequent steps of debugging.

3. With the appropriate credentials, SSH into the Network node. In our setup, it will be the Controller and Network node.

4. Start a shell that is connected to the namespace for the Router using the following command:

```
ip netns exec qrouter-<routers_id> exec bash.
```

The IP address configured on the external Network for this Router is `192.168.0.5`, which is shown in the following screenshot:

```
root@controller:~# ifconfig
lo        Link encap:Local Loopback
          inet addr:127.0.0.1  Mask:255.0.0.0
          inet6 addr: ::1/128 Scope:Host
          UP LOOPBACK RUNNING  MTU:65536  Metric:1
          RX packets:0 errors:0 dropped:0 overruns:0 frame:0
          TX packets:0 errors:0 dropped:0 overruns:0 carrier:0
          collisions:0 txqueuelen:0
          RX bytes:0 (0.0 B)  TX bytes:0 (0.0 B)

qg-7b2664a2-79 Link encap:Ethernet  HWaddr fa:16:3e:f4:d7:76
          inet addr:192.168.0.5  Bcast:192.168.0.255  Mask:255.255.255.0
          inet6 addr: fe80::f816:3eff:fef4:d776/64 Scope:Link
          UP BROADCAST RUNNING  MTU:1500  Metric:1
          RX packets:0 errors:0 dropped:0 overruns:0 frame:0
          TX packets:17 errors:0 dropped:0 overruns:0 carrier:0
          collisions:0 txqueuelen:0
          RX bytes:0 (0.0 B)  TX bytes:1210 (1.2 KB)

qr-fce5f263-b1 Link encap:Ethernet  HWaddr fa:16:3e:a6:c2:23
          inet addr:20.20.21.1  Bcast:20.20.21.255  Mask:255.255.255.0
          inet6 addr: fe80::f816:3eff:fea6:c223/64 Scope:Link
          UP BROADCAST RUNNING  MTU:1500  Metric:1
          RX packets:0 errors:0 dropped:0 overruns:0 frame:0
          TX packets:11 errors:0 dropped:0 overruns:0 carrier:0
          collisions:0 txqueuelen:0
          RX bytes:0 (0.0 B)  TX bytes:874 (874.0 B)
```

5. Use the `iptables -t nat -L -n` command to view the **Source Network Address Translation** (**SNAT**) configuration:

```
neutron-l3-agent-float-snat  all  --  0.0.0.0/0         0.0.0.0/0
SNAT        all  --  0.0.0.0/0         0.0.0.0/0          to:192.168.0.5
SNAT        all  --  0.0.0.0/0         0.0.0.0/0          mark match ! 0x2 ctstate DNAT to:192.168.0.5
```

You should be able to see the SNAT rules similar to the one in the preceding figure. When any VM connected to this Router tries to communicate with the outside world, the iptables rules use the external IP address on the Router to replace the source address of the packets going out. In this example, the external IP on the Router is `192.168.0.5` and it is used as the external IP for SNAT.

How it works...

The default L3 plugin on OpenStack provides external access to the VM instances using SNAT. It implements SNAT using iptables rules in the virtual Router. To enable SNAT on the Router, the tenant must set a gateway on the Router by connecting it to an external Network.

The gateway IP of the virtual Router is used to translate packets going out to the external world.

Troubleshooting a VM not reachable from external Networks

A tenant can associate a floating IP address to a VM in order to make it externally reachable. In this recipe, we will look at the possible reasons that block the access to the VM from external Networks.

External access to the VM works by providing **Destination Network Address Translation** (**DNAT**) at the virtual Router. To accomplish this, the following points must be taken care of:

- ► Your VM must be connected to a virtual Router
- ► You must have an external Network available to provide a floating IP
- ► You must associate a floating IP to your VM

Getting ready

The following information is required for this recipe:

- ► SSH-based login credentials for the Controller and Network node
- ► SSH-based login credentials for the Compute node

How to do it...

The following steps will show you how to troubleshoot a VM that is not accessible from the external Networks:

1. On Horizon, navigate to **Project | Network | Router** and make sure that the Router has its gateway set.

2. On Horizon, navigate to **Project | Compute | Instances** and find the floating IP associated to the VM. For this example, we have associated a floating IP of `192.168.0.4` to the VM instance with an internal IP of `20.20.21.6`:

	Instance Name	Image Name	IP Address	Size
☐			20.20.21.6	
☐	Chapter11_vm1	cirros-0.3.2-x86_64-rootfs	Floating IPs: 192.168.0.4	m1.tiny

Displaying 1 item

3. With the appropriate credentials, SSH into the Network node. In our setup, it will be the Controller and Network node.

4. Start a shell connected to the Router's namespace using the `ip netns exec qrouter-<routers_id> exec bash` command and check the iptables configuration for the NAT rules in the namespace with the following command:

```
Iptables -t nat -L -n
```

You should be able to see the NAT rules for the floating IP association:

```
Chain neutron-l3-agent-float-snat (1 references)
target     prot opt source            destination
SNAT       all  --  20.20.21.6        0.0.0.0/0          to:192.168.0.4

Chain neutron-l3-agent-PREROUTING (1 references)
target     prot opt source            destination
REDIRECT   tcp  --  0.0.0.0/0         169.254.169.254    tcp dpt:80 redir ports 9697
DNAT       all  --  0.0.0.0/0         192.168.0.4        to:20.20.21.6
```

5. If the VM has multiple network interfaces, make sure that the default route is set to the Network gateway for the interface that has the floating IP associated.

The NAT rules redirect the traffic arriving at the floating IP of `192.168.0.4` to the internal IP of `20.20.21.6`. It also changes the source IP of any packet from the VM to the outside world to the floating IP `192.168.0.4`.

How it works...

To make a VM externally accessible, a floating IP must be associated with it. A floating IP is an externally accessible IP address and is allocated from an external Network of the tenant.

When a floating IP is associated with a VM, Neutron configures the virtual Router to map the destination address of the incoming traffic on the floating IP to the VM's internal IP. Configuring the DNAT rules using iptables on the virtual Router can accomplish this.

Checking the status of the Neutron service

The first step towards troubleshooting OpenStack Networks would be to make sure that the Neutron service is running. In this recipe, we will look at ways to make sure that the Neutron server is running without any errors.

Getting ready

For this recipe, you will need the following information:

▶ SSH-based login credentials for the Controller and Network node

How to do it...

The following steps will show you how to check whether the Neutron service is running with the proper configurations:

1. With the appropriate credentials, SSH into the node where the Neutron server is running. In our setup, it will be the Controller and Network node.

2. In the `/etc/neutron/neutron.conf` file, make sure that you have correct `core_plugin` and `service_plugins` configured. For example, in the case of the ML2 plugin, the Neutron configuration is as follows:

   `core_plugin = ml2`

   The `service_plugins` should include a list of advanced services such as a Router, Firewall, and lbaas, depending on your deployment:

   `service_plugins = router,firewall,lbaas`

   Make sure that the packages for these service plugins are installed and configured.

3. You may wish to enable verbose and debug level logging for the Neutron server in the `neutron.conf` file for troubleshooting. Keep in mind that enabling the debug and verbose log will produce extensive logging, which will use the disk space. Therefore, it is best to enable it only for the required duration of troubleshooting:

   ```
   verbose = True
   debug = True
   ```

4. If you are using the ML2 plugin, check the ML2 configuration files in the `/etc/neutron/plugins/ml2` directory as well. The `ml2_conf.ini` file is the main configuration file that includes the type and mechanism driver settings.

5. Depending on your ML2 driver setting, you may need to review the configuration file that is specific to the driver. All the ML2 configuration files are located in the `/etc/neutron/plugins/ml2` directory. Please refer to previous chapters to learn more about the configuration of the ML2 type and mechanism drivers that are appropriate for your deployment.

6. Execute the following command to find out the status of the Neutron server:

   `service neutron-server status`

7. If you have made any changes to the configuration files, restart the Neutron server in order to load the new configuration by executing the following command:

   `service neutron-server restart`

8. The Neutron server logs are present in `/var/log/neutron/server.log`. In case the Neutron server fails to start, the Neutron logs can help in troubleshooting.

How it works...

The Neutron server configuration allows verbose logging that can help in troubleshooting. The main configuration file for Neutron is `neutron.conf` and it contains the core and service plugin configurations. The Neutron server runs as a Linux service on the OpenStack Controller node and you can use the service commands to restart them if any configuration has been changed.

Checking the MAC address table on a virtual switch

As the devices connected to the virtual Network start to communicate with each other, the virtual switch on the Compute node learns the MAC addresses of the network interfaces. In this recipe, we will learn how to view the MAC address table of a virtual switch on an OpenStack Compute node.

Getting ready

For this recipe, you will require the following information:

> ▶ SSH-based login credentials for the Compute node

How to do it...

The following steps will show you how to check the MAC address table on the virtual switch:

1. With the appropriate credentials, SSH into the Compute node.

2. Use the `ovs-appctl fdb/show` command to view the MAC addresses learned by the Open vSwitch instance:

```
ovs-appctl fdb/show br-int
```

```
openstack@controller:~$ sudo ovs-appctl fdb/show br-int
port  VLAN  MAC                Age
   4     2  fa:16:3e:e2:a8:14   43
   6     2  52:f4:cc:65:d3:56   35
   6     2  1a:44:73:4b:8b:59   35
   6     2  fa:16:3e:d0:33:58    1
```

3. For a Linux bridge-based deployment, follow the recipe *Viewing virtual interface information on the Compute node* in *Chapter 2, Using Open vSwitch for VLAN-Based Networks* to find the bridge name for the virtual Network. Use the `brctl showmacs` command with the bridge name to view the MAC addresses learned by a Linux bridge instance, for example, for a bridge, `brq1e023dc6-7a`, use the following command:

```
brctl showmacs brq1e023dc6-7a
```

```
openstack@compute1:~/devstack$ brctl show
bridge name       bridge id              STP enabled       interfaces
qbr4adb838e-11   8000.1a44734b8b59         no              eth1.1002
                                                           tap4adb838e-11

stack@compute1:~/devstack$ brctl showmacs qbr4adb838e-11
port no mac addr                   is local?       ageing timer
   2      1a:44:73:4b:8b:59        yes                 0.00
   1      52:f4:cc:65:d3:56        yes                 0.00
   2      fa:16:3e:d0:33:58        no                 35.32
```

The MAC address on the virtual switch corresponds to the MAC address of the network interface in the attached VMs.

How it works...

When the devices on the OpenStack Network communicate with each other, the virtual switches such as the Open vSwitch or Linux bridge will start learning the Layer 2 address (MAC address) of the devices connected to the Ports of the virtual Network by looking at the packets that traverse the switch. Learning how to view these MAC addresses on the virtual switch can help in understanding the flow of packets between devices such as the VM instances, Virtual Routers, and so on that the OpenStack tenants create.

12
Advanced Topics

In this chapter, we will look at some of the advanced networking concepts in OpenStack Neutron in the following recipes:

- ▶ Configuring Neutron for VPN as a service
- ▶ Testing VPN as a service on Neutron
- ▶ Using link aggregation on the compute node
- ▶ Integrating networking in a Heat template

Introduction

We will discuss VPN, link aggregation on the compute node, and integration with OpenStack Heat project in this chapter. The Heat project in OpenStack provides you with an orchestration service to spawn resources such as VMs, Routers, and load balancers along with their Network connectivity.

To implement these recipes, we will use an OpenStack setup as described in the following image:

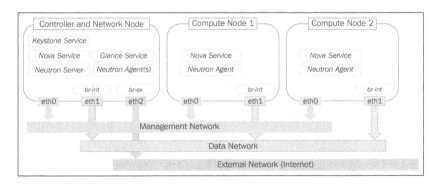

This setup has two compute nodes and one node for the controller and networking services.

Configuring Neutron for VPN as a service

A **Virtual Private Network** (**VPN**) connects two endpoints on different Networks over a public Internet connection in such a way that the endpoints appear to be directly connected to each other. VPNs also provide you with the confidentiality and integrity of the transmitted data.

VPN connectivity between two Networks can be implemented at different layers of an OSI stack. A VPN that connects the endpoints at Layer 2 is called L2 VPN while a VPN that connects the endpoints at Layer 3 (for example, an IP layer) is called L3 VPN.

Neutron provides a service plugin that enables OpenStack users to connect two Networks using a VPN. The reference implementation of the VPN plugin in Neutron uses Openswan to create an IPSEC based L3 VPN. IPSEC is a suite of protocols that provides a secure connection between two endpoints by encrypting each IP packet transferred between them. An IPSEC endpoint consists of the following two parts:

> ▸ A daemon to negotiate session keys between the peer endpoints
> ▸ A component that uses the session keys to encrypt/decrypt the packets

IPSEC uses the **Internet Key Exchange** (**IKE**) protocol in order to establish an authenticated session key. IPSEC can use various techniques for the authentication; OpenStack VPNaaS uses **Pre-Shared Keys** (**PSK**) as the authentication mechanism.

Getting ready

In this recipe, we will configure Neutron to use the reference VPNaaS plugin. For this recipe, you will need the following information:

> ▸ SSH-based login to the Controller and Network node

How to do it...

The following steps will show you how to install the VPN service plugin with Neutron:

1. With the appropriate credentials, SSH into the node where the Neutron server is running. In our setup, it will be the Controller and Network node.

2. Install the packages required to provide VPN services using a package manager such as yum or apt:

   ```
   openstack@controller:~$ sudo apt-get install python-neutron-vpnaas
   neutron-vpn-agent openswan
   ```

3. Open the neutron.conf configuration file using your desired editor. For example, the command for the vi editor will be as follows:

   ```
   openstack@controller:~$ sudo vi /etc/neutron/neutron.conf
   ```

4. In the `[DEFAULT]` section of the file, configure `vpnaas` as the service plugin for Neutron. If `service_plugins` is already configured, add the VPN service configuration to the list separated by a comma:

   ```
   [DEFAULT]
   ...
   service_plugins = vpnaas
   ```

5. Open the `/etc/neutron/vpnaas_agent.ini` configuration file and update the `device_driver` and `interface_driver` settings:

   ```
   interface_driver =
     neutron.agent.linux.interface.OVSInterfaceDriver
   vpn_device_driver=neutron.services.vpn.device_drivers.ipsec.
   OpenSwanDriver
   ```

6. To configure the Horizon dashboard for VPNaaS, open the `/usr/share/openstack-dashboard/openstack_dashboard/local/local_settings.py` file and set the `enable_vpn` option in the `OPENSTACK_NEUTRON_NETWORK` setting:

   ```
   'enable_vpn' = True
   ```

7. Restart `neutron-server`, `neutron-vpn-agent`, and `apache2` or `http server` for the changes to take effect:

   ```
   service neutron-server restart
   service neutron-vpn-agent restart
   ```

   On a RedHat- or CentOS-based system, restart apache, as follows:

   ```
   service httpd restart
   ```

   On Ubuntu, the following command restarts apache:

   ```
   service apache2 restart
   ```

Once the changes take effect, log in to Horizon and verify that the VPN support has been enabled by navigating to **Project** | **Network** | **VPN**.

How it works...

OpenStack Neutron provides VPN as a service. To enable this feature, the VPN plugin must be installed and configured on the Controller and Network node. The configuration of Horizon must also be updated in order to enable support for the VPN service.

Testing VPN as a service on Neutron

This recipe simulates a VPN connection between two data center sites connected over a public Network. We will create a private Network connected to a Router to simulate a data center. The VPN service provided by Neutron will be configured between two such Routers in order to connect the two private Networks.

Getting ready

The following table describes the infrastructure required for testing the VPN service:

Router	Private Network	Subnet	CIDR	VM	Location
Chapter12_Router1	Chapter12_Network1	Chapter12_SubNet1	10.10.10.0/24	VM1	Site1
Chapter12_Router2	Chapter12_Network2	Chapter12_SubNet2	10.10.20.0/24	VM2	Site2

In addition to this, we will use an external Network called public in order to simulate the Internet. The VPN connection will be made over the Internet (the public Network in this recipe) to connect the two Routers.

The external Network, public, uses a CIDR of `192.168.0.0/24`.

The virtual Network components are connected in a topology described in the following figure:

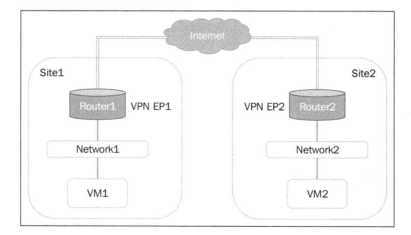

Follow the *Creating Network and Subnet using Horizon* recipe in *Chapter 1, Getting Started with OpenStack Networking* to create the Networks Chapter12_Network1 and Chapter12_Network2 with Subnets and CIDR as described in the preceding table. Launch two VMs, VM1 and VM2, connected to Chapter12_Network1 and Chapter12_network2, respectively.

Follow the recipes in *Chapter 6, Using Routing Services in Neutron* to create the two Routers, Chapter12_Router1 and Chapter12_Router2. The Networks, Chapter12_Network1 and Chapter12_network2, are added to the Routers, Chapter12_Router1 and Chapter12_Router2, respectively.

Next, set the gateway on both the Routers. Setting a gateway on the Routers will connect the Routers to the public Network and assign an IP address to the Router interface connected to the public Network. Once these steps have been completed, the **Network Topology** should look as follows:

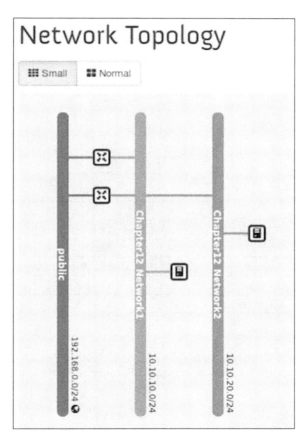

Note the IP addresses assigned to VM1 and VM2 once they have booted.

The Router's public IP addresses are used to set up the VPN. The external IP of the Routers must be noted. To find the external IP of the Router, navigate to **Project** | **Network** | **Router** and click on the desired Router. The external IP of the Router can be found in the **Router Details** tab:

Router Details

Overview   Interfaces

Name	Chapter12_Router1
ID	1b883a02-0472-4ea4-b6a9-dcd77aedc3c1
Project ID	bfd02b5c180f4765b6ff2a4ba3636413
Status	ACTIVE
Admin State	UP

External Gateway

Network Name	public
Network ID	5507d585-cb44-45c5-a53c-385069e2b5b1
External Fixed IPs	**Subnet ID** 1c9a1620-68d9-4fbb-bd92-bea531919809
	IP Address 192.168.0.4
SNAT	Enabled

The following table shows the IP addresses allocated to the Routers in our setup:

Router	Public IP address
Chapter12_Router1	192.168.0.4
Chapter12_Router2	192.168.0.5

How to do it...

The following steps will show you how to create a VPN service in order to test the VPN service plugin:

1. Log in to Horizon with the appropriate credentials.

2. In the left navigation menu, navigate to **Project** | **Network** | **VPN**.

3. In the **IKE Policies** tab, click **Add IKE Policy**.

4. On the **Add IKE Policy** screen, add **Name** and **Description** for the policy:

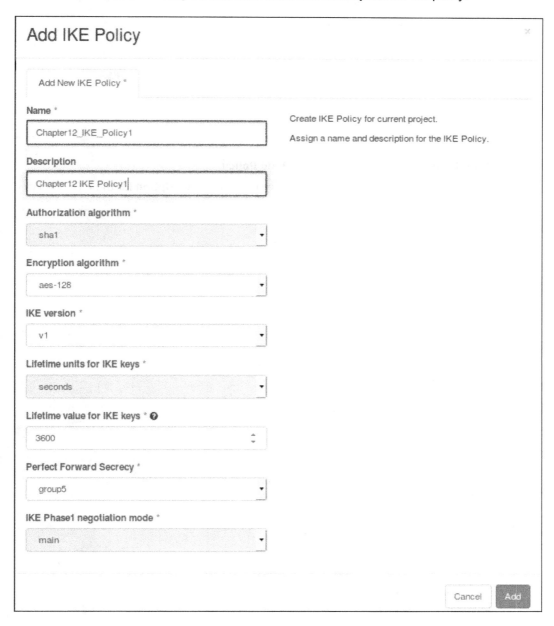

5. The **Add IKE Policy** screen also allows changing the IKE options such as Encryption, Authorization, and so on. We will use the default settings.

6. Click **Add** to create the IKE policy:

7. In the **IPSec Policies** tab, click **Add IPSec Policy**.
8. On the **Add IPSec Policy** screen, provide **Name** and **Description** for the IPSEC policy:

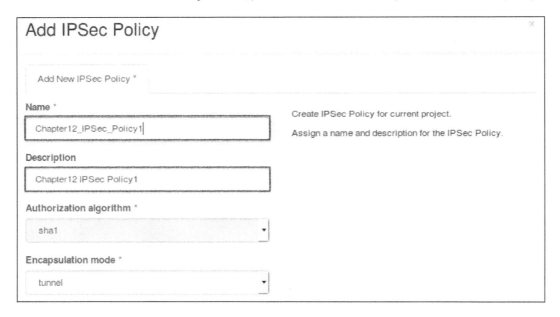

9. We will use the default settings for the rest of the options.

10. Click **Add** to create the IPSEC policy:

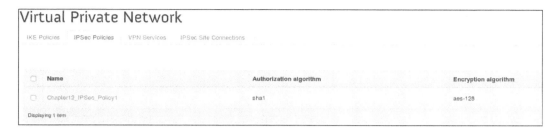

11. Next, we will create the VPN service.
12. In the **VPN Services** tab, click **+Add VPN Service**.
13. On the **VPN Service** screen, provide **Name** and **Description** for the VPN service:

14. In the **Router** drop-down menu, select the first Router, that is, **Chapter12_Router1**.
15. In the **Subnet** selection menu, choose the Subnet that has been added to the first Router, that is, Chapter12_SubNet1 with a CIDR of **10.10.10.0/24**.

16. Click **Add** to create the VPN service:

17. Repeat these steps to create another VPN service for the second Router with the Subnet, Chapter12_SubNet2, with a CIDR of **10.10.20.0/24**:

Name	Description	Subnet	Router
Chapter12_VPN2	Chapter12 VPN2	10.10.20.0/24	Chapter12_Router2
Chapter12_VPN1	Chapter12 VPN1	10.10.10.0/24	Chapter12_Router1

18. In the **IPSec Site Connections** tab, click **+Add IPSec Site Connection**.

19. On the **IPSec Site Connection** screen, provide **Name** and **Description** for the connection; we will use Chapter12_IPSec_Connection1 and Chapter12 IPSec Connection1, respectively.

20. Choose **VPN Service associated with this connection** from the drop-down menu; we will choose **Chapter12_VPN1**.

21. Choose **IKE Policy associated with this connection** and **IPSec Policy associated with this connection** as **Chapter12_IKE_policy1** and **Chapter12_IPSec_Policy1**.

22. In **Peer Gateway public IPv4/IPv6 Address or FQDN** and **Peer Router Identity for authentication (Peer ID)**, provide the external IP of the peer Router. For our example, the external IP for the peer Router Chapter12_Router2 is **192.168.0.5**.

23. In **Remote peer subnet(s)**, provide the target Subnet that this VPN will connect to; for our example, we will use this VPN to connect to Chapter12_SubNet2, which has a CIDR of 10.10.20.0/24.

24. Finally, we will need to provide **Pre-Shared Key (PSK) string** that will be used by the connection; for this example, we will use `Chapter12_Secret`:

25. Create another IPSEC site connection for the second Router. Choose **Chapter12_VPN2** as the VPN service and **Chapter12_IKE_policy1** and **Chapter12_IPSec_Policy1** for the IKE and IPSEC policy, respectively. (As we will use the same cloud installation to implement the VPN connections, we can share the policies between the two VPN configurations.) Provide the external IP of `Chapter12_Router1` for the peer Router's external IP or FQDN and `10.10.10.0/24` (the CIDR of `Chapter12_SubNet1`) as the remote peer Subnet(s):

IKE Policies	IPSec Policies	VPN Services	IPSec Site Connections		
☐ **Name**			**VPN Service**	**IKE Policy**	**IPSec Policy**
☐ Chapter12_IPSec_Connection2			Chapter12_VPN2	Chapter12_IKE_Policy1	Chapter12_IPSec_Policy1
☐ Chapter12_IPSec_Connection1			Chapter12_VPN1	Chapter12_IKE_Policy1	Chapter12_IPSec_Policy1

26. Test the VPN connections by executing a `ping` command to the instances across the VPN connection. In this example, our VMs have an IP address of `10.10.10.3` for VM1 and `10.10.20.3` for VM2:

```
login as 'cirros' user. default password: 'cubswin:)'. use 'sudo' for root.
chapter12-vm1 login: cirros
Password:
$ ifconfig
eth0      Link encap:Ethernet  HWaddr FA:16:3E:00:5C:66
          inet addr:10.10.10.3  Bcast:10.10.10.255  Mask:255.255.255.0
          inet6 addr: fe80::f816:3eff:fe00:5c66/64 Scope:Link
          UP BROADCAST RUNNING MULTICAST  MTU:1500  Metric:1
          RX packets:91 errors:0 dropped:0 overruns:0 frame:0
          TX packets:123 errors:0 dropped:0 overruns:0 carrier:0
          collisions:0 txqueuelen:1000
          RX bytes:9381 (9.1 KiB)  TX bytes:11992 (11.7 KiB)

lo        Link encap:Local Loopback
          inet addr:127.0.0.1  Mask:255.0.0.0
          inet6 addr: ::1/128 Scope:Host
          UP LOOPBACK RUNNING  MTU:65536  Metric:1
          RX packets:0 errors:0 dropped:0 overruns:0 frame:0
          TX packets:0 errors:0 dropped:0 overruns:0 carrier:0
          collisions:0 txqueuelen:0
          RX bytes:0 (0.0 B)  TX bytes:0 (0.0 B)
$ ping 10.10.20.1
PING 10.10.20.1 (10.10.20.1): 56 data bytes
64 bytes from 10.10.20.1: seq=0 ttl=63 time=2.579 ms
64 bytes from 10.10.20.1: seq=1 ttl=63 time=1.039 ms
--- 10.10.20.1 ping statistics ---
2 packets transmitted, 2 packets received, 0% packet loss
round-trip min/avg/max = 1.039/1.809/2.579 ms
$ ping 10.10.20.3
PING 10.10.20.3 (10.10.20.3): 56 data bytes
64 bytes from 10.10.20.3: seq=0 ttl=62 time=4.529 ms
64 bytes from 10.10.20.3: seq=1 ttl=62 time=3.058 ms
64 bytes from 10.10.20.3: seq=2 ttl=62 time=3.946 ms
```

The VPN connections are now functional between the two Routers and the instances on the two Networks can communicate with each other.

How it works...

The private networks, `Chapter12_Network1` and `Chapter12_network2`, are connected to their respective Routers. The Routers are assigned a public IP address by executing a set gateway operation. In our case, the Routers get a public IP from the CIDR `192.168.0.0/24` associated with the external Network, public.

In this recipe, we configured an IPSEC-based VPN and connected the private Networks, `Chapter12_Network1` and `Chapter12_Network2`. The Routers act as the VPN endpoints. While creating VPN site connections, information about the peer Router and the remote Subnet must be provided. The VPN service and site connection should be created for both the endpoints.

The VPN service configuration uses a secret key, PSK, that is shared by both the peers.

Using link aggregation on the compute node

Link aggregation or bonding is a way to combine multiple physical network links to a logical link.

Link aggregation is used as a means to provide higher bandwidth and redundancy against link failure. In this recipe, we will see how to configure link aggregation in order to connect the virtual switch on an OpenStack node to the physical switch.

We will assume that the virtual switch used on the OpenStack node is Open vSwitch and configure link aggregation with **Link Aggregation Control Protocol** (**LACP**):

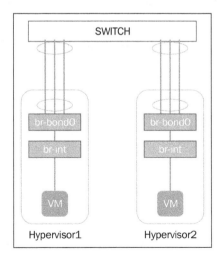

Getting ready

For this recipe, we will need the following information:

  ▶ SSH-based login for the Compute and Network node
  ▶ Details of the Network interface to use for link aggregation

How to do it...

The following steps will show you how to configure link aggregation on a Compute or a Network node and update Neutron to use the bonded interface for the tenant data traffic:

1. With the appropriate credentials, SSH into the Compute node.
2. Add a bridge on the Open vSwitch using the `ovs-vsctl add-br` command:

    ovs-vsctl add-br br-bond0

3. Next, we will create the bonded interface on this bridge with the `ovs-vsctl add-bond` command:

    ovs-vsctl add-bond br-bond0 bond0 eth1 eth2

4. Then, enable LACP on the bonded interface:

    ovs-vsctl set port bond0 lacp=active

5. Update the physical switch configuration to enable the LACP-based link aggregation interface. Consult your switch documentation to get the exact configuration.
6. Open the `/etc/neutron/plugins/ml2/ml2_conf.ini` configuration file using your desired editor. For example, the command for the vi editor will be as follows:

    openstack@controller:~$ sudo vi /etc/neutron/plugins/ml2/ml2_conf.ini

7. In the `[ovs]` section, update `bridge_mappings` in order to use the newly created bridge for the tenant traffic:

    ```
    [ovs]
    bridge_mappings = physnet1:br-bond0
    ```

8. Restart the Open vSwitch L2 agent for the configuration change to take effect:

    service neutron-plugin-openvswitch-agent restart

9. Repeat these steps on all the Compute and Network nodes that need to use link aggregation.

How it works...

Link aggregation provides both redundancy and a higher bandwidth by combining multiple physical Network links in a logical link.

Integrating networking in a Heat template

Nowadays, the installation of any nontrivial application spans more than one machine. Different machines provide specialized functions such as database servers, web servers, and many more. Heat is an OpenStack project that provides the users of OpenStack with the ability to start a group of connected resources such as VMs, Networks, Routers, and so on in order to create a complete infrastructure for deploying applications.

The tenant communicates with the orchestration system using the Heat client. A Heat template describes the stack of infrastructure resources requested by the user. A template consists of the following sections:

- **Version**: This provides a version of the template format
- **Description**: This describes the purpose of the template
- **Parameters**: This section describes the user-defined parameters that are used in the template; it can describe the parameter type and validation logic for the parameters
- **Resources**: The resources section describes the resources that the template tries to create
- **Outputs**: The output section describes the output to be printed after the orchestration is complete

The client submits the orchestration request using the Heat API on behalf of the user. The Heat engine parses, validates, and assigns user-specified values to the variables in the template. It then creates the resources defined in the template using various OpenStack clients in order to interact with individual services, as described in the following figure:

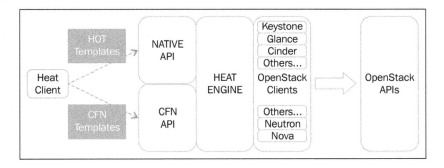

In this recipe, we will learn about the Heat template constructs to manage the Network resources.

Getting ready

The following steps will show you how to use Heat to create a simple stack consisting of a newly created Network attached to a Router. To deploy this topology, we will need a Heat template. We will use the following template for our example:

```yaml
heat_template_version: 2013-05-23

description: >
  Heat template to create a new neutron network, a router and adding the network to the router.

parameters:
  My_net1_name:
    type: string
    description: Name of the network to be created
  My_net1_cidr:
    type: string
    description: Network address (CIDR notation)


resources:
  Chapter12_net1:
    type: OS::Neutron::Net
    properties:
      name: { get_param: My_net1_name }

  Chapter12_subnet1:
    type: OS::Neutron::Subnet
    properties:
      network_id: { get_resource: Chapter12_net1 }
      cidr: { get_param: My_net1_cidr }

  Chapter12_router:
    type: OS::Neutron::Router

  Chapter12_router_interface:
    type: OS::Neutron::RouterInterface
    properties:
      router_id: { get_resource: Chapter12_router }
      subnet_id: { get_resource: Chapter12_subnet1 }


outputs:
```

This file is available on GitHub at `https://github.com/reachsrirams/packt-openstack-networking-cookbook/blob/master/Chapter12/Chapter12_Stack1.yaml`. Clone this repository to your local machine. We will be using the `Chapter12_Stack1.yaml` file for our recipe.

How to do it...

The following steps will show you how to create a simple stack of infrastructure using a Heat template:

1. Log in to Horizon with the appropriate credentials.

2. In the left navigation menu, navigate to **Project** | **Orchestration** | **Stacks**:

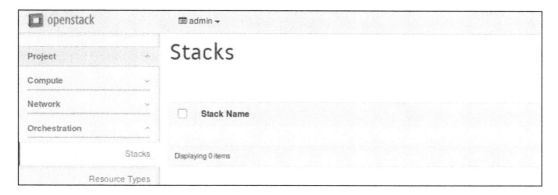

3. Click on **+Launch Stack**.

4. On the **Select Template** screen, select **Template Source** as **File**. Templates can be provided as a direct input, as a URL or file. For this example, we will use a **File**-based input:

5. Next, click on **Browse** to locate and upload the Heat template file,
    `Chapter12_Stack1.yaml`, that we created earlier.

6. Click **Next**.

7. The **Launch Stack** screen is created based on the parameters described in the
    template file:

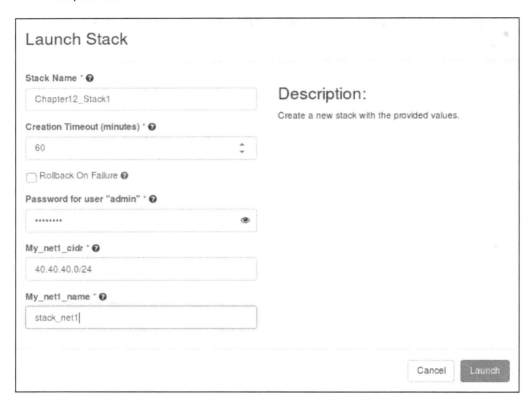

8. Click **Launch** to start the orchestration process:

9. Click on Stack Name to see the details of the stack.

10. The **Topology** tab shows the OpenStack resources created by Heat.

11. The **Overview** tab shows details such as **Status** of the stack, **Stack Parameters**, **Outputs**, and so on:

Stack Details: Chapter12_Stack1

Topology   Overview   Resources   Events   Template

Stack Overview

Information

Name	Chapter12_Stack1
ID	8e00d77d-f689-4e51-bf62-356ea4a1ef58
Description	Heat template to create a new neutron network, a router and adding the network to the router.

Status

Created	0 minutes
Last Updated	Never
Status	Create_Complete: Stack CREATE completed successfully

Outputs

Stack Parameters

My_net1_cidr	40.40.40.0/24
OS::project_id	06d8970c26624c1688ea5d18af212a8e
OS::stack_name	Chapter12_Stack1
OS::stack_id	8e00d77d-f689-4e51-bf62-356ea4a1ef58
My_net1_name	stack_net1

Launch Parameters

Timeout	60 Minutes
Rollback	Disabled

12. The **Resources** tab shows the resources used by the stack.

How it works...

The Heat engine parses, validates, and assigns values to the attributes in the template. Once the Heat template completes the validation process, the engine uses the OpenStack project clients to create the resources described in it. For example, for the Network-related resources, Heat uses the Neutron client in order to create the appropriate resources.

Index

A

allotted VLAN
viewing, for Network 29, 30
API requests
processing, for Network 214-217
processing, for Port 219-221
processing, for Subnet 217-219

C

Ceilometer 2
Classless Inter-Domain Routing (CIDR) 143
CLI
used, for adding load balancer health
    monitor 185, 186
used, for configuring security group
    rules 145, 146
used, for creating load balancer pool 176
used, for creating security group 144, 145
used, for creating Virtual IP 189, 190
Compute node
link aggregation, using 249, 250
virtual interface, viewing for GRE
    tunnels 94-97
virtual interface information, viewing 50-55
virtual interface information, viewing for
    VXLAN tunnels 86-89
virtual interface information, viewing 36-41

D

DB-Access-Network 67, 68
DB-VM 67, 68
DHCP server
starting, on specific Network node 108-110
Distributed Virtual Routing (DVR) 120

E

External Network
about 116
creating, Horizon used 63-66

F

Firewall
creating 161-163
Neutron, configuring 154, 155
policies, creating 159-161
rules, creating 156-158
rules, verifying on Network node 164-167
rules, viewing on Network node 164-167
Flat Network
about 48
creating, Horizon used 57-60
Neutron, configuring 56, 57
floating IP address
associating, to virtual machine 132-134
creating, Neutron CLI used 130-132
deleting, Neutron CLI used 130-132

G

Generic Routing Encapsulation (GRE) 92
GRE tunnels
virtual interface, viewing on Compute
    node 94-97
GRE type driver
Neutron, configuring 92, 93

H

Heat template
networking, integrating 251-255

Thank you for buying
OpenStack Networking Cookbook

About Packt Publishing

Packt, pronounced 'packed', published its first book, *Mastering phpMyAdmin for Effective MySQL Management*, in April 2004, and subsequently continued to specialize in publishing highly focused books on specific technologies and solutions.

Our books and publications share the experiences of your fellow IT professionals in adapting and customizing today's systems, applications, and frameworks. Our solution-based books give you the knowledge and power to customize the software and technologies you're using to get the job done. Packt books are more specific and less general than the IT books you have seen in the past. Our unique business model allows us to bring you more focused information, giving you more of what you need to know, and less of what you don't.

Packt is a modern yet unique publishing company that focuses on producing quality, cutting-edge books for communities of developers, administrators, and newbies alike. For more information, please visit our website at www.packtpub.com.

About Packt Open Source

In 2010, Packt launched two new brands, Packt Open Source and Packt Enterprise, in order to continue its focus on specialization. This book is part of the Packt open source brand, home to books published on software built around open source licenses, and offering information to anybody from advanced developers to budding web designers. The Open Source brand also runs Packt's open source Royalty Scheme, by which Packt gives a royalty to each open source project about whose software a book is sold.

Writing for Packt

We welcome all inquiries from people who are interested in authoring. Book proposals should be sent to author@packtpub.com. If your book idea is still at an early stage and you would like to discuss it first before writing a formal book proposal, then please contact us; one of our commissioning editors will get in touch with you.

We're not just looking for published authors; if you have strong technical skills but no writing experience, our experienced editors can help you develop a writing career, or simply get some additional reward for your expertise.

Learning OpenStack Networking (Neutron)

ISBN: 978-1-78398-330-8   Paperback: 300 pages

Architect and build a network infrastructure for your cloud using OpenStack Neutron networking

1. Build a virtual switching infrastructure for virtual machines using the Open vSwitch or Linux Bridge plugins.

2. Create networks and software routers that connect virtual machines to the Internet using built-in Linux networking features.

3. Scale your application using Neutron's load-balancing-as-a-service feature using the haproxy plugin.

OpenStack Cloud Computing Cookbook
Second Edition

ISBN: 978-1-78216-758-7   Paperback: 396 pages

Over 100 recipes to successfully set up and manage your OpenStack cloud environments with complete coverage of Nova, Swift, Keystone, Glance, Horizon, Neutron, and Cinder

1. Updated for OpenStack Grizzly.

2. Learn how to install, configure, and manage all of the OpenStack core projects including new topics like block storage and software defined networking.

3. Learn how to build your Private Cloud utilizing DevOps and Continuous Integration tools and techniques.

Please check **www.PacktPub.com** for information on our titles

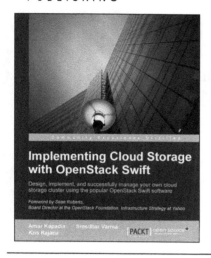

Implementing Cloud Storage with OpenStack Swift

Implementing Cloud Storage
with OpenStack Swift

Design, implement, and successfully manage your own cloud
storage cluster using the popular OpenStack Swift software

Foreword by Sean Roberts,
Board Director at the OpenStack Foundation, Infrastructure Strategy at Yahoo

Amar Kapadia   Sreedhar Varma
Kris Rajana

Implementing Cloud Storage with OpenStack Swift

ISBN: 978-1-78216-805-8   Paperback: 140 pages

Design, implement, and successfully manage your own cloud storage cluster using the popular OpenStack Swift software

1. Learn about the fundamentals of cloud storage using OpenStack Swift.

2. Explore how to install and manage OpenStack Swift along with various hardware and tuning options.

3. Perform data transfer and management using REST APIs.

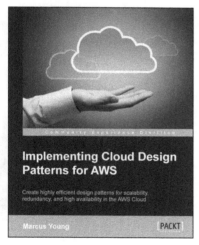

Implementing Cloud Design
Patterns for AWS

Create highly efficient design patterns for scalability,
redundancy, and high availability in the AWS Cloud

Marcus Young

Implementing Cloud Design Patterns for AWS

ISBN: 978-1-78217-734-0   Paperback: 228 pages

Create highly efficient design patterns for scalability, redundancy, and high availability in the AWS Cloud

1. Create highly robust systems using cloud infrastructure.

2. Make web applications resilient against scheduled and accidental down-time.

3. Explore and apply Amazon-provided services in unique ways to solve common problems.

Please check **www.PacktPub.com** for information on our titles